The Color of Precision Medicine

Will genome-based precision medicine fix the problem of race/ethnicity-based medicine? To answer this question, Sun and Ong propose the concept of racialization of precision medicine, defined as the social processes by which racial/ethnic categories are incorporated (or not) into the development, interpretation, and implementation of precision medicine research and practice.

Drawing on interview data with physicians and scientists in the field of cancer care, this book addresses the following questions: Who are the racializers in precision medicine, how and why do they do it? Under what conditions do clinicians personalize medical treatments in the context of cancer therapies? The chapters elucidate different ways in which racialization occurs and reveal that there exists an inherent contradiction in the usage of race/ethnicity as precision medicine moves from bench to bedside. The relative resources theory is proposed to explain that whether race/ethnicity-based medicine will be replaced by genomic medicine depends on the resources available at the individual and systemic levels. Furthermore, this book expands on how racialization happens not only in pharmacogenomic drug efficacy studies, but also in drug toxicity studies and cost-effectiveness studies.

An important resource for clinicians, researchers, public health policymakers, health economists, and journalists on how to deracialize precision medicine.

Shirley Sun is an associate professor of sociology at the Nanyang Technological University (NTU), Singapore. Her research areas are medical sociology and sociology of science, knowledge, and technology. She is the author of "Socio-economics of Personalized Medicine in Asia" (2017, London and New York: Routledge).

Zoe Ong is a PhD candidate from the Interdisciplinary Graduate Program at the Wee Kim Wee School of Communication and Information, Nanyang Technological University (NTU), Singapore. With an MSc in biological sciences, her research interests include cancer and genetics, digital health, health communication, and health literacy.

Routledge Studies in Science, Technology and Society

50 **The Policies and Politics of Interdisciplinary Research**
Nanomedicine in France and in the United States
Séverine Louvel

51 **Public Communication of Research Universities**
'Arms Race' for Visibility or Science Substance?
Marta Entradas, Martin W. Bauer

52 **Emotion in the Digital Age**
Technologies, Data and Psychosocial Life
Darren Ellis, Ian Tucker

53 **Distributed Perception**
Resonances and Axiologies
Natasha Lushetich, Iain Campbell

54 **Rousseau and the Future of Freedom**
Science, Technology and the Nature of Authority
Eric Deibel

55 **The Socio-Material Construction of Users**
3D Printing and the Digitalization of the Prosthetics Industry
David Seibt

56 **How Citizens View Science Communication**
Pathways to Knowledge
Carolina Moreno-Castro, Aneta Krzewińska and Małgorzata Dzimińska

57 **The Color of Precision Medicine**
Shirley Sun and Zoe Ong

For the full list of books in the series: www.routledge.com/Routledge-Studies-in-Science-Technology-and-Society/book-series/SE0054

The Color of Precision Medicine

Shirley Sun and Zoe Ong

LONDON AND NEW YORK

First published 2024
by Routledge
4 Park Square, Milton Park, Abingdon, Oxon, OX14 4RN

and by Routledge
605 Third Avenue, New York, NY 10158

Routledge is an imprint of the Taylor & Francis Group, an informa business

© 2024 Shirley Sun and Zoe Ong

The right of Shirley Sun and Zoe Ong to be identified as author of this work has been asserted in accordance with sections 77 and 78 of the Copyright, Designs and Patents Act 1988.

All rights reserved. No part of this book may be reprinted or reproduced or utilised in any form or by any electronic, mechanical, or other means, now known or hereafter invented, including photocopying and recording, or in any information storage or retrieval system, without permission in writing from the publishers.

Trademark notice: Product or corporate names may be trademarks or registered trademarks, and are used only for identification and explanation without intent to infringe.

British Library Cataloguing-in-Publication Data
A catalogue record for this book is available from the British Library

Library of Congress Cataloging-in-Publication Data
Names: Sun, Shirley Hsiao-Li, author. | Ong, Zoe, author.
Title: The color of precision medicine / Shirley Sun and Zoe Ong.
Other titles: Routledge studies in science, technology, and society
Description: Abingdon, Oxon ; New York : Routledge, 2024. | Series: Routledge studies in science, technology and society | Includes bibliographical references and index. | Contents: Using race to overcome race : an inherent contradiction in precision medicine — Trans-national colors : race, ethnicity and genomic science in the United States of America, Canada and Singapore — The "relative resources" model : heterogeneity of resources and the racialization of precision medicine — Pharmacogenetic/pharmacogenomic drug toxicity studies, race/ethnicity and managing adverse drug reactions in the clinic : ongoing tensions.
Identifiers: LCCN 2023055436 (print) | LCCN 2023055437 (ebook) | ISBN 9781032565583 (hardback) | ISBN 9781032565637 (paperback) | ISBN 9781003436102 (ebook)
Subjects: MESH: Precision Medicine | Race Factors
Classification: LCC R723 .S844 2024 (print) | LCC R723 (ebook) | NLM WB 102.7 | DDC 610.1—dc23/eng/20231220
LC record available at https://lccn.loc.gov/2023055436
LC ebook record available at https://lccn.loc.gov/2023055437

ISBN: 978-1-032-56558-3 (hbk)
ISBN: 978-1-032-56563-7 (pbk)
ISBN: 978-1-003-43610-2 (ebk)

DOI: 10.4324/9781003436102

Typeset in Galliard
by Apex CoVantage, LLC

For Our Global Families

Contents

Acknowledgments   xi

1 Introduction   1

Precision medicine (PM): A global phenomenon 1
What is precision medicine? Definitions, sites, and scale 2
Precision medicine as an alternative to race-based medicine 4
   What is race-based medicine and racial profiling in
      medicine? 4
   Problems with race-based medicine/racial profiling in
      medicine 5
   Is genome-based precision medicine really the answer? 6
Addressing the debate: Racialization as the key concept 6
   Racialization of national census categories 8
   Racialization in science (or, scientific racism) in colonial
      contexts 9
   Racialization of medicine in colonial contexts 10
   Racialization in medicine in contemporary times 12
In the (post-)genomic era: Racialization of human genomic
   science 14
What is the future of genome-based precision medicine? An
   empirical examination in cancer care in three postcolonial
   societies 17
Chapter outline 20

2 Using race to overcome race: An inherent contradiction in precision medicine   28

Introduction 28
Using race to overcome race: Understanding an inherent
   contradiction in translational precision medicine 33

viii *Contents*

    First domain: Searching for the genetic biomarker in
        scientific research 34
    Second domain: Recruiting suitable human subjects for
        clinical trials 37
    Third domain: Medical decision-making in the clinic 40
  Conclusion 43
  Notes: Coding of participants for table 1 45

3 **Transnational colors: Race, ethnicity, and genomic science in the United States of America, Canada, and Singapore**   49

  Introduction 49
  Is race biological or socially constructed? A brief overview 49
  Where and how does racialization happen in genomic
     science? 52
    Materials for racialization of a population sample and/or
        patient 52
    Issues with the different ways of racialization 55
  Perspectives from the genomic science community about the
     relationship between race and genetics 57
    Genetic differences between ethnoracial population
        groups 58
    No clear genetic distinction between ethnoracial
        population groups 58
    Genetic heterogeneity within an ethnoracial population
        group 59
    Race as a social construct 60
    If race is socially constructed, why are there differences
       in frequencies of genetic alleles between racial/ethnic
       groups? 62
    If not race, what drives human genomic diversity? 65
  Conclusion 66

4 **The "relative resources" model: Heterogeneity of resources and the racialization of precision medicine**   71

  Introduction 71
  The "personalized medicine" versus "racialized medicine"
     debate 71
  "Race is really the poor man's genomic test": The relative
     resources model 74

Financial resources 75
　　Human and informatics resources 78
　　Legal and infrastructural resources 80
　Implications of the relative resources model 82
　Conclusion 83

5 **Pharmacogenetic/pharmacogenomic drug toxicity studies, race/ethnicity, and managing adverse drug reactions in the clinic: Ongoing tensions**   88

　Introduction 88
　Examples of racialized pharmacogenomic studies in the US, Canada, and Singapore 89
　　Allopurinol 89
　　5-Fluorouracil (5-FU) 91
　　Cost-effectiveness studies, race/ethnicity, and precision medicine 92
　Who is Asian and who is Caucasian? 93
　Debating race/ethnicity-based pharmacogenetic toxicity data in the clinic 95
　　Subjective interpretation of drug toxicity risks 96
　　Toxicity is a multifactor phenomenon and is not just about genetics 97
　Pharmacogenetics/pharmacogenomics studies and pharmaceutical companies are at odds 98
　Conclusion 100

6 **Conclusion**   105

　What is known on the topics of race-based medicine, precision medicine, and the molecularization of race? 105
　What does this book add to the existing state of the art? 107
　What are the arguments and findings in each chapter? 109
　How might this study affect research, practice, or policy? 112
　　Research 112
　　Practice 113
　　Policy 114
　　Science communication by scientists and journalists 115
　　Medical education 116
　What should different stakeholders take away from this book? 116
　　Scientists 116

  Physicians/medical doctors 117
  Public policymakers 117
  Health economists 118
 What are the theoretical and empirical contributions of this book? 118
  On "racialization" 118
  On the nexus of relative resources and racialization of precision medicine 119
  On differential racialization 120
 What are the tensions with the usage of race/ethnicity in genomic science with medical and public health implications? 121
 What are some of the limitations of this study? 122
 What are some of the future research projects based on this book? 122

Appendix A	*128*
Appendix B	*132*
Index	*138*

Acknowledgments

We owe many people our utmost gratitude. The following paragraphs gratefully acknowledge just some of those colleagues and friends.

We appreciate very much the feedback of the manuscript we received from Francis Khek Gee Lim, Hallam Stevens, Ann Hui Ching, and Troy Duster. We are also grateful for the professional, constructive, and insightful comments of the editors and anonymous reviewers from the journals, including, but not limited to, *International Sociology*, *Science, Technology & Human Values*, *Science as Culture*, *Sociology of Health and Illness*, and *New Genetics and Society*.

Portions of this book were presented at a few conferences and seminars by the first author, and we are grateful for the questions and comments received. Partial draft of Chapter 2 was presented at the ELSI (ethical, legal, and social implications of genetics) seminar series, organized by Professor Paul Appelbaum, Center for Research on Ethical, Legal, and Social Implications of Genetics at Columbia University (October 2021). Partial draft of Chapter 3 was presented at the workshop "Post-truth politics and public health: Dis- and misinformation crises and media challenges" at Harvard University (March 2023), organized by Trisha Lin, professor of radio and television, National Chengchi University, Taiwan; and visiting scholar, Harvard-Yenching Institute 2022–2023. Chapter 4 was presented at Columbia University's Precision Medicine: Ethics, Politics, and Culture Project (PMEPC) seminar series in December 2019, co-organized by Professors Maya Sabatello and Gil Eyal. Draft of Chapter 5 was presented at the international symposium "Ordering the Human: Global Science and Racial Reason," organized by Professor Dorothy Roberts and held at the University of Pennsylvania (April 2018), as well as in a seminar titled "Precision Medicine, Race/Ethnicity, and Managing Adverse Drug Reactions in the Clinic," at the Institute for Society and Genetics, University of California–Los Angeles (March 2023).

We are also indebted to Professor Emeritus Troy Duster (UC–Berkeley and New York University) and Professor Aaron Panofsky at University of California–Los Angeles (UCLA) for their generous support of the first author's visiting research scholar position in 2023 at the Institute for Society and Genetics, UCLA, which facilitated the writing of this book.

Our appreciation also goes to the Singapore Ministry of Education and the College of Humanities, Arts, and Social Sciences at the Nanyang Technological University (NTU) for the research grant (AcRF Tier 1 grant RG161/17). We are very grateful for the superb research assistance provided by Ann Hui Ching, Pei Xuan Goh, Yanru Lek, Nadiya Nesseer, Nurul Zahidah Binte Abdullah, Hemavalli Padmanathan, Jin Yi Chua, Cheryl Ong Siew Bin, Lee Wen Ling Patricia, Atiqa Mashhood Dar, Lee Wen Xuan Trena, and Danny Chiam Yee Yeow.

Of course, this project would not have been possible without the generosity and kindness of the 46 physicians and scientists, and we thank them very much for sharing their rich experiences, views, and opinions, amid their extremely busy schedule. Last but not least, our heartfelt thanks go to our global family and friends, Alexander Sun, Francis Lim, Chen-Feng Shen, Bin Sun, Annie Park, Tony Park, Vickie Kuo, Randy Kuo, Becky Yeh, Jia Jia Teo, Yulan Wang, Troy Duster, Grace Hoe, Alex Li, Moses Li, Yanru Lek, May Lwin, and the late Maria Hsiao-Mei Liu.

1 Introduction

This book is about genetics, precision medicine, and race/ethnicity. Is race/ethnicity a useful proxy for genetics? Will genome-based precision medicine fix the problem of racial profiling in medicine? What are the implications of using race/ethnicity in human genome variation studies for patients – and society? We answer these questions and build new knowledge in the field of genomic science and precision medicine. Specifically, we define the concept of racialization of precision medicine as the social processes by which racial/ethnic categories are incorporated (or not) into the development, interpretation, and implementation of precision medicine research and practice. We seek to illuminate such processes by drawing on substantial primary data collected through semi-structured face-to-face interviews with practicing professionals (physicians and researchers) involved in cancer precision medicine in Asia (Singapore) and North America (United States and Canada).[1]

Precision medicine (PM): A global phenomenon

On 26 June 2000, it was announced at a White House event that a draft of the map of the entire human genome had been achieved. During this event, then-president of the United States Bill Clinton stated, "In coming years, doctors increasingly will be able to cure diseases like Alzheimer's, Parkinson's, diabetes and cancer by attacking their genetic roots," paving the way for the concept of precision medicine (National Human Genome Research Institute, 2000). At this time, Mr. Clinton also famously stated that "in genetic terms, all human beings, regardless of race, are more than 99.9 percent the same." His remark was echoed by Dr. Francis Collins, who said, "I'm happy that today, the only race we are talking about is the human race." The Human Genome Project, which started in 1990, was eventually declared completed in 2003 with the generation of an "essentially complete human genome sequence, which was significantly improved from the draft sequence" (National Human Genome Research Institute, 2022). The prospect of incorporating genomics into clinical practice has continued to attract significant attention and interest since then.

2 Introduction

In 2015, then-president of the United States Barack Obama scaled up the genomic transformation in healthcare when he launched the genome-based Precision Medicine Initiative with a USD 215 million government investment. He stated, "That's the promise of precision medicine – delivering the right treatments, at the right time, every time to the right person" (The White House Office of Press Secretary, 2015). While the precision medicine movement is arguably spearheaded by the United States, it has since become a global phenomenon. According to marketing research firm Market.us's estimate, the global precision medicine market size was USD 83.4 billion in 2022 and is projected to reach USD 254 billion by 2032 (Global Newswire, 2023). As Au and da Silva (2021: 193) noted,

> PM [Precision Medicine] is in the process of becoming a scientific bandwagon where large numbers of people, laboratories, and organizations commit their resources to one approach to a problem. . . . The PM scientific bandwagon is beginning to spread globally. . . . Actors in China and Brazil have launched their own PM initiatives, such as the Million Chinese Genomes Project (MCGP), the China Precision Medicine Project, and the Brazilian Precision Medicine Initiative (BPMI).

What is precision medicine? Definitions, sites, and scale

Genome-based precision medicine has transformed the practice of medicine from a "one-size-fits-all" approach to the use of DNA sequencing for individualized medical treatments. As Hunt and Kreiner (2013: 227) described, "The idea is that by scanning a person's genome, it will be possible to tailor health care based on the individual's genetic risk for developing various diseases, and their genetically governed reactions to specific medications." There is, however, no universal definition of precision medicine. In a broad sense, the US National Research Council defined it as such:

> An emerging approach for disease treatment and prevention that takes into account individual variability in genes, environment, and lifestyle for each person. It is in contrast to a one-size-fits-all approach, in which disease treatment and prevention strategies are developed for the average person, with less consideration for the differences between individuals.
> (Wang and Wang, 2023)

This definition considers not just treatment of a disease but also preventive health care. An initiative that reflects this broader definition of precision medicine is the "All of US" research program, which is a part of the US Precision Medicine Initiative launched in 2015, that aims to enroll over one million participants to share the data generated or captured over more than ten years from genome sequencing, electronic medical records, personal reported information, and digital health technologies (Ginsburg and Phillips, 2018).

In a narrow sense, precision medicine refers to "the use of genetic information about people and diseases for better targeted drug therapies" (Kohler, 2018). "The age of precision medicine is upon us," Dr. Ian McCaffery at the pharmaceutical company AbbVie has remarked, "where using genetic and other molecular data, and ultimately companion diagnostic tests, can help us target medicines to patients who we think could respond to them" (Abbvie, 2022). Indeed, precision medicine has already led to new US FDA-approved treatments, including in-vitro diagnostics, "that are tailored to specific characteristics of individuals, such as a person's genetic makeup, or the genetic profile of an individual's tumor" (U.S. Food and Drug Administration, 2018).

All over the world, a vast range of projects, initiatives, and collaborative programs in the field of precision medicine are currently underway or scheduled. In Canada, for example, the Canadian Institutes for Health Research (CIHR, 2023) has launched the Personalized Medicine Signature Initiative to "enhance health outcomes through patient stratification approaches by integrating evidence-based medicine and precision diagnostics into clinical practice." On the research front, GenomeCanada is a large-scale research initiative comprising several platforms which support a precision medicine structure. On one platform, The Terri Fox Research Institute, it is estimated that a total investment of $3 million was made in precision medicine research in 2021/2022 (Terri Fox Research Institute, n.d).

Similarly, major countries in the Asia-Pacific region, the fastest-growing precision medicine market in the world, are adopting DNA technologies in the healthcare settings at a rapid pace. According to the World Economic Forum (2017),

> nearly 40 countries have their own version of a precision medicine initiative, but, China's is the largest. The United States Precision Medicine Initiative started at $215 million in 2016. For every $1 the United States plans to spend on its initiative, China is spending $43.

The China Precision Medicine Project, which was announced in 2016, has an expected investment of RMB 60 billion yuan (or more than USD $9 billion) for research. As part of China's precision medicine efforts, a large-scale Chinese genome database derived from whole-genome sequencing data of 141,431 unrelated healthy Chinese individuals, the Chinese Millionome Database (CMDB), has been developed (Li et al., 2023).

In East and Southeast Asia, Singapore has also launched its National Precision Medicine strategy with precision medicine listed as part of the nation's Research, Innovation, and Enterprise (RIE) 2025 strategic goal that is aimed at transforming the nation's health care. This plan intends to accelerate biomedical research, improve health outcomes, and enhance opportunities for economic value across sectors. The government has set up Precision Health Research, Singapore (PRECISE), to coordinate its ten-year National Precision Medicine (NPM) strategy. The NPM strategy consists of three key phases.

4   *Introduction*

Phase One intends to lay the groundwork by establishing a 10,000 Singaporean reference database and partnering with industries as co-investors in the program. The genomes of 100,000 healthy Singaporeans and 50,000 persons with specific diseases will be generated in Phase Two, which will test the clinical use of precision medicine techniques and build data infrastructure for linking genetic data to electronic health records and other forms of data. In Phase Three, precision medicine will be implemented on a wide scale, with genetic data linked to clinical and lifestyle data to construct comprehensive Singapore-centric databases. Doctors and scientists are expected to be able to use these valuable resources to gain better knowledge of how illnesses emerge and find enhanced strategies to prevent and cure them in the long run (Precision Health Research, Singapore, 2023).

Precision medicine as an alternative to race-based medicine

In addition to improving on the traditional one-size-fits-all approach, precision medicine has been seen as an alternative to race-based medicine (Chakravarti, 2015). As Bonham et al. (2016: 2005) put it, "if the major challenges can be overcome, precision medicine could lead the way in reducing and ultimately eliminating the use of crude racial and ethnic census categories in drug prescribing." For instance, in research on warfarin pharmacogenomics in Asia, Chan et al. (2012: 317) discovered that "information from genetic testing is superior to clinical biomarkers and self-reported population/ethnic membership for predicting warfarin dose requirements."

What is race-based medicine and racial profiling in medicine?

When physicians use race/ethnicity as a proxy for a biological or medical trait to guide medical treatments for patients, they are practicing race-based medicine or engaging in the act of racial profiling in medicine. As Dorothy Roberts pointed out in a TEDMED talk titled "The problem with race-based medicine" (2018: 410), "race runs deeply throughout all of medical practice. It shapes physicians' diagnoses, measurements, treatment, prescriptions, even the very definition of diseases." Indeed, American psychiatrist Dr. Sally Satel made a public statement exemplifying this as the author of "I am a Racial Profiling Doctor" published in *The New York Times* (Satel, 2002).

> Almost every day at the Washington drug clinic where I work as a psychiatrist, race plays a useful diagnostic role. When I prescribe Prozac to a patient who is African-American, I start at a lower dose, 5 or 10 milligrams instead of the usual 10-to-20 milligram dose. I do this in part because clinical experience and pharmacological research show that blacks metabolize antidepressants more slowly than Caucasians and Asians.

Problems with race-based medicine/racial profiling in medicine

While racial profiling in medicine is pervasive, using race as a proxy for a patient's biological traits in medicine has resulted in substandard health care. One of the oft-cited examples is the misdiagnosis of a friend of Dr. Richard Garcia, a pediatrician:

> My childhood friend Lela wasn't diagnosed with cystic fibrosis until she was 8 years old. Over the years, her doctors had described her as a "2-year-old black female with fever and cough . . . 4-year-old black girl with another pneumonia." Had she been a white child, or had no visible "race" at all, she would probably have gotten the correct diagnosis and treatment much earlier. Only when she was eight did a radiologist, who had never seen her face to face, notice her chest radiograph and ask, "Who's the kid with CF?"
>
> (Garcia, 2004)

Another example is that autism in ethnic minority children tends to be misdiagnosed. For instance, unwillingness among Asian children to engage in direct eye contact has been attributed to autism by White doctors, whereas Black children's autism symptoms have been dismissed as behavioral problems (Waltz, 2011, 2013). More recently, in a webinar titled "Race and Genetics: Perspectives on Precision Medicine," Dr. Hilliard gave examples of two men dying from malaria in Africa, because physicians thought Black men had genetic protection against malaria and missed the opportunity to treat them properly (Baylor College of Medicine, 2023).

Moreover, broadly speaking, there is a wealth of literature on how "health care disparities arise from a complex interplay of economic, social, and cultural factors" (Adigbli, 2020; Chaturvedi and Eastwood, 2020; Ward et al., 2005; Edwards et al., 2020). Ward et al. (2005: 79), for example, suggested that

> socioeconomic factors influence cancer risk factors such as tobacco use, poor nutrition, physical inactivity, and obesity. Income, education, and health insurance coverage influence access to appropriate early detection, treatment and palliative care. Poor and minority communities are selectively targeted by the marketing strategies of tobacco companies, may have limited access to fresh foods and healthy nutrition, and are provided with fewer opportunities for safe recreational physical activity. . . . Cultural factors also play a role in health behaviors, attitudes toward illness.

This is particularly relevant in the field of cancer, with only 5–10% of all cancer cases attributed to genetic defects and 90–95% caused by environmental and lifestyle factors (Anand et al., 2008; Vijayvergia and Delinger, 2015). Fujimura and Rajagopalan (2011) suggested that there are more meaningful characteristics, such as social class and access to health care, than race/ethnicity to delineate a population in human genetic/genomic research concerning health and illness. Shostak and Moinester (2015) urged us to move beyond geneticization of health and take the social determinants of health seriously.

Race-based medicine and racial profiling in medicine have resulted in many problems well-documented in the literature, including but not limited to, diagnostic errors, differential treatments, lack of personalized medical treatment, prejudice toward and stereotyping of patients of color, racialized health disparities, lack of a holistic view of disease etiology, and misallocation of resources (Beal et al., 2006; Curtin et al., 2022; Epstein, 2007; Goodman and Brett, 2021). In recognition of these problems, there are currently efforts to move away from race-based medicine, with the United States at the forefront of this movement. In 2020, for example, the American Medical Association issued a policy statement titled "Elimination of Race as a Proxy for Ancestry, Genetics, and Biology in Medical Education, Research and Practice" (American Medical Association, 2020), emphasizing that race is socially constructed, rather than biologically determined. Similarly, in 2022, the American Academy of Pediatrics also issued a policy statement titled "Eliminating Race-Based Medicine" (Wright et al., 2022).

Is genome-based precision medicine really the answer?

As suggested previously, genome-based precision medicine is seen as a solution to the problem of race-based medicine. As Root (2003) put it:

> Given advances in genetic technology, physicians may soon have access to a patient's genetic transcript. Should she have his transcript, the doctor will not need to infer from his race or even his ancestry whether he is genetically disposed to certain diseases or respond better to medical treatments.

However, even when this technology is available, doctors may have access to some but not all patients' genetic profiles. To some scholars, race is a useful proxy for genetics, whereas to others, race does not correlate with genetic diversity (Adigbli, 2020; Callier, 2019; Caulfield et al., 2009; Edwards et al., 2020; Hernandez-Boussard et al., 2023; Krainc and Fuentes, 2022; Mamdani and Schwartz, 2020; Martschenko and Young, 2022; Mensah et al., 2019; Roman, 2022). To yet other scholars, race serves as a stepping stone to overall personalized treatment and individualized care tailored to one's socio-biological makeup (Wolinsky, 2011). So the debate regarding the role of race in medicine continues.

Addressing the debate: Racialization as the key concept

In order to address the debate surrounding the usage of race/ethnicity in the era of precision medicine, we believe that the concept of racialization is key. As Gonzalez-Sobrino and Goss (2019: 506) explained, the use of the concept of racialization was a way "not to reify the idea of race as biological or natural category, and to highlight the ways that racialization is corporeal and goes hand-in-hand with the creation of racial categories."

Racialization is defined differently by different authors (Murji and Solomos, 2005, 2014). For instance, Banton (1977: 18) utilized the concept of racialization narrowly to refer to the use of the idea of "race" to structure people's perceptions of the world's population. In comparison, Omi and Winant (1986: 13) defined racialization broadly as "the extension of racial meaning to a previously racially unclassified relationship, social practice, or group." Miles and Brown (2003: 101) focused on interactional occurrences and used the concept of racialization "to denote those instances where social relations between people have been structured by the signification of human biological characteristics in such a way as to defined and construct differentiated social collectivities." Finally, Lan (2005: 1) defined racialization as "a social process through which groups are marked by physical or cultural differences that become naturalized as essential" (p. 1, see also Lie, 2001). Each definition of racialization has its particular emphasis. For example, Omi and Winant's definition emphasizes racial meaning, while Miles and Brown's definition focuses on the relationship between biological features and social relations. As our study is particularly interested in the meaning attributed to race and ethnicity, we have combined the definitions provided by Omi and Winant (1986) and Lan (2005). That is, we draw on the concept of racialization as social processes and practices through which stratified others/racial categories are created and/or become essentialized, as well as the extension of racial meaning into previously race-neutral social processes and practices.

Baluran (2023) further developed the notion of "differential racialization," referring to

> the discordance between existing "official" understandings of group membership . . . and how these understandings are remolded and deployed to classify people in social interactions. At the micro-level, differential racialization refers to the process whereby individuals do away with the existing national-level and state-recognized racial-ethnic taxonomy in exchange for one that draws on national as well as localized understandings of racial-ethnic boundaries to assess and classify others', and their own, racial group membership.
>
> (p. 220–221)

Baluran's (2023) analysis points to the importance of level of analysis (e.g., individual, group, state, international) in providing a more nuanced understanding of racialization.

In this book, conceptually, we define the racialization of precision medicine as the social processes by which racial/ethnic categories are incorporated into the development, interpretation, and implementation of precision medicine research and practice. Empirically, we examine how scientists and clinicians

8 *Introduction*

think about race and how racial meanings are attached (or not) to a series of practices – genomic studies, clinical trials, and medical decision-making – in the context of precision medicine. That said, the process of racialization started before the genomic era, and we will now turn to these earlier developments.

Racialization of national census categories

One of the ways that racialization occurs is with national census categories. The racialized national census can influence scientific research and medical practice. Race is often a component of national census categories, but it is socially constructed and its meaning changes over time. As Ossorio and Duster (2005: 119) put it, "race is a complex but empirically demonstrable stratifying practice that creates identity and hierarchy through social interaction." A clear example is the changing definition of "White" in the United States. Irish and Jewish persons were not considered White prior to World War II but were accepted as being White later on (Lopez, 2006). Almaguer (2012: 146) also noted that, in the 1930s, the Mexican population "were summarily removed from the White category and placed in a separate racial designation as 'Mexican' . . . but by 1940 . . . the Mexican population was once again redefined as part of the 'White' population." Various racial categories were introduced into the censuses of countries at different historical points. For instance, "Hispanic or Latino" was not offered as a racial category until the 2000 US census. Rumbaut (2009: 16–17) noted that

> the groups subsumed under that label [i.e. Hispanic or Latino] – Mexicans, Puerto Ricans, Cubans, Dominicans, Salvadorans, Guatemalans, Colombians, Peruvians, Ecuadorians, and the other dozen nationalities from Latin American and even Spain itself – were not "Hispanics or Latinos" in their countries of origin; rather, they only became so in the United States.

Historically, if a child was biracial, the US administration assigned the paternal race to the child (Beal et al., 2006).

The ways in which race and racialization operate may vary, for example, in the United States versus in Canada and Singapore. Moreover, these racial/ethnic categories are not commensurable across different settings. For instance, in Canada, the language of race has been avoided in the Canadian census; instead, the term used is "visible minority." Equality rights and a commitment to multiculturalism were enshrined in the Canadian Charter of Rights and Freedoms in 1982, followed by a Special Committee on the Status of Visible Minorities in Canadian Society in 1983. The Employment Equity Act in 1986 defines visible minority as "persons, other than aboriginal peoples, who are non-Caucasian in race and non-White in colour." In 2007, the United Nations Committee on the Elimination of Racial Discrimination recorded concern that the term implied whiteness as the norm and therefore constructed racial minorities as the perpetual other. The term "visible minority" also assumed that non-Whites were equally racialized (Thompson, 2013).

In Southeast Asia, the Republic of Singapore is a city-state of slightly over 710 square kilometers located near the bottom of Peninsula Malaysia. According to PuruShotam (1998), the first census in Singapore, produced in 1871, consisted of 33 ethnic categories:

> Europeans and Americans, Armenians, Jews, Eurasians, Abyssinians, Achinese, Africans, Andamese, Arabs, Bengalis and other natives of India not particularized, Boyanese, Bugis, Burmese, Chinese, Cochin Chinese, Dyaks, Hindoos, Japanese, Javanese, Jaweepekans, Klings, Malays, Manilamen, Mantras, Parsees, Persians, Siamese, Singhalese, Military – British, Military – Indian, Prisoners – Local, Prisoners – Transmarine.
> (PuruShotam, 1998: 61)

In the census of 1881, a decade later, there were 47 ethnic categories. These categories were

> reclassified . . . under six main categories . . . these six categories were "European and Americans," "Eurasians," "Chinese," "Malays and Other Natives of the Archipelago," "Tamils and other natives of India," and "Other Nationalities." Once instituted in this way, these six divisions were retained in this form for the following two censuses.
> (PuruShotam, 1998: 61–62)

The censuses of 1921 and 1931, which identified 56 and over 70 races respectively. It should also be noted that with the exception of "Eurasians," further differentiations were made in all five other race categories. Comparing Singapore and Malaysia, Daniel Goh (2019: 192) suggested that "patronage multiracialism was institutionalized in Malaysia, and corporatist multi-racialism in Singapore, aligned with economic policy to promote *bumiputra* and statist capital accumulation respectively." The Singapore census eventually evolved to have only four race categories – Chinese, Malay, Indians, and Others. As of June 2023, over a third of Singapore's 5.9 million population are noncitizens. Among the citizen population, 75.6% are Chinese, 15.1% are Malays, 7.6% are Indians, and 1.7% are Others (Department of Statistics, Ministry of Trade and Industry, Singapore, 2023).

In short, the introduction of race/ethnic categories into the national census in some countries has resulted in the racialization of the national census. The racialization of national census categories is driven by the prevailing sociopolitical climate – as the sociopolitical climate changes over time, the race categories available in the national census also change.

Racialization in science (or, scientific racism) in colonial contexts

It is important to be aware that, "prior to the advent of racial slavery in the colonial Americas, the concept of race – defined as a way to divide and rank peoples of the world – does not exist in Europe. The primary measure of difference is religion" (Goodman et al., 2012).

The idea of race – that there exist, in the natural world, human population groups marked by biological and thus innate differences – originated in Europe. Or as Goodman et al. (2012: 10) put it, race is "a system of ideas, identities, and material relations that emerged slowly in the context of Western European imperialism and colonial expansion beginning in the 15th century."

The notion of race shaped scientific research by influencing how scientists saw and interpreted the world. According to Miles and Brown (2003: 39), starting in the eighteenth century, "'race' increasingly came to refer to a biological type of human being, and science purported to demonstrate the number and characteristics of each 'race', and a hierarchical relationship between them." For example, in 1758, Carolus Linnaeus published *Systema Naturae*, in which he classified four basic races of humans (i.e., American, European, Asian, and African) and attributed behavioral traits to each race (Goodman et al., 2012: 20). Linnaeus' classification has remained influential since its invention. Indeed, ever since the invention of the idea of race, there have been numerous attempts in the field of science to find empirical evidence trying to prove that racial groups were biologically determined and that being "White" was biologically superior; this is a phenomenon known as "scientific racism." Prominent examples of racism in the scientific fields include, but are not limited to, craniology and phrenology, polygenism, and the measurement of human intelligence via the socially constructed IQ scores. Such attempts have been discredited by careful scientific studies. For example, in relation to craniology, or the study of human skulls, Boas (1912) reported significant changes in cranial shape and size between Italian and Jewish immigrants and their United States–born children and revealed that cranial development was responsive to environmental conditions (as opposed to being a stable type due to heredity). Gould (1982) also showed the biases and errors of the statistical measurement of human intelligence by race.

In short, the racialization of science started with colonial expansion. Scientific racism spreads the idea of innate biological differences between racial groups, with some of such studies reinforcing such differences. But it is important to remember, as geneticist Richard Lewontin reminds us, that "race was imported into science from social practice and not vice versa" (Goodman et al., 2012: 26).

Racialization of medicine in colonial contexts

The formation of racial categories and groups is a function of the social process of "Othering" (Said, 2003), and medicine plays an important role in this process. As McCleery (2015: 155) put it, "modern colonial medicine is seen as a tool enabling colonization; a method of creating 'others' in the colonies and of 'othering' the colony itself." Suggesting the term "race-medicine" as a complement to the more familiar "race-science," Suman Seth argued that historians should look beyond European scientists and toward colonial medical practitioners in the eighteenth century to understand the development of racial theories (Seth, 2018). To that end, Seth traced a shift from medical discourses that emphasized the importance of environment to theories that relied increasingly on racial difference during the latter decades of the eighteenth century. Skin color, in other words, became a causal rather than correlational factor in medical assessments of health and illness in the eighteenth century. Seth argued that this change from place to race in medical texts demonstrates the importance of colonial medicine to emerging conceptions of race in the British Empire. In postcolonial contexts, one example of race-based medicine is how Black men in the USA who protested against social injustice were more often diagnosed with the psychotic disorder of schizophrenia, which was often associated with violence (Sebring, 2021).

Racial categories have also been used by social actors to determine access to medical resources. As Amster (2022: E709–E710) observed, "In a colonial health care system, race is the basis for resource allocation. . . . Race-based medicine produced segregated hospitals – well-funded, modern hospitals for colonizers and underfunded, inferior hospitals for the colonized." Examples of such could be seen in America where the segregation of all lepers was mandated under the Leprosy Repression Act of 1891. This act, however, was exercised differently for Black and White leprosy patients, with the difference in treatment justified using racial and cultural differences that seemingly affected the occurrence of this disease (Deacon, 2000). Physicians advocated that White leprosy patients could benefit more from home segregation with the help of their family rather than being institutionalized, as Black leprosy patients were, since exposure to the unfavorable climate of the colony resulted in White leprosy patients being more susceptible to severe forms of leprosy that tended to affect them psychologically rather than physically (Deacon, 2000).

In Canada, Johnson (2012: ii) argued that

> the racialization of medicine began as early as 1707 with the colonial writings of British physician Hans Sloane. While this initial racialization process did not overtly express any value judgements, it did suggest that Negros should be treated differently – if only in medical terms.

Another example of racialization of medicine in Canada is how tuberculosis was believed to be hereditary in aboriginal communities, and this belief was used to account for First Nations' high infection and death rates. Physicians and officials were convinced that "simply being an Aboriginal person meant one was inherently susceptible to tuberculosis" (McMillen, 2021: 1666).

The racialization of illness and medicine also happened in the Asian region. In British Malaya, Asians were seen by colonial administrators as biologically inferior to Europeans and more susceptible to tuberculosis. Moreover, different "races" at that time were believed to have different levels of immunity towards the disease. The Chinese "race," for instance, were subcategorized into Straits Chinese and Mainland China–born Chinese. The elite Straits Chinese were seen as resistant toward the disease (Loh and Hsu, 2020). In India, local Indians were not only seen as carriers of diseases but also were deemed more susceptible to mental illnesses as a result of their racial inferiority, which rendered their mental capacity poorer compared to Europeans (Levine, 1994; Chatterjee, 2015). Under the Spanish Empire, smallpox was deadly for some subgroups of the Filipino population (such as those located in the Bicol region), and the colonizers believed that this was because they had a naturally racially low immunity to the smallpox (Newson, 2011).

As we have shown through the various examples noted in the previous section, similar to the racialization of science, the racialization of medicine occurred during colonial times. Consequently, the practice of medicine, which was originally race-neutral, became imbued with racial meaning.

Racialization in medicine in contemporary times

Race was introduced to the US medical curriculum by Benjamin Rush in 1790, including the notion that blackness was a distinct type of leprosy (Ioannidis et al., 2021). To this day, race is still deeply ingrained in medical practices, with clinicians still assessing a patient's disease risk and selecting appropriate treatment options based on race. In fact, clinicians are taught to consider a patient's racial and ethnic identity. For example, in Hunt and Kreiner's (2013: 231–232) study, 86% of clinicians interviewed mentioned that they were taught to prescribe anti-hypertensive medicine differently based on a patient's race, and most of them did as told (p. 231–232). In addition, Smart and Weiner (2018) have shown that clinical guidelines factor in an individual's race and thus contribute to physicians' differential recommendations for treatment based on race. In medical school training, the frequent use of racial classifications for population stratification found in study materials has allowed for the cultivation of a mindset that utilizes race as a diagnostic shortcut (Anderson, 2008; Brooks, 2015). The following are a few examples of the ways race has been used as a proxy in the context of postcolonial modern medicine.

Duffy antibody

Race was used as a proxy for antibodies in the blood. It was believed that there was a difference in the distribution of Duffy antibody alleles amongst those of African and European descent, which resulted in a recommendation for ranking order of preferred blood donors. One of the preferences was for "compatible blood from donors of the same ethnic group as the patient's" (Kenny, 2006: 461). This policy was heavily criticized and finally removed (Kenny, 2006).

Risk estimation of hyperbilirubinemia

Maternal medical race records, based on the mother's assigned race, were used to predict the risk of hyperbilirubinemia in newborns, with African Americans deemed to be at the lowest risk (Beal et al., 2006). However, Beal et al. (2006)

found that "For numerous mothers in each category of race, medical record-documented race differs from [the] mother['s] self-reported race" (p. 7):

> Of mothers documented as white in the medical record, only 64% self-reported as white, whereas 13% self-reported as Hispanic, 3% Middle Eastern, and 11% as more than or equal to 2 races. Of 427 mothers documented as black in the medical record, 70% self-reported as black and 23% as more than or equal to 2 races. We also found poor agreement between medical record-documented and mother self-reported race in the Asian and Middle Eastern categories (only 35% and 50% agreement, respectively).

This discrepancy highlights one of the many issues with race-based medicine. Moreover, when we consider how national census racial categories change over the course of time (as we have discussed previously), this also calls into question how accurate or reliable race-based approach is. For example, how were maternal records of Hispanics before the year 2000 filed? Newborns may not be properly diagnosed for hyperbilirubinemia as a result of race-based medicine.

While healthcare professionals' explicit racial/ethnic biases are now being challenged or removed in medical practice, their implicit biases are much more difficult to spot and manage. Under what conditions are implicit racial biases against patients most likely to occur? Studies in the United States show that physicians' implicit biases influence judgement in high-stress environments such as in emergency departments (Dehon et al., 2017). A systematic review published in Academic Emergency Medicine examining studies using the Implicit Bias test found that medical providers tend to be biased towards White patients, regardless of specialty. Patients of color were more likely to have longer waiting times and less likely to be admitted compared to White patients (Dehon et al., 2017). Black patients are also less likely to receive electrocardiographs and chest x-rays if suspected to have Acute Coronary Syndrome (ACS), while those who do are less likely to receive immediate care (Pezzin et al., 2007; Musey et al., 2016). Emergency medicine and internal medicine residents who showed an implicit bias for White patients were also more likely to treat them over Black patients with thrombolysis for myocardial infarction (Dehon et al., 2017). In short, racial profiling in clinical care is not uncommon even in contemporary times.

When the implicit bias is built into the machine

Problems with race-based medicine go beyond the level of physicians using race as a proxy, as some biomedical tools – for example, diagnostic algorithms – are already designed to take into account the patient's race; this is alternatively known as "race correction." For example, the American College of Cardiology's Cardiovascular Disease Risk Estimator (a clinical tool to help doctors

14 *Introduction*

prescribe anti-cholesterol medication) has differing risk estimations for African Americans, Whites, and Others (Beal et al., 2006).

In addition, spirometry is a medical tool that is frequently used for diagnosis and treatment of various respiratory diseases, as well as identifying chronic obstructive respiratory disease (Braun, 2015). Lundy Braun discovered that operators were sometimes unaware that the spirometry has been racialized since race as a variable was added by the manufacturer. It is known that there are differences in lung function depending on the time, geographical region, between populations, and between individuals. Due to this, standardization practices are put in place to adjust for these differences (Braun, 2015). One such standardized, but problematic, practice is "race correction" or "ethnic adjustment" wherein spirometers use "a scaling factor for all the people not considered to be 'White' or by applying population specific norms" (Braun, 2015: 99–101). In such "race correction" or "ethnic adjustment," the operator must select the race of the individual by either asking them or by guessing.

As with lung function, race is used as a proxy for muscle mass in nephrology to measure kidney function (Tsai, 2018), specifically the estimated Glomerular Filtration Rate (eGFR). Using a mathematical equation, the amount of creatinine can be measured. Creatinine is a waste product produced by normal wear and tear of the body's muscles as well as from food consumption. This mathematical equation, the Chronic Kidney Disease Epidemiology Collaboration (CKD-EPI), includes a race correction for African Americans based on research indicating that they have higher levels of creatinine in their blood, possibly attributed to their increased muscle mass (Cerdeña et al., 2020; Roberts, 2021). In spite of proponents of the equation warning that eliminating race adjustment in estimating glomerular filtrate rate (eGFR) might lead to overdiagnosis and overtreatment of African American patients, the reverse is also true: race adjustments can delay specialist care or transplantation and lead to a worse outcome when there are already higher rates of end-stage kidney disease and kidney failure in the African American community than in the general population (Vyas et al., 2020).

In sum, race-based medicine takes many forms, including but not limited to, physicians' implicit or explicit bias, systemic racism influencing healthcare providers' judgement, and algorithm biases (e.g., Adigbli, 2020; Bayne et al., 2023; Geneviève et al., 2020; Hernandez-Boussard et al., 2023). However, as Hunt and Kreiner (2013: 226) warned, whatever the cause, when patients receive medication based on the presumption of racial and ethnic identity instead of individualized care which considers their specific situations and needs, it will result in suboptimal health care and "essentialized racial/ethnic identity."

In the (post-)genomic era: Racialization of human genomic science

Despite the advent of genomic technology, race is still frequently used as a means of classification in human genetics/genomics research (e.g., Ferryman, 2023; James et al., 2021). Its role was discussed in Phimister (2003): "it seems unwise to abandon the practice of recording race when we have barely begun to understand the architecture of the human genome." Even when genome-based studies were conducted in a race-neutral setting, race/ethnicity remained to be used as a classification tool in analyzing and presenting results (Prainsack, 2015; Weigmann, 2006). This has led to race being re-inscribed as a biological entity at the molecular level (Phelan et al., 2013). The persistence of using race can be attributed in part to its ability to serve as a "residual category" that are used to account for differences in drug efficacy between populations that genetics cannot capture (Kahn, 2004), but there are also other larger social forces outside of scientific practices.

For instance, continued use of racial categories in science is also motivated by ideas of representativeness and social justice (Schaefer et al., 2020). As Morning (2011) showed, while social scientists view race/ethnicity as a social construct, some scientists in the field of biomedical and life sciences do not necessarily agree. Those from the biomedical sciences who argue that race/ethnicity is meaningful often emphasize on inclusivity and, in fact, are usually people of color. Burchard (Burchard et al., 2003), for example, is convinced that racial and ethnic differences are biologically meaningful and is relevant in the causes and expression of diseases. In sharp contrast, medical ethnographers are concerned that such racially, ethnically based inclusion of human subjects in human genetics/genomic research may, ironically, recreate the medical exclusions (Outram et al., 2022).

There are also various types of activism that aim to ensure that women and minorities are included in medical research in the United States (Epstein, 2007). Such activism has resulted in policies governing the use of racial/ethnic categories in genetic research (Duster, 2006; Fullwiley, 2007; Roberts, 2008), such as the 1993 National Institute of Health (NIH) Revitalization Act. This act mandates that women and minorities be included as participants in any NIH-funded clinical studies. The purpose of these guidelines is to guarantee that everyone, regardless of sex/gender or race/ethnicity, benefits fully from biological discoveries (Geller et al., 2018). Though such policies were initially intended to increase minority participation in clinical research and reduce racial disparities in health, they have, ironically, encouraged the framing of studies and findings along racial/ethnic lines. This, in turn, encouraged the belief that racial inequalities in health may be traced back to genetic differences (Duster, [1990] 2003, 2006; Fullwiley, 2007; Roberts, 2011). Moreover, race and ethnicity continue to be a basis for bioscientific discoveries, and such racialized/ethnicized data is normalized through subsequent research designs (Montoya, 2011).

Indeed, institutional forces shape the way genomic science research is conducted. An ethnographic study by Fujimura and Rajagopalan (2011) engaging with geneticists conducting genome-wide association studies (GWAS) using EIGENSTRAT technology to find genetic markers for disease showed that some geneticists agree with the critique on race and thus attempt to avoid that use of race categories. However, the study concluded that

> scientists make decisions about how to do the research based on their assessments of scientific accuracy, new technologies, disciplinary

commitments, political expediency, and personal politics. Although we have identified new actors . . . working to avoid the use of race categories in biomedical genetics research, it is not clear how much they can change the *institutionalized and historical practices within the larger assemblage.*
(Fujimura and Rajagopalan, 2011: 22, emphasis ours)

Market forces also contribute to the persistence of race in genomic science. In *The Genealogy of a Gene*, Jackson (2015) discussed the debates surrounding the use of race/ethnicity in population-based genomic studies. He provided perspectives from both camps of the debate, namely, the essentialists (those who believe that race is biological) and constructivists (those who believe that race is a social construct). He also acknowledged the good intentions of government initiatives (FDA and NIH policies to include race/ethnicity in research) but noted that this use of race/ethnicity can become problematic when companies and Big Pharma use race to market their product. This is especially so when "private interests are increasingly determining how scientific knowledge is constructed" (Jackson, 2015: 187). Pharmaceutical companies initially viewed FDA requirements as "unwarranted meddling of the government in private industrial affairs" (Jackson, 2015: 163). However, these drug companies became compliant after realizing the potential of using race to generate new markets. Also, pharmaceutical companies now can offer legitimate excuses to not cut the costs of prescription drugs because "one size does not fit all" (Jackson, 2015: 165). Similarly, Caulfield (2011) identified market pressures as one of the dominant forces that reinforce biological views of race, as pharmaceutical companies are inclined to use an existing classification system that generates the largest market.

Political factors also have a role in the persistence of racial/ethnic categories in precision medicine. Through attribution of variations in health status to genetics rather than socioeconomic or societal factors, governmental responsibilities can be reduced (Prainsack, 2015). Furthermore, an increasing number of governments throughout the world (including Mexico and India) are asserting genomic sovereignty over their citizens' DNA. Some countries argue that establishing genomic sovereignty prevents bio-piracy by the pharmaceutical business. However, referring to a country's genomes as physiologically unique from those of others further institutionalizes biological meanings of racial/ethnic labels (Benjamin, 2009; Duster, 2015).

The use of race as a temporary proxy for genetics by multiple stakeholders in precision medicine (Fullwiley, 2007; Rajagopalan and Fujimura, 2012) has allowed for the geneticization of race and ethnicity (Wade, 2017). However, "it is possible to make arbitrary groupings of populations defined by geography, language, self-identified faiths, other identified physiognomy and so on and still find statistically significant allelic variations between these groupings" (Duster, 2006: 434). This is seen in Takezawa et al.'s (2014: 3) study wherein it is described that "even among mainland Japanese, statistically meaningful genetic differentiation was found among individuals in different regions, such as Tohoku, Kanto, Kinki, and Kyushu." Hence, it is inaccurate and unreliable to infer that allelic frequency variations represent intrinsic biological distinctions across racial or ethnic populations.

If people believe that race/ethnicity is biologically real or genetically determined, then such belief is real in its consequences. Simon Crompton (2007) described the tendency among physicians to believe that sickle cell anemia is prevalent among African Americans because of genetics. However, studies have shown that the specific gene that predisposes an individual to sickle cell anemia is common among diverse ethnic groups, including Latin Americans, Indians, Greeks, and Italians. Another example is the prenatal genetic tests offered to prospective parents. Amy Harmon (2004) described the problems that Karen Coveler, an Ashkenazi Jew, encountered. Karen Coveler's doctor prescribed a total of ten genetic tests to her on the basis of her ethnicity to determine if there was a risk of her child inheriting a particular disease. All of these tests turned out to be negative, but her child was born deaf. Though tests are certainly available to assess the genetic predisposition to deafness, Ms. Coveler was not offered any tests outside of the ten "ethnically based" ones. This case suggests that the decision to limit genetic tests for individuals on the basis of ethnicity is unsound.

The continued use of racial categories in human genomic research and medicine also has resulted in unintended social consequences in non-medical aspects of society, including, but not limited to identity politics (Nelson, 2008, 2016; TallBear, 2013; Roth and Ivemark, 2018) and patent applications and approvals (Kahn, 2017).

What is the future of genome-based precision medicine? An empirical examination in cancer care in three postcolonial societies

Precision medicine is becoming an increasingly significant part of the healthcare system globally. A core component that is rapidly evolving in precision medicine is pharmacogenomics (Gammal et al., 2021; Kisor and Farrell, 2019), which is the utilization of a patient's genome to determine the most effective medication while minimizing the risk of adverse drug reactions (Kisor and Farrell, 2019). Scientific and clinical efforts in pharmacokinetics and pharmacodynamics have enabled genetic testing to be adopted into standard clinical practice in oncology and molecular oncology, resulting in wide adoption of pharmacogenomics in the field of cancer care (Raheem et al., 2020).

The current model of the precision oncology practice are molecular tumor boards that serve as a pathway for the clinical implementation of genomic medicine (Raheem et al., 2020, Walko et al., 2016). These molecular tumor boards include individuals from many disciplines, who will interpret the results of next-generation sequencing and study tumor cases at the molecular level, directing patient-specific targeted therapy. Oncology provides a unique opportunity for precision medicine with somatic mutations being both causes of cancer and therapeutic targets (Kolesar and Vermeulen, 2021; Walko et al., 2016). These targeted therapies have been shown in clinical trials to be more effective and less harmful than traditional chemotherapy (Kolesar and Vermeulen, 2021). In a study by Walko et al. (2016), patients with lung cancer with an activating mutation in the epidermal growth factor receptor (EGFR) have the option of being treated with EGFR inhibitors, which is a form of targeted therapy. These EGFR inhibitors were both more effective and less toxic than the standard cytotoxic chemotherapy.

What does race/ethnicity have to do with genome-based precision medicine? The common reason cited for the persistent reliance on race in scientific research and medicine despite claims of genome-based precision medicine is the high cost of genetic sequencing (Schwarze et al., 2020). While genomics presents an alternative to understanding and managing human health, the high costs associated with it can be prohibitive. However, as genomic technology continues to advance and costs of genetic sequencing continue to lower, personalized precision medicine tailored to an individual's unique genetic profile seems to be becoming closer to reality. This raises questions such as: What is the future of precision medicine? Will it truly be personalized or continue to be ethnoracialized? We attempt to provide answers to these questions by engaging with practitioners in cancer precision medicine from US, Canada, and Singapore. The majority of existing studies of precision medicine have been single-country studies (Reardon, 2022; Ackerman, 2022; Darling et al., 2022; Gordon and Koenig, 2022; James and Joseph, 2022; Outram et al., 2022; Rapp and Outram, 2022; Hedgecoe, 2004; Ong, 2016). However, given the global scale of genomic science and precision medicine, we believe it is important to understand clinicians' experiences in different settings. As such, we used qualitative research methods, specifically, semi-structured interviews, to provide contexts and grounded understanding of the clinicians' views and opinions, in places where precision medicine is more advanced (the USA and Canada), and those to which it has disseminated (i.e., Singapore).

We aim to evaluate the promise and claim by proponents of precision medicine that advances in genomics will replace the harmful practices of race-based medicine and race/ethnicity-adjusted algorithms to decide on how to best treat a patient. By integrating an individual's genomic information in making medical decisions about clinical care, precision medicine proponents argue that race is no longer needed. In this book, we argue that, in the genomic era, the "molecular reinscription of race" is only half the story; the other half is racialization of precision medicine.

While conceptions of race are socially constructed and context-dependent, the public perception of race as having biological roots persists, despite decades of work disproving the biological determinism of race. As noted earlier and as will be demonstrated later in our interview data, geneticists contribute to such perception through the usage of race in human genetic/genomic studies, in what has been termed the "molecular reinscription of race" (Duster, 2006), "molecularization of race" (Fullwiley, 2015), and the "biomedicalization" of race (Bliss, 2015) in the existing literature. Drawing on semi-structured interviews, we put forth the relative resources theory and make the argument that whether, when, and how race/ethnicity is used in medicine is a function of the relative resources available and accessible to the physicians and the patients.

We present data on how researchers think about various racial/ethnic categories, including but not limited to "Asian," "Caucasian," "Chinese," "African American," and "Hispanic/Latino." Of note, although race and ethnicity are, by definition, different concepts (Sheldon and Parker, 1992), we have used them interchangeably in this book. According to Sheldon and Parker (1992: 105), race is a "biological concept which categorizes humanity by means of sets of phenotypical features that appear to distinguish between varieties of people and are passed on between generations" and "indicates differences between people or groups which are fixed and imposed from outside," whereas ethnicity "refers more to shared cultural characteristics and national identity," with "notions of self-definition and group identification defined from within." However, our interviewees generally used these two terms interchangeably. In many instances, for example, interviewees may refer to the race "Asian" (Goodman et al., 2012) as "ethnicity" instead. To understand whether there are implicit differences in our interviewees' perception of "race" and "ethnicity," we analyzed when each term is used by our interviewees. Our analysis revealed that differences in the use of these terms occurred in the context of describing population *strata*: when only one level of stratification is required, "race" and "ethnicity" are used interchangeably, but when more than one level of stratification is necessary, ethnicity tends to be used as a lower-level category. Nonetheless, given that "race" and "ethnicity" are generally used interchangeably by our interviewees, we use "race" and "ethnicity" interchangeably as well in this book.

What are the implications of using race/ethnicity in genome-based precision medicine? In this book, we show that the racialization of precision medicine, due to broader societal and financial constraints, contributes to the persistence of racial profiling in medicine.

What, then, can stakeholders – that is, clinicians as healthcare providers, scientists as influencers and public health policymakers (including health economists) as governors – do to help physicians practice personalized precision medicine and avoid racialized precision medicine? We delineate the various solutions required to implement personalized precision medicine in the clinic to achieve its fullest promise. In the following chapters, we focus on the novel setting of clinical care for cancer to highlight voices of physicians and clinicians treating patients as well as propose and articulate a new conceptual framework – the relative resources model – to understand the social conditions under which precision medicine will be personalized. We communicate directly to stakeholders and discuss topics of interest to these stakeholders in separate chapters.

Chapter outline

To recap, in this chapter, we have introduced the problem of racial profiling in medicine and provided a brief history of the racialization of science and medicine. We have also articulated the promise of precision medicine to fix the problem of racial profiling in medicine in the genomic era.

In Chapter 2, we address the question "why racialization happens" and demonstrate that there is an inherent contradiction regarding the usage of race/ethnicity from bench to bedside in precision medicine. In Chapter 3, we focus on "how racialization happens" and elaborate on the idea of differential racialization in precision medicine and the implications of such differential racialization. In Chapter 4, we propose the relative resources theory to explain when and why racialization of precision medicine happens and to articulate the social conditions under which patients are more likely to receive personalized precision medicine, as opposed to racialized precision medicine, in cancer treatment. In Chapter 5, we explore the racialization of pharmacogenetic/pharmacogenomic studies and cost-effectiveness studies concerning drug toxicity (as opposed to the issue of drug efficacy in the previous chapters) and delineate the controversial role of using race and ethnicity in the domain of medical decision-making concerning adverse drug reactions (ADRs). In Chapter 6, we elaborate on the contributions and implications of our findings and arguments in the fields of sociology (especially the subfields of racial and ethnic studies, medical sociology, sociology of science, knowledge and technology, sociology of health and illness), science communication, health services, public health policy and bioethics (e.g., ethical, legal, and social implications of genetic/genomic studies), and science and technology studies (STS).

Note

1 While rich qualitative data provide the readers of this book a valuable window into a field that is difficult to access, we do not claim that the data is representative of any given population. The interviewee profile is provided in Appendix A.

References

Abbvie (2022) Why isn't medicine one size fits all? Available at: www.abbvie.com/who-we-are/our-stories/why-isnt-medicine-one-size-fits-all.html (accessed 16 October 2023).

Ackerman SL (2022) Promising precision medicine: How patients, clinicians and caregivers work to realize the potential of genomics-informed cancer care. *New Genetics and Society* 41(3): 196–215. DOI: 10.1080/14636778.2021.1997577.

Adigbli G (2020) Race, science and (im)precision medicine. *Nature Medicine* 26: 1675–1676.

Almaguer T (2012) Race, racialization, and latino populations in the United States. In: HoSang D, LaBennett O and Pulido L (eds) *Racial Formation in the Twenty-First Century*. Berkeley: University of California Press, pp. 143–161.

American Medical Association (2020) Elimination of race as a proxy for ancestry, genetics, and biology in medical education, research and clinical practice

H-65.953. Available at: https://policysearch.amaassn.org/policyfinder/detail/racism?uri=%2FAMADoc%2FHODxml-H-65.953.xml (accessed 16 October 2023).
Amster EJ (2022) The past, present and future of race and colonialism in medicine. *Canadian Medical Association Journal* 194(20): E708–E710.
Anand P, Ajaikumar BK, Sundaram C, et al. (2008) Cancer is a preventable disease that requires major lifestyle changes. *Pharmaceutical Research* 25(9): 2097–2116.
Anderson W (2008) Teaching "race" at medical school: Social scientists on the margin. *Social Studies of Science* 38(5): 785–800.
Au L and da Silva RGL (2021) Globalizing the scientific bandwagon: Trajectories of precision medicine in China and Brazil. *Science, Technology, & Human Values* 46(1): 192–225.
Baluran DA (2023) Differential racialization and police interactions among young adults of Asian descent. *Sociology of Race and Ethnicity* 9(2): 220–234. DOI: 10.1177/23326492221125121.
Banton M (1977) *The Idea of Race*. London: Tavistock Publications Ltd.
Baylor College of Medicine (2023) In race and genetics: Perspectives of percision medicine 2023. Available at: www.bcm.edu/departments/molecular-and-human-genetics/engagement-and-equity/evenings-with-genetics/events (accessed 16 October 2023).
Bayne J, Garry J and Albert MA (2023) Brief review: Racial and ethnic disparities in cardiovascular care with a focus on congenital heart disease and precision medicine. *Current Atherosclerosis Reports* 25(5): 189–195. DOI: 10.1007/s11883-023-01093-3.
Beal AC, Chou S-C, Palmer RH, et al. (2006) The changing face of race: Risk factors for neonatal hyperbilirubinemia. *Pediatrics* 117(5): 1618–1625.
Benjamin R (2009) A lab of their own: Genomic sovereignty as postcolonial science policy. *Policy and Society* 8(4): 341–355.
Bliss C (2015) Biomedicalization and the new science of race. In: Bell S and Figert AE (eds) *Reimaging (Bio)Medicalization, Pharmaceuticals and Genetics: Old Critiques and New Engagements*. New York and London: Routledge, pp. 175–196.
Boas F (1912) Changes in the bodily form of descendants of immigrants. *American Anthropologist* 14(3): 530–562.
Bonham, VL, Callier SL and Royal CD (2016) Will precision medicine move us beyond race? *The New England Journal of Medicine* 374(21): 2003–2005.
Braun L (2015) Race, ethnicity and lung function: A brief history. *Canadian Journal of Respiratory Therapy* 51(4): 99–101.
Brooks KC (2015) A silent curriculum. *Journal of the American Medical Association* 313(19): 1909–1910.
Burchard EG, Ziv E, Coyle N, et al. (2003) The importance of race and ethnic background in biomedical research and clinical practice. *The New England Journal of Medicine* 348(12): 1170–1175.
Callier SL (2019) The use of racial categories in precision medicine research. *Ethnicity & Disease* 29(Supp 3): 651–658.
Canadian Institutes of Health Research (2023) Personalized medicine. Available at: https://cihr-irsc.gc.ca/e/43627.html (accessed 16 October 2023).
Caulfield T (2011) Public representations of genetics: Reifying race? In: Maheu L and MacDonald RA (eds) *Challenging Genetic Determinism: New Perspectives on the Gene in Its Multiple Environments*. Montreal: McGill-Queen's University Press.
Caulfield T, Fullerton SM, Ali-Khan SE, et al. (2009) Race and ancestry in biomedical research: Exploring the challenges. *Genome Medicine* 1(1): 8.
Cerdeña JP, Plaisime MV and Tsai J (2020) From race-based to race-conscious medicine: How anti-racist uprisings call us to act. *The Lancet* 396(10257): 1125–1128.

Chakravarti A (2015) Perspectives on human variation through the lens of diversity and race. *Cold Spring Harbor Perspectives in Biology* 7(9): a023358.

Chan S, Suo C, Lee S, et al. (2012) Translational aspects of genetic factors in the prediction of drug response variability: A case study of warfarin pharmacogenomics in a multi-ethnic cohort from Asia. *The Pharmacogenomics Journal* 12(4): 312–318.

Chatterjee S (2015) Healing the body: Colonial medical practice and the corporeal context. *Proceedings of the Indian History Congress* 76: 546–554.

Chaturvedi N and Eastwood S (2020) Prescribing by ethnicity: (Im)precision medicine? *Diabetes Care* 43(8): 1687–1689.

Crompton S (2007) Medicine that's only skin deep. *The Times*. Available at: www.thetimes.co.uk/article/medicine-thats-only-skin-deep-w2qmktpms3v.

Curtin M, Somayaji D and Dickerson SS (2022) Precision medicine testing and disparities in health care for individuals with non-small cell lung cancer: A narrative review. *Oncology Nursing Forum* 49(3): 257–272.

Darling KW, Kohut M, Leeds S, et al. (2022) "Doing good" in U.S. cancer genomics? Valuation practices across the boundaries of research and care in rural community oncology. *New Genetics and Society* 41(3): 254–283.

Deacon H (2000) Racism and medical science in South Africa's Cape Colony in the mid- to late nineteenth century. *Osiris* 15: 190–206.

Dehon E, Weiss N, Jones J, et al. (2017) A systematic review of the impact of physician implicit racial bias on clinical decision making. *Academic Emergency Medicine* 24(8): 895–904.

Department of Statistics, Ministry of Trade and Industry, Singapore (2023) Population trends 2023. Available at: www.singstat.gov.sg/-/media/files/publications/population/population2023.ashx (accessed 23 October 2023).

Duster T ([1990]2003) *Backdoor to Eugenics*. New York and London: Routledge.

Duster T (2006) The molecular reinscription of race: Unanticipated issues in biotechnology and forensic science. *Patterns of Prejudice* 40(4–5): 427–441.

Duster T (2015) A post-genomic surprise: The molecular reinscription of race in science, law and medicine. *The British Journal of Sociology* 66(1): 1–27.

Edwards TL, Breeyear J, Piekos JA, et al. (2020) Equity in health: Consideration of race and ethnicity in precision medicine. *Trends in Genetics* 36(11): 807–809.

Epstein S (2007) *Inclusion: The Politics of Difference in Medical Research*. Chicago: University of Chicago Press.

Ferryman K (2023) Bounded justice, inclusion, and the hyper/invisibility of race in precision medicine. *The American Journal of Bioethics* 23(7): 27–33. DOI: 10.1080/15265161.2023.2207515.

Fujimura JH and Rajagopalan R (2011) Different differences: The use of "genetic ancestry" versus race in biomedical human genetic research. *Social Studies of Science* 41(1): 5–30.

Fullwiley D (2007) The molecularization of race: Institutionalizing human difference in pharmacogenetics practice. *Science as Culture* 16(1): 1–30.

Fullwiley, D (2015) Race, genes, power. *The British Journal of Sociology* 66: 36–45.

Gammal RS, Lee YM, Petry NJ, et al. (2021) Pharmacists leading the way to precision medicine: Updates to the core pharmacist competencies in genomics. *American Journal of Pharmaceutical Education* 86(4): 269–275.

Garcia RS (2004) The misuse of race in medical diagnosis. *Pediatrics* 113(5): 1394–1395.

Geller SE, Koch AR, Roesch P, et al. (2018) The more things change, the more they stay the same. *Academic Medicine* 93(4): 630–635.

Geneviève LD, Martani A, Shaw D, et al. (2020) Structural racism in precision medicine: Leaving no one behind. *BMC Medical Ethics* 21(17): 1–13.

Ginsburg GS and Phillips KA (2018) Precision medicine: From science to value. *Health Affairs* 37(5): 694–701.

Global Newswire (2023) Precision medicine market size (USD 254 Bn by 2023, at 12.1% CAGR) globally: Analysis by market.us. *GlobeNewswire News Room*. Available at: www.globenewswire.com/en/news-release/2023/03/06/2620711/0/en/Precision-Medicine-Market-Size-USD-254-Bn-by-2032-at-12-1-CAGR-Globally-Analysis-by-Market-us.html (accessed 16 October 2023).

Goh D (2019) Arrested multiculturalisms: Race, capitalism, and state formation in Malaysia and Singapore. In: Goh DPS and Gabrielpillai M et al. (eds) *Race and Multiculturalism in Malaysia and Singapore*. London and New York: Routledge.

Gonzalez-Sobrino B and Goss DR (2019) Exploring the mechanisms of racialization beyond the black-white binary. *Ethnic and Racial Studies* 42(4): 505–510.

Gordon DR and Koenig BA (2022) If relatives inherited the gene, they should inherit the data: Bringing the family into the room where bioethics happens. *New Genetics and Society* 41(1): 23–46.

Goodman AH, Moses YT and Jones JL (2012) *Race: Are We So Different?* West Sussex: Wiley-Blackwell.

Goodman CW and Brett AS (2021) Race and pharmacogenomics – personalized medicine or misguided practice? *Journal of the American Medical Association* 325(7): 625–626.

Gould SJ (1982) *The Mismeasure of Men*. New York: W. W. Norton & Company.

Harmon A (2004) As gene test menu grows, who gets to choose? *The New York Times*, 21 July: A1–A15.

Hedgecoe A (2004) *The Politics of Personalized Medicine: Pharmacogenetics in the Clinic*. Cambridge: Cambridge University Press.

Hernandez-Boussard T, Siddique SM, Bierman AS, et al. (2023) Promoting equity in clinical decision making: Dismantling race-based medicine. *Health Affairs* 42(10): 1369–1373.

Hunt LM and Kreiner MJ (2013) Pharmacogenetics in primary care: The promise of personalized medicine and the reality of racial profiling. *Culture, Medicine and Psychiatry* 37(1): 226–235.

Ioannidis JPA, Powe NR and Yancy C (2021) Recalibrating the use of race in medical research. *Journal of the America Medical Association* 325(7): 623–624.

Jackson M (2015) *The Genealogy of a Gene: Patents, HIV/AIDS, and Race*. Cambridge, MA: MIT Press.

James JE and Joseph G (2022) "It's personalized, but it's still bucket based": The promise of personalized medicine vs. the reality of genomic risk stratification in a breast cancer screening trial. *New Genetics and Society* 41(3): 228–253.

James JE, Riddle L, Koenig BA, et al. (2021) The limits of personalization in precision medicine: Polygenic risk scores and racial categorization in a precision breast cancer screening trial. *PloS One* 16(10): e0258571.

Johnson HR (2012) *Distempers peculiar to negros: Colonial physicians, etiological investigations, and the racialization of medicine in the eighteenth-century British West Indies*. MA Thesis, University of British Columbia, Canada.

Kahn J (2004) How a drug becomes "ethnic": Law, commerce, and the production of racial categories in medicine. *Yale Journal of Health Policy, Law, and Ethics* 4(1): 1–46.

Kahn J (2017) Revisiting racial patents in an era of precision medicine. *Case Western Reserve Law Review* 67(4): 1153–1169.

Kenny MG (2006) A question of blood, race, and politics. *Journal of the History of Medicine and Allied Sciences* 61(4): 456–491.

Kisor DF and Farrell CL (2019) Expanding pharmacist and student pharmacist access to genetics/genomics/pharmacogenomics competency education. *Journal of Medical Education and Curricular Development* 6.

Kohler S (2018) Precision medicine – moving away from one-size-fits-all. Available at: www.ehidc.org/sites/default/files/resources/files/precision%20medicine.pdf (accessed 16 October 2023).

Kolesar JM and Vermeulen LC (2021) Precision medicine: Opportunities for health-system pharmacists. *American Journal of Health-System Pharmacy* 78(11): 999–1003.
Krainc T and Fuentes A (2022) Genetic ancestry in precision medicine is reshaping the race debate. *Proceedings of the National Academy of Sciences of the United States of America* 119(12): e2203033119.
Lan PC (2005) Stratified otherization: Recruitment, training and racialization of migrant domestic worker. *Taiwanese Journal of Sociology* 34: 1–57.
Levine P (1994) Venereal disease, prostitution, and the politics of empire: The case of British India. *Journal of the History of Sexuality* 4(4): 579–602.
Li Z, Jiang X, Fang M, et al. (2023) CMDB: The comprehensive population genome variation database of China. *Nucleic Acids Research* 51(D1): D890–D895.
Lie J (2001) *Multiethnic Japan*. Cambridge: Harvard University Press.
Loh KS and Hsu LY (2020) Introduction In: *Tuberculosis – The Singapore Experience, 1867–2018: Disease, Society and the State*. London and New York: Routledge, pp. 1–9.
Lopez IH (2006) *White by Law: The Legal Construction of Race*. New York: New York University Press.
Mamdani H and Schwartz AG (2020) Genomic characterization of NSCLC in African Americans: A step toward "race-aware" precision medicine. *Journal of Thoracic Oncology: Official Publication of the International Association for the Study of Lung Cancer* 15(12): 1800–1802.
Martschenko DO and Young JL (2022) Precision medicine needs to think outside the box. *Frontiers in Genetics* 13: 795992.
McCleery I (2015) What is "colonial" about medieval colonial medicine? Iberian health in global context. *Journal of Medieval Iberian Studies* 7(2): 151–175.
McMillen C (2021) Indigenous peoples, tuberculosis research and changing ideas about race in the 1930s. *Canadian Medical Association Journal* 193(43): E1666–E1668.
Mensah GA, Jaquish C, Srinivas P, et al. (2019) Emerging concepts in precision medicine and cardiovascular diseases in racial and ethnic minority populations. *Circulation Research* 125(1): 7–13.
Miles R and Brown M (2003) *Racism*. London and New York: Routledge.
Montoya M (2011) *Making the Mexican Diabetic*. Oakland, CA: University of California Press.
Morning A (2011) *How Scientists Think and Teach about Human Difference*. Oakland, CA: University of California Press.
Murji K and Solomos J eds. (2005) *Racialization: Studies in Theory and Practice*. Oxford: Oxford University Press.
Murji K and Solomos J eds. (2014) *Theories of Race and Ethnicity: Contemporary Debates and Perspectives*. Cambridge: Cambridge University Press.
Musey PI, Studnek JR and Garvey L (2016) Characteristics of ST elevation myocardial infarction patients who do not undergo percutaneous coronary intervention after prehospital cardiac catheterization laboratory activation. *Critical Pathways in Cardiology: A Journal of Evidence-Based Medicine* 15(1): 16–21.
National Human Genome Research Institute (2000) June 2000 white house event. Available at: www.genome.gov/10001356/june-2000-white-house-event (accessed 16 October 2023).
National Human Genome Research Institute (2022) Human genome project. Available at: www.genome.gov/about-genomics/educational-resources/fact-sheets/human-genome-project (accessed 16 October 2023).
Nelson A (2008) Bio science: Genetic genealogy testing and the pursuit of African ancestry. *Social Studies of Science* 38(5): 759–783.
Nelson A (2016) *The Social Life of DNA: Race, Reparation and Reconciliation after the Genome*. Boston, MA: Beacon Press.

Newson LA (2011) *Conquest and Pestilence in the Early Spanish Philippines*. Manila, Philippines: Ateneo de Manila University Press.
Omi M and Winant H (1986) *Racial Formation in the United States*. London and New York: Routledge.
Ong A (2016) *Fungible Life: Experiment in the Asian City of Life*. Durham, NC: Duke University Press.
Ossorio P and Duster T (2005) Race and genetics: Controversies in biomedical, behavioral, and forensic sciences. *American Psychologist* 60(1): 115–128.
Outram S, Ackerman S, Norstad M, et al. (2022) The challenge of recruiting diverse populations into health research: An embedded social science perspective. *New Genetics and Society* 41: 1–11.
Pezzin LE, Keyl PM and Green GB (2007) Disparities in the emergency department evaluation of chest pain patients. *Academic Emergency Medicine* 14(2): 149–156.
Phelan JC, Link BG and Feldman NM (2013) The genomic revolution and beliefs about essential racial differences: A backdoor to eugenics? *American Sociological Review* 78(2): 167–191.
Phimister EG (2003) Medicine and the racial divide. *New England Journal of Medicine* 348(12): 1081–1082.
Prainsack B (2015) Is personalized medicine different? *The British Journal of Sociology* (66): 28–35.
Precision Health Research, Singapore (2023) Our story. Available at: www.npm.sg/ (accessed 13 October 2023).
Purushotam NS (1998) *Negotiating Language, Constructing Race: Disciplining Difference in Singapore*. Berlin and New York: Mouton De Gruyter.
Raheem F, Kim P, Grove M, et al. (2020) Precision genomic practice in oncology: Pharmacist role and experience in an ambulatory care clinic. *Pharmacy* 8(1): 32. https://doi.org/10.3390/pharmacy8010032 (accessed 16 October 2023).
Rajagopalan R and Fujimura JH (2012) Will personalized medicine challenge or reify categories of race and ethnicity? *The Virtual Mentor* 14(8): 657–663.
Rapp R and Outram S (2022) Building the airplane while flying it: Tracking the transformation of novel sequencing practices into clinical services. *New Genetics and Society* 41(3): 284–291.
Reardon J (2022) The pathos of precision. *New Genetics and Society* 41(3): 187–195. DOI: 10.1080/14636778.2022.2115352.
Roberts DE (2008) Is race-based medicine good for us? African American approaches to race, biomedicine, and equality. *Journal of Law, Medicine & Ethics* 36(3): 537–545.
Roberts DE (2011) *Fatal Invention: How Science, Politics, and Big Business Re-Create Race in the Twenty-First Century*. New York: New Press.
Roberts DE (2018) 46. The problem with race-based medicine. In: Obasogi OK and Darnovsky M (eds) *Beyond Bioethics: Toward a New Biopolitics*. Berkeley: University of California Press, pp. 410–414.
Roberts DE (2021) Abolish race correction. *Lancet* 397(10268): 17–18.
Roman Y (2022) The United States 2020 Census data: Implications for precision medicine and the research landscape. *Personalized Medicine* 19(1): 5–8.
Root M (2003) The use of race in medicine as a proxy for genetic differences. *Philosophy of Science* 70(5): 1173–1183.
Roth W and Ivemark B (2018) Genetic options: The impact of genetic ancestry testing on consumers' racial and ethnic identities. *American Journal of Sociology* 124(1): 150–184.
Rumbaut RG (2009) Pigments of our imagination: On the racialization and racial identity of "Hispanics" and "Latinos". In: Cobas JA, Duany J and Feagin JR (eds) *How the United States Racializes Latinos: White Hegemony and Its Consequences*. Boulder, CO: Paradigm.

Said EW (2003) *Orientalism: Penguin Modern Classics*. London, England: Penguin Classics.
Satel S (2002) I am a racially profiling doctor. *The New York Times*, 5 May. Available at: www.nytimes.com/2002/05/05/magazine/i-am-a-racially-profiling-doctor.html (accessed 16 October 2023).
Schaefer GO, Tai ES and Sun SH (2020) Navigating conflicts of justice in the use of race and ethnicity in precision medicine. *Bioethics* 34(8): 849–856.
Schwarze K, Buchanan J, Fermont JM, et al. (2020) The complete costs of genome sequencing: A microcosting study in cancer and rare diseases from a single center in the United Kingdom. *Genetic Medicine* 22: 85–94.
Sebring JC (2021) Towards a sociological understanding of medical gaslighting in Western Health Care. *Sociology of Health and Illness* 43(9): 1951–1964.
Seth S (2018) *Difference and Disease: Medicine, Race, and the Eighteenth-Century British Empire*. Cambridge: Cambridge University Press.
Sheldon TA and Parker H (1992) Race and ethnicity in health research. *Journal of Public Health Medicine* 14(2): 104–110.
Shostak S and Moinester M (2015) Beyond geneticization: Regimes of perceptibility and the social determinants of health. In: Bell S and Figert A (eds) *Reimaging (Bio)Medicalization, Pharmaceuticals and Genetics: Old Critiques and New Engagements*. New York and London: Routledge, pp. 216–238.
Smart A and Weiner K (2018) Racialised prescribing: Enacting race/ethnicity in clinical practice guidelines and in accounts of clinical practice. *Sociology of Health and Illness* 40(5): 843–858.
Takezawa Y, Kato K, Oota H, et al. (2014) Human genetic research, race, ethnicity and the labeling of populations: Recommendations based on an interdisciplinary workshop in Japan. *BMC Medical Ethics* 15(33): 1–5.
TallBear K (2013) *Native American DNA: Tribal Belonging and the False Promise of Genetic Science*. Minneapolis: University of Minnesota Press.
Terri Fox Research Institute (n.d.) Precision medicine: Understanding the importance of investing in precision medicine. Available at: www.tfri.ca/about-cancer/cancer-topics/cancer-topic/precision-medicine (accessed 16 October 2023).
Thompson D (2013) Racial formations: Canada. In: Mason PL (ed) *Encyclopedia of Race and Racism*. New York: MacMillan Reference USA, pp. 370–373.
Tsai J (2018) What role should race play in medicine? *Scientific American Blog Network*. Available at: https://blogs.scientificamerican.com/voices/what-role-should-race-play-in-medicine/ (accessed 16 October 2023).
U.S. Food and Drug Administration (2018) Precision medicine. Available at: www.fda.gov/medical-devices/in-vitro-diagnostics/precision-medicine (accessed 16 October 2023).
Vijayvergia N and Delinger C (2015) Lifestyle factors in cancer survivorship: Where we are and where we are headed. *Journal of Personalized Medicine* 5(3): 243–263.
Vyas DA, Eisenstein LG and Jones DS (2020) Hidden in plain sight – Reconsidering the use of race correction in clinical algorithms. *New England Journal of Medicine* 383: 874–882.
Wade P (2017) *Degrees of Mixture, Degrees of Freedom: Genomics, Multiculturalism, and Race in Latin America*. Durham, NC: Duke University Press.
Walko C, Kiel PJ and Kolesar J (2016) Precision medicine in oncology: New practice models and roles for oncology pharmacists. *American Journal of Health-System Pharmacy* 73(23): 1935–1942.
Waltz M (2011) Autism and race. *Community Care*, 3 March. Available at: www.sciesocialcareonline.org.uk/autism-and-race/r/a1CG0000000GWhvMAG (accessed 16 October 2023).
Waltz M (2013) *Autism: A Social and Medical History*. London: Palgrave McMillan.

Wang RC and Wang Z (2023) Precision medicine: Disease subtyping and tailored treatment. *Cancers (Basel)* 15(15): 3837.

Ward E, Jemal A, Cokkinides V, et al. (2005) Cancer disparities by race/ethnicity and socioeconomic status. *CA: A Cancer Journal for Clinicians* 2004(54): 78–93.

Weigmann, K (2006) Racial medicine: Here to stay? *EMBO Reports* 7(3): 246–249.

The White House Office of Press Secretary (2015) Available at: https://obamawhitehouse.archives.gov/the-press-office/2015/01/30/remarks-president-precision-medicine (accessed 16 October 2023).

Wolinsky H (2011) Genomes, race and health. *EMBO Reports* 12(2): 107–109. DOI: 10.1038/embor.2010.218.

World Economic Forum (2017) 3 ways China is leading the way in precision medicine. Available at: www.weforum.org/agenda/2017/11/3-ways-china-is-leading-the-way-in-precision-medicine/ (accessed 13 October 2023).

Wright JL, Davis WS, Joseph MM, et al. (2022) Eliminating race-based medicine. *Pediatrics* 150(1): e2022057998.

2 Using race to overcome race
An inherent contradiction in precision medicine

"The phenotypic marker of race and ethnicity, is really only a phenotypic marker . . . the whole point of genetic testing is you get away from these phenotypic looks."
– Interviewee Dr.20 (USA)

Introduction

As noted in the previous chapter, the completion of the Human Genome Project in 2003 was thought to be the end of race-based medicine. Yet even now using race as a proxy for human genetic variation remains a controversial practice. This is a critical issue as it not only affects health and illness management today, but also bears a "ripple effect" on the future of medicine (Acquaviva and Mintz, 2010: 702). As James and Joseph (2022: 228) argued in their analysis of a clinical trial of risk-based breast cancer screening, there can be a "fundamental tension between the promissory ideals of personalized medicine, and the reality of implementing risk-stratified care on a population scale." While some purport that the use of racial categories is essential in pursuing scientific discoveries and making medical decisions, others suggest that race should not be used. Why are there such different opinions on this issue? In this chapter, we first provide a succinct review of the existing literature regarding arguments against the use of race as a proxy for genetics, before looking at the reasons supporting it.

One key argument highlighted by those who object to the usage of race as a proxy for genetics is the "lack of concrete evidence" of its utility and validity (Acquaviva and Mintz, 2010: 703). Using race to determine disease diagnosis/prognosis and treatment is deemed "enticingly simple solutions to complex questions of disease" (Braun, 2006: 563). As argued by Schwartz (2001: 1392), "[a]ttributing differences in a biologic end point to race is not only imprecise but also of no proven value in treating an individual patient," and race is deemed "inappropriate . . . as a central diagnostic tool for an individual patient" (Braun et al., 2007: 1426).

This is in part due to the arbitrariness of race. In the words of Braun (2006: 567): "There is no single conception of race that produces the same categories of people in all contexts." Travassos and Williams (2004) echoed this observation. This, in turn, limits the comparability and application of race-based

DOI: 10.4324/9781003436102-2

human genetics study results. Moreover, at a genetic level, "there are no alleles that define . . . a unique population or race" (Schwartz, 2001: 1393). Although the prevalence of certain alleles may correlate with racial categories, it has been found that "ancestral alleles [that] affect disease rates and medication efficacy . . . do not align neatly with commonly used racial groupings" (Schwartz, 2001; Tsai et al., 2016: 916). In other words, an allele may be found more frequently in a particular racial group, but it also exists in other racial groups, albeit at lower frequencies. Phenomena like migration and interracial marriages further complicate matters as they result in greater "genetic intermingling" and admixtures that cannot be accounted for by existing racial categories (Gravlee, 2009; Tsai et al., 2016; Schwartz, 2001: 1393). As such, using race as a proxy for genetics is problematic (Acquaviva and Mintz, 2010).

There are also issues with how an individual's racial identity is determined. Such determination typically occurs via self-reports or visual assessments, which are arbitrary. Self-reports are "not a reliable indicator of race" as the racial category self-selected by an individual may vary from one circumstance to another depending on the options available (Root, 2003: 1179). Visual assessments of phenotypes are also vulnerable to inaccuracies given their subjective nature and ambiguities. There may also be a disjuncture between a physician's assessment of a patient's race and the patient's self-identified race, as well as between the physician's assessment and the definition of race used in a particular genetic study physicians rely on to inform their medical decisions for the patient (Root, 2003; Tsai et al., 2016). Given the random assignment of race, race-based probabilities of disease occurrence or drug response assigned to patients run the risk of being biologically inaccurate (Acquaviva and Mintz, 2010; Travassos and Williams, 2004).

Not surprisingly, another reason for opposing the use of race as a proxy for genetics is the danger of errors in diagnosis and treatment decisions that can, in turn, result in substandard care for patients (Acquaviva and Mintz, 2010; Bowser, 2001; Braun et al., 2007; Root, 2003; Tsai et al., 2016). Indeed, those who oppose the use of race as a proxy for genetics contend that instead of helping the medical treatment process, "[b]oth historical evidence and contemporary genetic research suggest that 'racial profiling' in medicine can lead to serious medical errors" (Braun et al., 2007: 1423). Beyond the possibility of capricious assignment of race as mentioned previously, medical errors may result from physicians' "racialized implicit biases" (Tsai et al., 2016: 916), as well as reliance on racial profiling as "the simplest, lowest-transaction-cost route to diagnosis and treatment" (Bowser, 2001: 120) and treating all individuals from a particular racial group the same way to the detriment of those who "present outside of simplified racial paradigms" (Tsai et al., 2016: 917). Physicians may "miss clinically relevant information or assume the presence or absence of genetic or cultural factors that, in fact, may or may not be present" (Bowser, 2001: 119), be "blind to diagnoses considered uncommon in patients of the presumed race or ethnicity" (Acquaviva and Mintz, 2010: 703), and/or be "less inclined to recommend a procedure if the literature states that the odds are low that the treatment will be successful" simply because of the patient's racial profile (Bowser, 2001: 117). In other words, there is a lack of individualized prognosis and treatment when racial profiling is used because "the utility of a given procedure is often decided *a priori*, without an individualized assessment of the patient's condition" (Bowser, 2001: 117).

The use of race as a proxy for genetics is also problematic as it distracts from a holistic view of diseases and hampers efforts to find out the specific (potentially non-genetic) cause of a disease. It is deemed a "naïve reductionism" approach that fails to "[acknowledge] the interplay of organisms and environments over the life course" (Gravlee, 2009: 51). When the emphasis is placed on race and genetics, other factors that may be responsible for a disease such as "[e]nvironmental exposures, family histories, the stress of dealing with racism, access to and quality of care may be left unexamined" (Braun et al., 2007: 1425). There is also a risk that the use of race as a proxy for genetics will "limit our thinking about what these biomedical differences suggest about health disparities and inequalities in general" (Lee, 2009: 1184), and that race and genetics will become an easy and convenient explanation for any health-related differences while real causative factors remain undiscovered (Brower, 2002; Schwartz, 2001). The focus on searching for the genetic cause of disease can also hinder efforts to reduce racial health disparities by "fuel[ing] a logic that would concentrate resources needed to redress disparities on pharmaceutical interventions that work at the molecular level rather than addressing larger issues of diet, behavior, racism, and economic inequality that also play significant roles" (Braun, 2006; Kahn, 2003: 479).

Long-term consequences also include opening "the door to a wider range of potentially devastating discriminatory practices" (Kahn, 2003: 479). Conducting medical genetic research along racial lines pathologizes race, which can in turn strengthen racial biases, stereotypes, stigmas, and prejudices against particular racial groups (Braun, 2006; Brower, 2002; Jenkins, 2015; Kahn, 2003; Tsai et al., 2016). This not only "distributes the risk of genetic discrimination unequally" between different racial groups (Root, 2003: 1177), but results in a "vicious cycle" as social inequalities leading to health disparities are further reinforced (Gravlee, 2009: 48; Root, 2003).

Finally, the continued use of race as a proxy for genetics despite its limitations can have problematic implications for the future of medicine. As pointed out by Acquaviva and Mintz (2010: 702), "the physicians of tomorrow are shaped by the physicians of today, who were molded by the physicians of the past." Negative outcomes resulting from the use of race as a proxy for genetics may thus persist, especially if "race is presented in a routinized way and students are not introduced to the nuances of the controversies over race in medicine" (Braun and Saunder, 2017: 522).

Given these arguments, why do some scientists/clinicians continue to use race as a proxy for genetics? On a fundamental level, they believed that "human populations tend to have a structure, with variations in allelic frequencies between different parts of the structure" (Lillquist and Sullivan, 2006: 4) and that "the greatest genetic structure that exists in the human population occurs at the racial level" (Risch et al., 2002: 4). It is not just the presence or absence of the risk allele that can differ across racial/ethnic groups but also the implications of having the allele (Bamshad et al., 2004; Burchard et al., 2003; Bustamante et al., 2011; Hindorff et al., 2018; Risch et al., 2002; Shah and Gaedigk, 2018). Examples of genes that have perceived racial variations include the set of type 2 diabetes susceptibility genes, wherein similar effects were found in "Asian" and "Mexican American" populations but not in "African" populations (Streicher et al., 2011), and the group of alleles associated with drug metabolizing enzymes (Shah and Gaedigk, 2018).

Another reason is the belief that the "potential costs [of linking race with genetics] are outweighed by the benefits in terms of diagnosis and research" (Burchard et al., 2003: 1174). Race is perceived as "geographic and sociocultural constructs with biological ramifications" – racial groups differ from each other not just in terms of genetics but also non-genetic factors such as socioeconomic status, that can have interactive effects on disease occurrence and health outcomes (Burchard et al., 2003: 1171; Burchard et al., 2005; Risch et al., 2002; Shah and Gaedigk, 2018). Since racial categories capture both genetic and non-genetic influences, they are purported to be helpful in "generating and exploring hypotheses about environmental and genetic risk factors, as well as interactions between risk factors, for important medical outcomes" (Burchard et al., 2003: 1171) by serving as "a starting point for further investigation" (Risch et al., 2002: 2) and in "provid[ing] valuable input for prevention and treatment decisions" before specific causative factors are identified, or when better genetic information is not available (Risch et al., 2002: 2; Shah and Gaedigk, 2018).

In line with Duster's (2006: 435) argument that "molecular reinscription of race" happens during "the practical application of molecular genetics," support for the use of race as a proxy for genetics may also be motivated by pragmatic considerations. Such pragmatic racialism (Sun, 2020) is characterized as being action oriented, with decisions made mainly according to cost-based considerations and guided by practical considerations that "emphasiz[e] practical utility at the expense of scientific accuracy" (Kivetz and Tyler, 2007; Nelson et al., 2018: 227; Sun, 2020). Pragmatic advantages range from ostensibly helping to save time and money to increasing the probability of successfully conducting biomedical research, publishing in the highly competitive scholarly science community, and working with pharmaceutical companies' capital investments (Burchard et al., 2003; Nelson et al., 2018; Sun, 2017, 2020). Epstein (2007: 13) also showed that the "categorical alignment" of US Census racial categories with biomedical research has helped geneticists and others connect their science to multiple stakeholders.

Another reason for support is social justice (Bentley et al., 2017; Bliss, 2012). From this perspective, the use of race as a proxy for genetics is a form of anti-racist racialism driven by awareness of racial discrimination (Bliss, 2012, 2015; Epstein, 2007; Fullwiley, 2008). Scientists and physicians in this group are conscious of the lack of representation of minority groups in science and view the use of racial categories as a way of ensuring equitable representation in, and thereby gains from, their work across different racial/ethnic groups. As Burchard et al. (2003: 1174) noted, "If investigators ignored race and ethnic background in research studies and persons were sampled randomly, the overwhelming majority of participants in clinical studies in the United States would be White, and minority populations would never be adequately sampled." Without sufficient representation of people from minority populations, the "generalizability of results is severely compromised" (Hussain-Gambles et al., 2004: 386). This can perpetuate already considerable health disparities because only some people (usually from the majority populations) get to benefit from these studies (Bentley et al., 2017; Bustamante et al., 2011; Foster and Sharp, 2002; Popejoy and Fullerton, 2016; Sirisena and Dissanayake, 2017). Genetic testing based on studies that lack sufficient racial and ethnic diversity in the study population may result in ambiguous test results and false positives when applied to the general population (Popejoy and Fullerton, 2016; Hindorff et al., 2018). There are also concerns that "clinicians may rely too heavily on data obtained from Europeans to have clinical decisions for Africans and other non-European populations" even though results may not be directly applicable (Mersha and Abebe, 2015: 12). As such, within the scientific community, there has been a shift away from colorblindness to a cautiously curated paradigm of race-positivity, wherein race is used in the name of ensuring everyone stands to benefit, and particularly minority populations (Bliss, 2012).

In response to the argument that race should not be used as a proxy for genetics because of its arbitrariness as a social construct, proponents contended that even if race was not "a valid primary concept in human population genetics," it may still "be a useful proxy yielding reliable inferences or sound probabilistic reasoning in some specifically well-defined biomedical contexts" (Maglo, 2010: 362). Moreover, rather than hindering scientific discovery, some purport that it is precisely the "classificatory ambiguity" of racial/ethnic identities that "helps geneticists negotiate collaborations among researchers with competing demands, resist bureaucratic oversight, and build accountability with study populations" (Panofsky and Bliss, 2017: 59). In short, it is seen as still useful even if the definition of racial/ethnic categories are socially constructed and politically arbitrary.

The paragraphs in this section summarize the various reasons for and against the use of race as a proxy for genetics in the field of biomedical research and medicine. This debate sets an interesting background for examining the field of precision medicine. Despite precision medicine's promise of medical treatments tailored to the individual patient, it is important to empirically examine whether the use of race as a proxy for genetics still occurs in the various domains of precision medicine from scientific research to clinical trials and, subsequently, medical decision-making in the clinic. In this chapter, we aim to elucidate when and why race is used in precision medicine. In answering this question, we show that there is an inherent contradiction in such use.

Using race to overcome race: Understanding an inherent contradiction in translational precision medicine

Our analysis of the interview data reveals that the potential use of race and racialized statistics as a proxy for genetics is domain-specific. Across the three domains of translational precision medicine, the degree of acceptance in using race starts high in the scientific research domain but decreases as it moves along the translation process to clinical trials and subsequently clinical applications (see Figure 2.1). Specifically, some interviewees expressed support for using race in scientific research but rejected it in clinical trials and/or medical applications. When more is at stake (i.e., giving patients treatments that have life-or-death significance), it becomes less acceptable.

In the following sections, we examine the degree of acceptance in the context of activity occurring in each of these three domains. For each section, we present interviewees' reasons for rejecting the use of race in that domain before discussing reasons for acceptance.

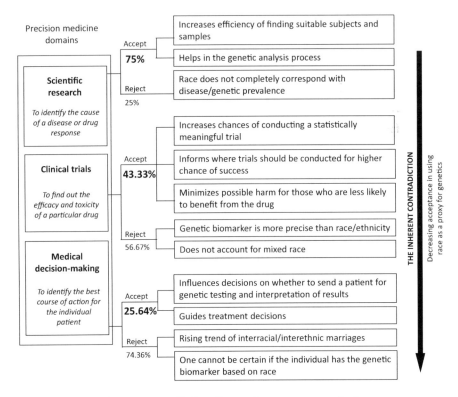

Figure 2.1 The inherent contradiction: Decreasing acceptance of using race as a proxy for genetics in three domains in precision medicine

34 *Using race to overcome race*

First domain: Searching for the genetic biomarker in scientific research

The main activity occurring in the scientific research domain is the search for potential disease-causing genetic biomarkers. Achieving this requires biological samples from subjects with the disease for genetic analysis. As shown in Table 2.1, of the 16 interviewees who responded to the

Table 2.1 Interviewees' stances regarding the use of race in three domains in precision medicine

		Scientific research				Clinical trials				Medical decision-making			
		YES		NO		YES		NO		YES		NO	
S/N	Category	Straight-forward	Nuanced	Straight-forward	Nuanced	Straight-forward	Nuanced	Straight-forward	Nuanced	Straight-forward	Nuanced	Straight-forward	Nuanced
Canada (11 interviewees)													
1	Physician						✓						✓
2	Scientist						✓					✓	
3	Physician	✓									✓		✓
4	Physician										✓		✓
5	Physician									✓			
6	Scientist				✓								
7	Physician										✓		
8	Physician												✓
9	Scientist	✓								✓			
10	Scientist	✓						✓		✓			
11	Scientist	✓				✓				✓			
USA (10 interviewees)													
12	Scientist					✓							✓
13	Physician										✓		✓
14	Physician												✓
15	Physician												✓
16	Physician										✓		
17	Physician												✓
18	Physician						✓				✓		
19	Physician									✓			✓
20	Physician									✓			✓
21	Scientist	✓											✓
Singapore (24 interviewees)													
22	Physician					✓				✓			
23	Physician									✓			✓
24	Researcher/Physician						✓						✓

Using race to overcome race 35

		Scientific research				Clinical trials				Medical decision-making			
		YES		NO		YES		NO		YES		NO	
S/N	Category	Straight-forward	Nuanced	Straight-forward	Nuanced	Straight-forward	Nuanced	Straight-forward	Nuanced	Straight-forward	Nuanced	Straight-forward	Nuanced
25	Scientist					✓							
26	Researcher/Physician												✓
27	Scientist					✓							✓
29	Physician											✓	
30	Researcher/Physician		✓			✓							✓
31	Scientist	✓						✓		✓			
32	Physician	✓								✓			
33	Physician												✓
34	Physician					✓							✓
35	Researcher/Physician	✓						✓			✓		
36	Researcher/Physician	✓									✓		
37	Scientist									✓			
38	Researcher/Physician					✓				✓			
39	Researcher/Physician	✓						✓					✓
40	Researcher/Physician		✓	✓							✓		
41	Researcher/Physician		✓					✓					
42	Researcher/Physician						✓						✓
43	Researcher/Physician	✓				✓							
44	Researcher/Physician									✓			✓
45	Researcher/Physician						✓						✓
46	Scientist		✓			✓							

Note: Interviewee Dr.28 from Singapore is excluded from this analysis because he is a health economist.

questions in the context of scientific research, a minority (4; 25%) were deeply concerned about the use of race. Of these four, three were completely against using race, arguing that race used in statistics was not helpful because racial/ethnic categories did not completely correspond with disease occurrence, and that genetic differences between racial/ethnic groups were actually small.

For instance, according to Dr.40 (Singapore), while nasopharyngeal cancer (NPC) was common in Southern China, it also occurred in Malays in Singapore, albeit at a lower frequency. Furthermore, Dr.19 (Singapore) emphasized the lack of sufficient genomic differences across ethnicities – in lung cancer, for example – and suggested that there must exist "a universal, nice, clever, elegant explanation that transcends ethnic boundaries" to explain disease occurrence. Instead of relying on race, these interviewees focus on genetics or use other "modifiable risk factors" (Dr.6, Canada) to study human disease.

A majority (12; 75%) supported using race because, to many of them, racialized statistics of disease prevalence guided their research:

> There is no reason why we should pick one ethnic group over the other, *unless we notice that a disease is much more common in one ethnic group compared to the other*. . . . If a disease is equally common in Indians, Malays, and Chinese, and Europeans, we want to study all [of them]. But if . . . the disease is very common in Chinese and Chinese only, [like] nasopharyngeal cancer [NPC], then of course, you just want to pick that ethnic group . . . you can't do nasopharyngeal cancer in Europeans. It's just not possible.
>
> (Dr.46, Singapore)

> We know that different ethnic groups have different susceptibilities to different diseases . . . [A]nd [for] lots of different disease conditions there seem to be predisposing alleles that have different impacts in an ethnic group. . . . [Y]ou have to know that the variant occurred in the ethnic group in order to be able to say that.
>
> (Dr.6, Canada)

Race becomes useful in this context because researchers believe such statistics help to identify populations in which researchers should "get deeper" (Dr.21, USA) in their research. They nudge scientists towards population(s) with a higher occurrence of the disease and increase the possibility of finding suitable subjects and samples for further studies.

Race is also perceived to be useful in the genetic analysis process. As shared by Dr.32 (Singapore), knowing race/ethnicity-based differences in genetics and disease susceptibility can aid the process of identifying disease biomarkers by "fine-map[ping] where the disease gene is." This is because there are "biologically critical" portions of our genes that do not differ between individuals of different ethnicities, and other portions that do, because of the hypothesized, but unproven, "founder effect" (Lee et al., 2001: 2).

In short, although respondents generally acknowledged that the genetic biomarker is the end goal, most were accepting of using race in the genomic research domain because it helps the search for the genetic biomarker by narrowing down not only the population in which relevant subjects (and therefore samples) to recruit, but also where the genetic biomarker is likely to be found.

Most interviewees, however, also emphasized the need to eventually move beyond race/ethnicity and identify the actual genetic driver of the disease or the drug response:

> It is important [to study genomic profiles in an ethnic or racial framework] because we are beginning to see that there is a difference between males and females, between the Caucasians and [people in] this part of the world [i.e. Asia]; like Epidermal Growth Factor Receptor [EGFR] mutant lung cancer is so common here compared to the West and it is important to know the reason why. . . . [I]f we can find it and we can prevent it, then [race is] probably not so important.
>
> (Dr.35, Singapore)

That is, scientists use racialized statistics to make the search for the genetic biomarker more efficient. However, they also believe that race/ethnicity is just a stepping stone towards the specific genetic cause (Kahn, 2009).

Second domain: Recruiting suitable human subjects for clinical trials

A total of 30 interviewees commented on the use of race in the domain of clinical trials, with 13 (43.33%) generally expressing support, and a majority of 17 (56.67%) expressing concern.

Interviewees who expressed concern emphasized the genetic biomarker as a more precise method for stratification. To them, such molecular precision constitutes an *objection* to the use of race:

> It really is going to be [genetic] driver-driven, not . . . race. . . . You're talking about . . . decisions made on very precise information. Race is not . . . precise information at all.
>
> (Dr.20, USA)

> Do I stratify for Asian or do I stratify for the molecular biomarker? So I think part of that depends upon the level of confidence you have in which is the better predictive factor. . . . Ethnicity is very fuzzy. . . . Ethnicity is not just molecular makeup; it's also your culture, what you eat, what's your diet, what are the practices. I guess one of the hopes is when you . . . go down to the DNA, it provides a . . . much cleaner way of discriminating. You either have the variant or you don't.
>
> (Dr.27, Singapore)

Dr.10 (USA) highlighted another issue that arises with the use of race – its inability to account for individuals of mixed race, who cannot fit neatly into any existing racial/ethnic groupings and, thus, might not be able to benefit from such race/ethnic-based study results.

In contrast, respondents who supported the use of race in clinical trials talked about pragmatic reasons. Firstly, using race was justified as a way to increase the chances of conducting a statistically meaningful – and thus, ethical – clinical trial:

> [L]et's say I'm examining this gene, which is . . . predominantly present in a particular population, say, the Chinese population. . . . Then I think it's very logical to restrict the analysis to. . . . Chinese, because you have no money to [study everybody]. If you're going to do all populations, you're not going to get result[s], and a failed . . . study of poor [statistical] power . . . is an unethical study.
>
> (Dr.43, Singapore)

Clinical trials are meant to assess the efficacy and toxicity of a drug. In the case of genomic medicine clinical trials, if there are insufficient participants with the disease and/or the genetic biomarker, it remains unclear whether there was a true lack of drug effectiveness, or whether the drug was actually effective in participants with a particular genetic biomarker, but had its overall effectiveness diminished after enrolling subjects without the biomarker. While this can be overcome by recruiting more participants to enable further analysis of different types of subgroups, as pointed out by Dr.43 (Singapore), that requires considerably more resources, which are not always available. As such, the availability of racialized statistics is perceived to allow researchers to identify target populations in which they are more likely to find participants with the disease and/or the genetic markers of interest without having to spend more resources.

Moreover, interviewees believed that racialized statistics could inform where clinical trials should be conducted for a higher chance of success, even when genetic markers are the key factor of interest:

> If you have an East Asian with lung cancer, you are more likely to find the EGFR mutation than [with a] counterpart in the West. So EGFR Tyrosine Kinase Inhibitors [TKI] trials will be more commonly conducted in this part of the world where it is more prevalent.
>
> (Dr.35, Singapore)

> Let's say there's a new drug with a new target and it is twice as common in Asian patients, it might be that they will screen or run more studies in Asia. This is in fact, quite common with EGFR studies as they are run first in Asia.
>
> (Dr.1, Canada)

> Any given Caucasian can be more genetically distinct from another Caucasian than they are from another person of Asian ethnicity. But in general, because . . . you had at certain times isolated populations that

basically became more homogenous . . . most of the genetic diversity is driven by . . . geography.

(Dr.12, USA)

We interpret the argument in the previous section to mean that interviewees are in support of using race to narrow down the target population because they believe that human subjects thus recruited are more likely to have the target gene and therefore more likely to respond to the drug. However, it is crucial to note that the interviewees also noted that the determining variable is genetic rather than the subject's racial/ethnic profile because the genetic biomarker is seen as a more precise indicator of potential drug efficacy. As the interview data shows, first, genetic markers are not race/ethnicity-specific, so people with the genetic biomarker of interest can be of different race/ethnicities. Second, the same disease can be a result of different genetic mutations, such that recruiting people by disease phenotype alone may be insufficient.

Thirdly, because of drug toxicity risks associated with clinical trials, Dr.23 (Singapore) pointed out that the use of race is also perceived to minimize possible harm:

We did not select this group of patients [based] on the fact [that] they were East Asians. We selected them based on the fact that the BIM [B cell lymphoma-2-like 11] polymorphism was only present in Asians, and the fact that a large proportion of the tumors . . . which was driven by . . . EGFR mutations were . . . present in Asia! . . . [W]e do not discriminate [against] anyone [by] going on a study by race . . . but . . . if there is a scientific rationale . . . if you already know that it's not going to be useful, then it would be unethical to subject them to such a test in the first place. That would constitute a natural exclusion.

In short, racialized statistics do not only suggest populations with a higher prevalence of the genetic biomarker; they also indicate which populations have a lower prevalence. As such, setting the eligibility criteria of participants based on racialized statistics is perceived as a form of ethical protection for populations less likely to benefit from the drug.

Overall, while there are different opinions, it appears that supporters and opponents of using race are driven by similar motivations of finding the best way to accomplish their work: to derive meaningful findings while maximizing possible benefits and minimizing potential harm to clinical trial participants. The difference lies in the preferred approach. Even for those who accept the use of race, we see that they are also aware of the need to go beyond race. However, they choose to first rely on racialized statistics to stratify the population and invest more after the drug has been shown to be effective, because they believe that, in doing so, they save resources. In comparison, those who reject the use of race in the domain of clinical trials prefer to directly test the hypothetically causal genetic biomarker, because such genetics-driven clinical trials, if successful, have the potential to benefit more people (as compared to only the particular racial/ethnic group that was recruited for the trial) more quickly (as the genetic biomarker has already been verified by the end of the trials).

Third domain: Medical decision-making in the clinic

For the context of medical decision-making, responses were gathered from a total of 39 interviewees. Relative to the other two contexts, a smaller percentage of respondents (10; 25.64%) supported the use of race, and a majority (29; 74.36%) objected to it in clinical practice.

Those who objected voiced a fundamental problem with racialized statistics. They argued that racialized statistics indicate the overall probability for a *population*, but when it comes to an *individual*, who is the focus in the clinical context, one cannot be certain if the individual truly has the genetic biomarker until testing has been conducted:

> [Race] is a short form. . . . It is not adequate and not precise enough for medication definitely . . . it's like, "Oh, you are Asian" and you might be accurate ninety-nine times out of hundred, but you are not accurate a hundred times out of hundred. Maybe it is good enough for general medicine but if it is a question of life and death, then . . . I don't think it's good enough.
>
> (Dr.2, Canada)

> Ethnicity alone may predispose you to certain genetic changes that are more prevalent in your particular race but it doesn't mean that just because you belong to that race, you should be automatically . . . ostracized from a treatment."
>
> (Dr.44, Singapore)

> I have a higher suspicion that it is going to be [EGFR] positive if I have a 40-year-old Asian, female, non-smoker. But as I am a scientist and I like the hard data, I want to see the tests all come out in the genomic testing rather than saying, demographically they probably have this mutation, because they might not.
>
> (Dr.16, USA)

Belonging to a racial/ethnic group with low prevalence of a genetic marker does not mean that the individual does not have the genetic marker, or vice versa (Ossorio and Duster, 2005). Generally, the impulse to treat all patients the same way (that is, to send all patients' biological samples for genetic testing) is driven by the desire to avoid ambiguity and its associated potential for medical misdiagnoses:

> All we know is that Indians have less lung cancer in general compared to the other ethnic groups. . . . But if the Indian patient comes down with lung cancer, we will still investigate along the . . . same line as other ethnic groups . . . We look for the mutations in everybody, we know that there is a difference in the incidence but the way we manage them will be the same.
> (Dr.35, Singapore)

> I think the percentages [of EGFR] are slightly higher in the Asian population but to me, that does not mean that a non-Asian is being ruled out for having an EGFR mutation – just because they are not Asian. So I err on the side of testing everybody.
> (Dr.16, USA)

> The phenotypic marker of race and ethnicity, is really only a phenotypic marker . . . the whole point of genetic testing is you get away from these phenotypic looks.
> (Dr.20, USA)

Essentially, a biomarker may occur less frequently in a particular racial/ethnic group, but that biomarker-driven disease, if present, should *not* be treated any differently in different racial/ethnic groups. By sending all patients for genetic testing to ascertain their genetic status, doctors overcome the ambiguity presented by racialized statistics and move one step closer to precision medicine.

Interviewees who supported using race shared how racialized statistics can influence clinical practice in different ways. The first involves deciding whether to send a patient for genetic testing based on race/ethnicity:

> The gene encoding this enzyme [UGT1A1] is very polymorphic. Now in a Caucasian, there is one promoter region which is the *28 which is very common, about 15%. In Asians, . . . Chinese and Malays only, the polymorphism is found in 2–4% of the populations. . . . Indians [are] similar to the Caucasians. It is about 15%. . . . [I]f you compare *6, it is completely absent in a Caucasian and . . . only present in an Asian, so that is where . . . ethnic group matters. . . . The [USA] FDA did not introduce *6 testing because it is totally absent in Caucasian[s] whereas [Singapore] HSA [Health Sciences Authority] introduce[d] both *6 and *28 testing. . . . [T]he prevalence of [a] certain [mutation] in [a] certain ethnic group is important.
> (Dr.37, Singapore)

42 Using race to overcome race

> I think that if we have more information about racial or ethnic background, that [will] probably impact [the] referral pattern.
>
> (Dr.17, USA)

The second involves interpreting results:

> Without knowing the ethnic background of the subject, you don't know whether to interpret [the results] as "Yes, this person has an increased risk" or "No, [for] this person, there is no difference."
>
> (Dr.10, Canada)

The third involves guiding treatment/therapeutic decisions, such as the dosage of a drug:

> [W]e know that . . . Caucasians . . . don't tolerate one particular oral chemotherapy called capecitabine . . . very well, so we usually reduce the dose for them, or we are more vigilant in observing them while they're [in] treatment.
>
> (Dr.44, Singapore)

> We can say that we are doing this because you are Asian [and] there is a higher probability [of toxicity] among Asians than Caucasians . . . and because of this toxicity we have to avoid it. That's harnessing a racial difference . . . for [the] good of the individual.
>
> (Dr.16, Canada)

To decide on a treatment plan, doctors need to be able to identify the medical condition and decide on the best course of action treating it. It is evident from the previous responses that racialized statistics can play a role in the clinical context, but some interviewees who support the use of race also admitted that it may no longer be as relevant in guiding clinical decisions with the rising trend of interracial/interethnic marriages, which can make population studies "complicated to interpret" (Dr.17, USA).

Interviewees who objected to the use of race in the clinic also used this line of argument. As Dr.22 (Singapore) shared, there is currently anecdotal knowledge to guide drug dosages for Asians vis-à-vis Caucasians, but it would be difficult to extend such knowledge to children of interracial/interethnic marriages, who will not have "a very neat categorization."

In other words, the use of race as a proxy for genetics in clinical applications hinges on the ability to correctly identify and sort patients into these racial/ethnic categories. With interracial/interethnic marriages, however, the next generation will have hyphenated identities that cannot be clearly classified. Accordingly, it will be difficult to use race/ethnicity-based probabilities for clinical decision-making.

Moreover, patient-centered care goes beyond considering the patient's genetic profile. Other factors such as patients' circumstances ("can the patients tolerate treatment; are they fit enough to tolerate either chemotherapy or targeted therapy; what are the patient's wishes in terms of what they want in terms of treatment[?]" (Dr.16, USA)) and availability of resources is also important. As such, while testing for the genetic biomarker remains the preferred approach for these critics of using race as a proxy for genetics, they also acknowledged that genetic testing may not always be feasible and that racialized statistics can be used to guide clinical decisions in such resource-poor situations:

> [Race/ethnicity is also] one of the reasons for testing someone . . . because if we were to test all squamous cell lung cancers, that would take up our whole testing budget.
> (Dr.11, Canada)

> They [race-based data] are helpful in the sense that, if we have no information, and we have these characteristics, it gives us an *a priori* probability that the treatment will work . . . this prevalence does not influence whether we biopsy or not. . . . But if we cannot get a result from biopsy, or a patient is not able to undergo biopsy, somebody who's really sick, and where the possibility of a pneumothorax would be devastating, we're not going to biopsy. We might treat empirically.
> (Dr.20, USA)

> Let's say I'm in a country where I don't have the ability to do the test . . . and I have a White patient and an Oriental patient with lung cancer. I can tell the White patient, "Look, if I give you this drug, there's a 10% chance it's going to work," and I can tell the Oriental patient, "There's a 50–70% chance this drug is going to work." That's using ethnicity. But I would rather be a 100% certain; I'd rather do the test.
> (Dr.24, Singapore)

What is ultimately relied on in the clinic – whether to use race or genetics – is influenced by a host of factors, including the availability of resources and the patient's preferences (Sun, 2020).

Conclusion

The primary research question addressed in this chapter is *when* and *why* racialization occurs in precision medicine, which consists of three empirical domains: genomic research, clinical trials, and clinical decision-making. We analyzed the qualitative data collected through 45 semi-structured face-to-face interviews with clinicians and clinician-scientists engaged in translational precision medicine in cancer treatment and prevention. We show that whether practitioners accept the use of race/ethnicity in translational precision medicine is, at least in part, a function of the specific domain logic. Use of race is more accepted in the scientific research domain but becomes less relevant and even problematized when knowledge moves to clinical trials and, subsequently, sites of clinical application. Moreover, we draw on interview data to understand the reasons underlying such a pattern and reveal the inherent contradiction in the usage of race in precision medicine, namely, that geneticists are using race in their research projects, but physicians treating patients think that usage of the racial identity of the patient is something to be overcome.

Even though the translational and precision medicine initiative is new, as today's science and technology studies (STS) scholars have suggested, some of the issues that this initiative has brought up remain the same; for example, is race important when we try to categorize people for genomic research, when we know that race/ethnicity is politically arbitrary and historically contingent? Is finding out more about genetics going to help improve racial and ethnic minorities' health when we know that their poorer health is mainly due to socioeconomic disadvantages? Regarding the issue of race, Shim (2014) showed that epidemiologists measure race, class, and gender as individual traits, but people of color living with heart disease know from their lived experiences that they suffer from heart disease because of the interactional and cumulative effects of inequality. Lee et al. (2001: 66) suggested that "holding scientists accountable for their use of racial categories and racialized populations in their research is a promising intervention" to avoid reifying race as biological. Epstein (2007) traced the political forces that created the "inclusion-difference" paradigm, and the NIH and FDA rule that investigators pursuing grants and conducting clinical trials must state their study recruitment targets by gender, race, and ethnicity. Embedded in such "inclusion-difference" political momentum in the early twentieth century, the scientists that Bliss (2012) interviewed suggested that their use of race/ethnicity is for fighting for social justice.

Our findings enable us to appreciate more fully the social significance of the scholarly literature on race and genomic science, in particular, the "molecular reinscription of race" (Duster, 2015) and the molecularization of race (Reardon, 2004; Koenig et al., 2008; Bliss, 2012; Fullwiley, 2007, 2008; TallBear, 2013; Wade et al., 2014; McGonigle and Benjamin, 2016; Nelson, 2017).

As we have shown, most clinicians do not think that race should be used as a proxy for the patient's genetic profile in the medical domain. It is also important to note that the data shows that, among our interviewees, there is little categorical acceptance of the usage of race; usually, an interviewee's stance is nuanced, accepting such usage only in particular situations or with particular exceptions.

Contrasting opinions among our interviewees also reveal an inherent contradiction regarding the use of race in precision medicine. Namely, we find that scientists say that they must use race in genomic science while medical doctors object to such usage. However, given that medicine uses findings from previous domains to guide clinical decision-making, even if doctors want to use genetic biomarkers, it would be difficult, if not impossible, if scientific research and clinical trials did not frame studies around genetic biomarkers.

Given our findings, we disagree with Burchard et al. (2003), Bustamante et al. (2011), Oh et al. (2015), Popejoy and Fullerton (2016), and Manolio's (2019) suggestion to use race/ethnicity as a proxy for genetic diversity and equity. One way to resolve the inherent contradiction noted previously would be to involve both geneticists and medical doctors to collaborate in translational precision medicine research projects. Otherwise, clinicians may find themselves overwhelmed with racialized drugs (Roberts, 2011; Kahn, 2013) and racialized guidelines (Smart and Weiner, 2018; Sun, 2017) to which they have voiced objections.

Notes: Coding of participants for table 1

We categorized the participants based on their stance towards the use of racialized statistics in each of the three contexts: scientific research, clinical trials, and medical decision-making. First, we read through each transcript and identified instances where the interviewee commented on the use of racialized statistics in scientific research, clinical trials, or medical decision-making. We then analyzed each instance to determine the stance expressed by the interviewee. In assessing each selected instance, we sought to answer the following question: "Based on what the interviewee is saying here, does he/she support the use of racialized statistics in this context?"

We initially intended to simply divide participants into two groups, namely, "Yes," which consists of interviewees who support the use of racialized statistics in that particular context, and "No," which consists of interviewees who object to the use of racialized in that particular context. However, our preliminary attempt at coding the transcripts revealed that these two groups alone were unable to fully capture the nuances of the participants' perspectives. Some interviewees' stances were not as clear-cut as simply "yes" or "no" because they also voiced out concerns. As such, we further divided the "Yes" and "No" groups into subgroups of "Straightforward" and "Nuanced" instead. This gave us a total of four different categories for each context.

We then defined the four groups in the following ways. Interviewees who shared that they used racialized statistics in that context without objections (even if they also demonstrated awareness of its limitations) were placed in the "Yes-Straightforward" group. Interviewees who used racialized statistics in that context but also mentioned the problems with using race or specified that their use of racial information is driven by considerations of genetics were placed in the "Yes-Nuanced" group. Interviewees who rejected the use of racialized statistics and/or voiced support for using factors other than race (e.g., genetics, family history) were placed in the "No-Straightforward" group. Interviewees who mainly used genetics but highlighted how they accept the use of racialized statistics in certain circumstances were placed in the "No-Nuanced" group.

To determine which group the interviewee belonged to for a particular context, we evaluated all the relevant quotes from that interviewee for that context holistically. For example, for Interviewee X, we compiled and looked at all the instances in which he/she commented on the use of racialized statistics in scientific research before arriving at a conclusion about his/her overall stance for scientific research. This process is then repeated for the clinical trials and medical decision-making contexts.

References

Acquaviva KD and Mintz M (2010) Perspective: Are we teaching racial profiling? The dangers of subjective determinations of race and ethnicity in case presentations. *Academic Medicine* 85(4): 702–705. DOI: 10.1097/acm.0b013e3181d296c7.

Bamshad M, Wooding S, Salisbury BA, et al. (2004) Deconstructing the relationship between genetics and race. *Nature Reviews Genetics* 5(8): 598–609.

Bentley AR, Callier S and Rotimi CN (2017) Diversity and inclusion in genomic research: Why the uneven progress? *Journal of Community Genetics* 8(4): 255–266.

Bliss C (2012) *Race Decoded: The Genomic Fight for Social Justice*. Stanford, CA: Stanford University Press.

Bliss C (2015) Science and struggle: Emerging forms of race and activism in the genome era. *The Annals of the American Academy of Political and Social Science* 661(1): 86–108.

Bowser R (2001) Racial profiling in health care: An institutional analysis of medical treatment disparities. *Michigan Journal of Race and Law* 7(1): 78–133.

Braun L (2006) Reifying human difference: The debate on genetics, race, and health. *International Journal of Health Services* 36(3): 557–573. DOI: 10.2190/8jaf-d8ed-8wpd-j9wh.

Braun L, Fausto-Sterling A, Fullwiley D, et al. (2007) Racial categories in medical practice: How useful are they? *PLoS Medicine* 4(9): 1423–1428. DOI: 10.1371/journal.pmed.0040271.

Braun L and Saunder B (2017) Avoiding racial essentialism in medical science curricula. *The American Medical Association Journal of Ethic* 19(6): 518–527. DOI: 10.1001/journalofethics.2017.19.6.peer1-1706.

Brower V (2002) Is health only skin-deep? Do advances in genomics mandate racial profiling in medicine? *EMBO Reports* 3(8): 712–714. DOI: 10.1093/embo-reports/kvf168.

Burchard EG, Borrell LN, Choudhry S, et al. (2005) Latino populations: A unique opportunity for the study of race, genetics, and social environment in epidemiological research. *American Journal of Public Health* 95(12): 2161–2168. DOI: 10.2105/AJPH.2005.068668.

Burchard EG, Ziv E, Coyle N, et al. (2003) The importance of race and ethnic background in biomedical research and clinical practice. *The New England Journal of Medicine* 348(12): 1170–1175.

Bustamante CD, De La Vega FM and Burchard EG (2011) Genomics for the world. *Nature* 475(7355): 163–165.

Duster T (2006) The molecular reinscription of race: Unanticipated issues in biotechnology and forensic science. *Patterns of Prejudice* 40(4–5): 427–441.

Duster T (2015) A post-genomic surprise: The molecular reinscription of race in science, law and medicine. *The British Journal of Sociology* 66(1): 1–27.

Epstein S (2007) *Inclusion: The Politics of Difference in Medical Research*. Chicago: University of Chicago Press.

Foster MW and Sharp RR (2002) Race, ethnicity, and genomics: Social classifications as proxies of biological heterogeneity. *Genome Research* 12(6): 844–850.

Fullwiley D (2007) The molecularization of race: Institutionalizing human difference in pharmacogenetics practice. *Science as Culture* 16(1): 1–30.

Fullwiley D (2008) The biologistical construction of race: "Admixture" technology and the new genetic medicine. *Social Studies of Science* 38(5): 695–735.

Gravlee CC (2009) How race becomes biology: Embodiment of social inequality. *American Journal of Physical Anthropology* 139(1): 47–57. DOI: 10.1002/ajpa.20983.

Hindorff LA, Bonham VL, Brody LC, et al. (2018) Prioritizing diversity in human genomics research. *Nature Reviews Genetics* 19(3): 175–185.

Hussain-Gambles M, Atkin K and Leese B (2004) Why ethnic minority groups are under-represented in clinical trials: A review of the literature. *Health and Social Care in the Community* 12(5): 382–388.

James JE and Joseph G (2022) "Its' personalized, but it's still bucket based": The promise of personalized medicine vs. the reality of genomic risk stratification in a breast cancer screening trial. *New Genetics and Society* 41(3): 228–253.

Jenkins K (2015) *I think therefore you are: Detecting the social construction of race in medicine*. Doctoral dissertation, University of Florida, US.

Kahn J (2003) Getting the numbers right: Statistical mischief and racial profiling in heart failure research. *Perspectives in Biology and Medicine* 46(4): 473–483. DOI: 10.1353/pbm.2003.0087.

Kahn J (2009) Beyond bidil: The expanding embrace of race in biomedical research and product development. *Saint Louis University Journal of Health Law and Policy* 3: 61–92.

Kahn J (2013) *Race in a Bottle: The Story of BiDil and Racialized Medicine in a Post-Genomic Age*. New York: Columbia University Press.

Kivetz Y and Tyler TR (2007) Tomorrow I'll be me: The effect of time perspective on the activation of idealistic versus pragmatic selves. *Organizational Behavior and Human Decision Processes* 102(2): 193–211.

Koenig B, Lee SA and Richardson S eds. (2008) *Revisiting Race in a Genomic Age*. New Brunswick, New Jersey and London: Rutgers University Press.

Lee C (2009) "Race" and "ethnicity" in biomedical research: How do scientists construct and explain differences in health? *Social Science & Medicine* 68(6): 1183–1190. DOI: 10.1016/j.socscimed.2008.12.036.

Lee SS, Mountain J and Koenig BA (2001) The meanings of "race" in the new genomics: Implications for health disparities research. *Yale Journal of Health Policy, Law, and Ethics* 1: 33–75.

Lillquist E and Sullivan CA (2006) Legal regulation of the use of race in medical research. *The Journal of Law, Medicine & Ethics* 34: 535–551. DOI: 10.1111/j.1748-720X.2006.00067.x.

Maglo KN (2010) Genomics and the conundrum of race: Some epistemic and ethical considerations. *Perspectives in Biology and Medicine* 53(3): 357–372.

Manolio TA (2019) Using the data we have: Improving diversity in genomic research. *The American Journal of Human Genetics* 105(2): 233–236.

McGonigle IV and Benjamin R (2016) *The Molecularization of Identity: Science and Subjectivity in the 21st Century*. Cambridge: Cambridge University Press.

Mersha TB and Abebe T (2015) Self-reported race/ethnicity in the age of genomic research: Its potential impact on understanding health disparities. *Human Genomics* 9(1): 1–15.

Nelson A (2017) *The Social Life of DNA: Race, Reparations, and Reconciliation after the Genome*. Boston: Beacon Press.

Nelson SC, Yu JH, Wagner JK, et al. (2018) A content analysis of the views of genetics professionals on race, ancestry, and genetics. *American Journal of Bioethics Empirical Bioethics* 9(4): 222–234. DOI: 10.1080/23294515.2018.1544177.

Oh SS, Galanter J, Thakur N, et al. (2015) Diversity in clinical and biomedical research: A promise yet to be fulfilled. *PLoS Medicine* 12(12): 1–20.

Ossorio P and Duster T (2005) Race and genetics: Controversies in biomedical, behavioral, and forensic sciences. *American Psychologist* 60(1): 115–128.

Panofsky A and Bliss C (2017) Ambiguity and scientific authority: Population classification in genomic science. *American Sociological Review* 82(1): 59–87. DOI: 10.1177/0003122416685812.

Popejoy AB and Fullerton SM (2016) Genomics is failing on diversity. *Nature* 538(7624): 161–164.

Reardon J (2004) *Race to the Finish: Identity and Governance in an Age of Genomics.* Princeton, NJ: Princeton University Press.

Risch N, Burchard E, Ziv E, et al. (2002) Categorization of humans in biomedical research: Genes, race and disease. *Genome Biology* 3(7): comment2007.1(2002). DOI: 10.1186/gb-2002-3-7-comment2007.

Roberts DE (2011) *Fatal Invention: How Science, Politics, and Big Business Re-Create Race in the Twenty-First Century.* New York: New Press.

Root M (2003) The use of race in medicine as a proxy for genetic differences. *Philosophy of Science* 70(5): 1173–1183. DOI: 10.1086/377398.

Schwartz R (2001) Racial profiling in medical research. *The New England Journal of Medicine* 344(18): 1392–1393.

Shah RR and Gaedigk A (2018) Precision medicine: Does ethnicity information complement genotype-based prescribing decisions? *Therapeutic Advances in Drug Safety* 9(1): 45–62. DOI: 10.1177/2042098617743393.

Shim JK (2014) *Heart-Sick: The Politics of Risk, Inequality, and Heart Disease.* New York: NYU Press.

Sirisena ND and Dissanayake VHW (2017) Focusing attention on ancestral diversity within genomics research: A potential means for promoting equity in the provision of genomics based healthcare services in developing countries. *Journal of Community Genetics* 8(4): 275–281.

Smart A and Weiner K (2018) Racialised prescribing: Enacting race/ethnicity in clinical practice guidelines and in accounts of clinical practice. *Sociology of Health and Illness* 40(5): 843–858.

Streicher SA, Sanderson SC, Jabs EW, et al. (2011) Reasons for participating and genetic information needs among racially and ethnically diverse biobank participants: A focus group study. *Journal of Community Genetics* 2(3): 153–163.

Sun S (2017) *Socio-Economics of Personalized Medicine in Asia.* London and New York: Routledge.

Sun S (2020) Clinical usefulness of genetic testing for drug toxicity in cancer care: Decision-makers' framing, knowledge and perceptions. *New Genetics and Society* 39(4): 359–384.

Tallbear K (2013) *Native American DNA: Tribal Belonging and the False Promise of Genetic Science.* Minneapolis, MN: University of Minnesota Press.

Travassos C and Williams DR (2004) The concept and measurement of race and their relationship to public health: A review focused on Brazil and the United States. *Cadernos De Saúde Pública* 20(3): 660–678.

Tsai J, Ucik L, Baldwin N, et al. (2016) Race matters? Examining and rethinking race portrayal in preclinical medical education. *Academic Medicine* 91(7): 916–920.

Wade P, Beltrán CL, Restrepo E, et al. (2014) *Mestizo Genomics: Race Mixture, Nation, and Science in Latin America.* Durham and London: Duke University Press.

3 Transnational colors

Race, ethnicity, and genomic science in the United States of America, Canada, and Singapore

Introduction

With the rising popularity of big data-driven precision medicine initiatives, datasets are increasingly being scrutinized (Hulsen et al., 2019; Schaefer et al., 2019). Recent headlines include: "How the genomics health revolution is failing ethnic minorities" (Mackley, 2017), "Lack of diversity in genomic databases may affect therapy selection for minority groups" (Gallagher, 2021), and "Lack of diversity in genomic research hinders precision medicine for non-White Americans" (University Communications, 2019). In addition, there are academic journal articles with titles such as "Lack of diversity in genomic databases is a barrier to translating precision medicine research into practice" (Landry et al., 2018), "The missing diversity in human genetic studies" (Sirugo et al., 2019), and "Prioritizing diversity in human genomics research" (Hindorff et al., 2018). Diversity in genetic research tends to be assessed based on race/ethnicity. The lack of biological specimens from racial and ethnic minority groups is perceived to be a problem and is primarily understood to be a function of lack of trust in the healthcare system by such minority groups (Kraft et al., 2018; Edwards et al., 2020), lack of consistent community engagement (Edwards et al., 2020), and fear of discrimination (Griffith, 2020; Canedo et al., 2018). Given this ongoing development, the primary research question that this chapter aims to address is, "In the context of basic research and clinical trials, how are race/ethnicity defined and what are the views of scientists, clinician-scientists or clinicians in the field of precision medicine regarding race and genetics?"

Is race biological or socially constructed? A brief overview

Race is often used to stratify populations in genomic science studies. However, one longstanding debate associated with the usage of race/ethnicity as a proxy for genetic diversity is whether race is biological or a social construct. In tracing the history of this debate, Rajagopalan et al. (2016: 350) underscored the importance of understanding it because of its larger implications for "struggles for power resources, political legitimacy, and health and human rights."

DOI: 10.4324/9781003436102-3

The idea that race is biological can be traced back as far as the seventeenth and eighteenth centuries when practitioners in the natural sciences demarcated morphological and physiological traits between races, which were used to support the idea of racial hierarchies. François Bernier, a French physician, was "among the first to try to classify peoples around the world into distinct races using morphological traits" (Rajagopalan et al., 2016: 351). Other attempts followed, including Carolus Linnaeus and Johannes Blumenbach's "proposed hierarchies of four and five major races . . . implicitly ranked along visible phenotypic attributes such as skin and hair color" (Rajagopalan et al., 2016: 351). Similar research continued to emerge over the next few centuries, resulting in "racial differences [being] essentialized – that is, cast as natural, innate, and immutable" (Rajagopalan et al., 2016: 351).

Over the years, various conceptualizations of biological race have emerged, ranging from "Kitcher's biological concept of race [based on the premise of reproductive isolation] . . . Dobzhansky's (1937) genetic race concept, Andreasen's (1998, 2000, 2005) cladistic race concept, and Pigliucci and Kapalan's ecological race concept" (Hardimon, 2013: 23), to Hardimon's (2013) populationist concept of race. The concept of "population" proposes that groups of people differ "not by the absolute presence or absence of different traits but by the statistical frequencies of . . . [genetic] variants or alleles" (Rajagopalan et al., 2016: 353). This notion has contributed to allowing the belief that race is biologically determined to persist in the genomic era because it has "shift[ed] discussions in the biological sciences [away] from earlier 'typological' views of race" and "laid the groundwork for a 'genetic race concept' [by] retaining the core idea of bounded, genetically differentiated groups" (Rajagopalan et al., 2016: 353).

In the genomic era, genetic/genomic research commonly cited as evidence that race is biological include observations that some diseases occur more frequently in particular racial/ethnic groups (e.g., Paul and Brosco, 2013; Wailoo and Pemberton, 2006), the discovery of genetic markers that appear to be able to distinguish populations with different ancestries (also known as population-specific alleles or ancestry informative markers (AIMs)) (e.g., Fullwiley, 2008; Rajagopalan and Fujimura, 2012), as well as genetic clustering studies that divide the human population into groups that seemed to reflect folk racial categories (e.g., Rosenberg et al., 2002).

In sharp contrast, several studies have demonstrated that race is a social construct. As summarized by Rajagopalan et al., (2016: 353–354):

> Scholars in sociology and anthropology, as well as evolutionary genetics, began to argue in the twentieth century that race and race categories were *not* durable, natural, biological, or innate groupings (Boaz, 1912; Du Bois, 1940; Gould, 1996; Lewontin, 1972; Montagu, 1942). . . . These scholars saw race and race categories as sociohistorical, dynamic, and specific to particular times and places, and produced relationally and

processually (Blumer, 1958; Duster, 1990; Hacking, 2005; Haraway, 1997; Stephan, 1986).

These scholars, thus, showed how the idea of race actually began as a sociopolitical construct to justify European colonization (Smedley, 2007). The concept of race only became biologized when "[r]acist sciences constructed biological research outcomes that underscored the very differences they were looking for, and these alleged biological differences were in turn mobilized as 'explanations' for still other alleged differences across race" (Rajagopalan et al., 2016: 351). Indeed, racial categories have been observed to vary across time and place, implying its nature as a social construct. Research to refute the idea that race is genetic have also emerged. For example, Livingstone (1962) argued that there is no biological characteristic (gene or phenotype) that is wholly exclusive to a human population group, and that genetic variability occurs clinally (i.e., that genetic profiles change gradually with distance, similar to the idea of a gradient) rather than by discrete racial groups. Additionally, Lewontin (1972) famously showed how genetic variation between people of the same race was much larger than genetic variation between people of different races. Interestingly, Rosenberg et al.'s (2002: 2381) genetic clustering study, which suggested that the existence of biological racial categories, has also been used by those who oppose the concept of biological race, as the same study also showed that "within-population differences among individuals account for 93 to 95% of genetic variation; differences among major groups constitute only 3 to 5%." This corroborates with Lewontin's (1972) research noted previously.

Scholars who believe that race is a social construct have also argued that claims of race being genetic (i.e., that race is biological) arise from a conflation of race and genetics. This phenomenon has been termed the "molecular reinscription of race" (Duster, 2006) or the "molecularization of race" (Fullwiley, 2007). In addition, as pointed out by Fujimura et al. (2008: 644), many genetic studies looking at the "genetics of difference" have been read as "genetics of race" because of the way samples were selected and the way results were framed. Rather than being evidence that race is biological, these scholars elucidated that the observed racial differences in disease occurrence and outcomes is a reflection of how "racial discrimination comes to be embodied in illness" (Hardimon, 2013: 16; Krieger, 2001; Root, 2003). To these scholars, racial differences in disease occurrence and outcomes are not derived from differences in biology, but differential experiences shaped by social determinants of health. Or as Omi and Winant (2015: 110) put it, "While it may not be 'real' in a biological sense, race is indeed real as a social category with definite social consequences."

In short, while "race" has long been one of the most contested concepts in the social and natural sciences, its position has changed significantly since the year 2000. During this period, it has been reclaimed by some geneticists as a term to describe discrete clusters of human genetic diversity in the population. Controversially, these clusters have been mapped onto historically embedded classification of "race." In turn, this has led to renewed debates about whether "race" is socially constructed and has no genetic or biological basis or whether it can legitimately be reconceptualized as a biological construct (Skinner, 2007). Reardon (2005: 17–44) contrasted this with the late twentieth century, which "witnessed a surge in claims about the biological meaninglessness of race, [whereas in] the early years of the new millennium . . . scientists moved to defend the use of race in biomedical research." Hartigan (2008: 166) has claimed that in the struggle between the social constructionists' and geneticists' conceptualization of race, the latter is "gaining in reality."

In Chapter 2, we showed that a majority of interviewees supported the use of race as a proxy for genetics in scientific research. In this chapter, our analysis of the interview data collected from speaking to geneticists, clinician-scientists, and clinicians in Singapore, Canada, and USA reveals the different ways in which racialization occurs in contemporary genomic science, as well as the different reasons one might believe race to be biological (which justifies its use in genomic science) or a social construct.

Where and how does racialization happen in genomic science?

In what follows, first, we elaborate on eight ways through which a population sample or a patient's identity may be racialized/ethnicized. In addition, we describe the criticisms of these methods raised by our interviewees.

Materials for racialization of a population sample and/or patient

1 Name/surname

One of the most common ways of determining an individual's racial category is by his/her name or surname. As Dr.34 (Singapore) admitted, "I can quite honestly tell you that . . . we just look at the [patient's] name and say that this is a Chinese, Indian or Malay." Similarly, Dr.6 (Canada) shared that "You can do it [based] on surname." Where databases and registries are concerned, Dr.13 (USA) explained that "they have an algorithm to define race and ethnicity by name." For example, in the USA, the National Cancer Institute's Surveillance, Epidemiology, End Results (SEER) program, "Hispanic ancestry . . . is identified through algorithms that identify Spanish surnames" (Bach et al., 2002). Likewise, in the California Cancer Registry, for certain race/ethnic groups, one of the criteria for extracting an individual's racial/ethnic identity is his/her surname, for example, whether it matches the designated lists of Spanish, Middle Eastern, or Vietnamese surnames (California Cancer Registry, 2018).

2   *Visual/appearance/look/phenotype*

Another way an individual's race/ethnicity may be assigned is based on his/her appearance. As Dr.32 (Singapore) put it, "Just look at appearance . . . they are different." Some interviewees from Canada and the USA concurred:

> You show up for your appointment, and the [hospital] admission staff, they have to check a box, and they don't wanna ask, nobody told them how they should collect the data, so then they just looked at you and they say, "Well, she looks like she's Chinese; okay, I'm going to check Chinese."
> (Dr.21, USA)

> By the [researchers] seeing them coming in and participating [in the study] . . . visual identification. So, let's say if you are of mixed racial origin, you will look more like one than the other.
> (Dr.2, Canada)

The underlying assumption for this method is that people of different races/ethnicities have differences in their appearances that have unchanging meanings which are obvious to others viewing them.

3   *National registration identity card (NRIC, only Singapore)*

One method unique to the Singapore context is the determination of an individual's racial/ethnic identity "based on the identity card [NRIC]" (Dr.45, Singapore). As Dr.37 (Singapore) remarked, "Because . . . the name, and I think the race is written there [on the NRIC]. That's their national registry, that's what they are supposed to be." In this way, the Singapore National Registration Identity Card (NRIC) serves as a simple and state-sanctioned way of assigning race/ethnicity to a population sample in the genetic studies or to a patient.

4   *Self-report (including ticking off a box on a form)*

Self-reporting is another way in which racialization occurs. Through this method, the race/ethnicity which the individual self-identifies becomes his/her racial/ethnic identity. Self-identification is a relatively straightforward process, wherein either "You ask them, whether they identify themselves as [a particular racial/ethnic group]" (Dr.40, Singapore) or patients "may have boxes to tick . . . a form to fill up so you can put down what your ethnicity is" (Dr.8, Canada).

5   *Parents/grandparents/ancestry – two generations, three generations, and/or more*

Another method considers not just the individual's self-reported racial/ethnic identity but also that of his/her progenitors, typically the individual's parents and/or grandparents, in deciding the race/ethnicity of the individual. This "generational descent" (Dr.23, Singapore) approach was mentioned by interviewees from Singapore and Canada:

> If the grandparents, parents and . . . the patient, or the human subject, all declare themselves as Malay, then the person is classified as Malay.
>
> (Dr.24, Singapore)

> You not only have your ethnicity, but you have the ethnicity of each of your grandparents. . . . [Y]ou can figure out your parents' [race/ethnicity] from your grandparents'.
>
> (Dr.6, Canada)

Three generations are considered in the former, whereas in the latter, only two generations are considered to infer the individual's parents' race/ethnicity. In other situations, the number of generations are not specified. Dr.17 (USA), for example, shared that she "will sometimes ask about whether they have African or Jewish heritage."

6 Country of (family) origin/nativity

Another way through which an individual's race/ethnicity is determined is based on their country of origin. This question of country of origin may be applied at the individual or family level:

> You ask this question: are you originally from India? Or Pakistan? Bangladesh? Anywhere from the . . . South Asian subcontinent . . . And all of them fulfil it, either they themselves are from there, as a first-generation immigrant, or their parents or grandparents are from there.
>
> (Dr.46, Singapore)

> The issue of ethnicity, family ancestry, country of family origin, is an interesting one . . . we do know that ancestry plays a role in genetic determinance [sic] . . . and precision medicine, [so] we ask the country of family origin . . . where is your family from?"
>
> (Dr.11, Canada)

Likewise, in the USA, studies may "have a separate question for . . . place of birth," and such studies based on country of origin are known as "studies of nativity" (Dr.21, USA).

7 Geography

For scientific research and clinical trials, racial/ethnic grouping can also be determined based on "geographical location on the world map" (Dr.46, Singapore) or "where they originate from" (Dr.15, USA):

Anything that is 6 hours flight from here [Singapore] I guess you [can define as Asian] . . . Thailand is Asia. South Korea is Asia . . . I would consider Japan Asia.

(Dr.27, Singapore)

Some trials . . . will group [e.g., Asians in Canada, Japanese, Korean, and Asians in Singapore] as all Asian, or some trials group it by region. . . . [They will] report it as . . . we had three hundred from Asia, two hundred from North America, one hundred from Europe.

(Dr.3, Canada)

8 Genotyping race/ethnicity based on genetics/ancestry informative markers

The most recent way of racializing a population sample and/or a patient that has emerged is through the use of genetics, "by trying to measure what we call [an] ancestry informative marker (AIM)" (Dr.32, Singapore). As noted previously, this is a minority view among our interviewees and stems from the belief that "we can actually identify ethnicity from the genotypes" (Dr.6, Canada) because "we can look in their DNA and tell where they're from" (Dr.11, Canada). Dr.21 (USA) elaborated:

Before we had the AIMs (Ancestry Informative Markers) toolbox available to us . . . the discourse, mostly among sociologists and social epidemiologists, [was] that race and ethnicity in this country is entirely a social construct. And which I agree with, because it is constructed socially here in this country, but they're based on ancestry . . . where people come from, and there is a biological component to that, and a genetic component to that. So, I think to say it's entirely a social construct, I don't actually agree with that . . . having the AIMs . . . helps us to maybe start to tease the two apart so we can get a better [sense of] what part of it is social, what part of it is genetic.

These eight different ways of race-making may be used alone or in combination. For example, as Dr.34 (Singapore) shared, if there are "patients who look Chinese but . . . have [a] Indian name or Malay name . . . we will have to verify that with their NRIC." Some interviewees also voiced preference for one method over the other. For example:

In the demographics box, they [i.e. patients] self-report. Honestly, I didn't really look at it. I will just talk to them and get a sense of what their cultural background is and who they identify themselves with.

(Dr.16, USA)

Issues with the different ways of racialization

Questioning racialization by name

Regarding the use of names as material for race-making, Dr.6 (Canada) qualified that while name/surname can be used for determining one's race, there are two main issues with this method because "people [get] married and . . . [t]hey use different names . . . some people will have the English name on it, and some the Chinese name, so it's [problematic]." Firstly, when people get married, they may, for example, adopt the surnames of their partners, which may not be deemed to be of the same race as they are. Indeed, a study by Bach et al. (2002) highlighted how in the SEER program, misclassification can occur frequently, particularly for females, because the surname-matching algorithm fails to account for "surname changes that can occur with marriage." Secondly, an individual may have more than one name, as is commonly the case among some Asian communities and children from mixed marriages, and this may affect the race he/she is judged to belong to if his/her different names are associated with different races.

Questioning racialization by NRIC

As Dr.38 (Singapore) pointed out, race-making via NRIC hinges upon collection of race-based data, but whether such data is collected is context-specific (i.e., whether such data is of interest in that country). Furthermore, the racial categories used for population stratification are socially constructed:

> [Race] is . . . a social construct of . . . immigrant countries because of . . . the need for [a] census. That's why we, we collect data on how many people are Malays, Indians and whatever. In countries where race is not part of their census' collections, these issues [of using race as a proxy for genetic diversity] are viewed quite differently.

Questioning racialization by generational descent

As Dr.45 (Singapore) questioned, "What is Chinese anymore? What is Indian anymore? . . . [Y]ou must be like, five generations of pure Chinese?" The number of generations required to classify someone as belonging to a particular racial/ethnic group in a study is a social decision made by the researchers.

Questioning racialization by genetics

Even if we accept the idea that AIMs can specify an individual's racial/ethnic composition in percentages, how we apply these values towards determining one's racial/ethnic identity is also a social decision:

> I think researchers have been increasingly careful in North America about ethnicity, because what percentage of you have to be Chinese before you can be considered Chinese?
>
> (Dr.1, Canada)

Inconsistencies between different ways of racialization

Another issue with these different ways of racialization is how they can yield different answers about an individual's race even when they are applied to the same individual. Dr.25 (Singapore) shared an example:

> One thing I am very careful of is with Indonesians. . . . [T]hey can be Chinese, they can be Indians. But all of them, their names are Malay, you know. So, I am very careful. If the Indonesian patient is clearly a Chinese, I mean, you can also see.

Due to cultural practices in naming conventions, using names and using visual identification to determine one's race/ethnicity can lead to different conclusions. Other interviewees also noted the incongruence that can occur between self-identification and other materials for race-making. One example shared by Dr.4 (Canada) is that between genetics and self-identification: "Some people who are genetically, ¾ White and ¼ Black, they identify [as] Black. Like Michael Jackson." Visual identification and self-identification can also be at odds with each other:

> We ask the patients, they may look Asian, and we say, What race do you have, and they say we are African American, that's what we go with. That's self-reported.
>
> (Dr.14, USA)

As seen in the quote, it appears that one way of resolving such incongruences when they occur is to prioritize one method of racialization over another.

In sum, drawing from our interview data, we have elucidated eight different ways through which racialization occurs in genomic science, and highlighted criticisms raised by interviewees concerning these different ways of race-making. Such empirical evidence lends support to the idea that race is socially constructed. Not surprisingly, Ross (2012) described how the American Congress of Obstetricians and Gynecologists (ACOG) faced difficulty in assigning a single ethnicity to individuals. Moreover, there are also instances in which results of different methods of racialization do not match. While interviewees were able to provide a way of resolving incongruences arising from the usage of different materials for race-making, that is, to prioritize one method of racialization over another, this nonetheless highlights the social construction of race/ethnicity.

Perspectives from the genomic science community about the relationship between race and genetics

Having illustrated the many different ways through which racialization occurs in genomic science, we move on to the next question: What do genomic science experts think about the relationship between race and genetics?

Genetic differences between ethnoracial population groups

Our interview data revealed that a minority of interviewees believe ethnoracial population groups to be genetically different. For example, Dr.46 (Singapore) said the following:

> There is a Singapore . . . Genome Variation Project. So, if you . . . [geno]type everyone for seven hundred thousand markers, you can actually see the differences. One of [the markers] could be [differentiating between] Chinese, Malays, and Indians. . . . If you compare from the genome scan, I can see exactly where you are. Are you really Chinese? Or you're halfway between, halfway between there. No problems. I can even guess whether or not you have European ancestry. So, this is extremely objective.

Similarly, Dr.10 (Canada) remarked that "Ethnicity is really based on your genetics. It's what makes you different from me, it's what your genes are, what your DNA sequence [is]." In other words, for these interviewees, there are real genetic differences between different ethnoracial population groups, such that "race is a proxy for different genetic backgrounds" (Dr.13, USA).

No clear genetic distinction between ethnoracial population groups

However, a majority of the interviewees were of the view that there is no clear genetic distinction between different ethnoracial population groups. Dr.11 (Canada), for example, highlighted that there is only one human race: "Of course, genetically, to call somebody African is kind of silly, because the reality is that's where the human race began." Likewise, Dr.32 (Singapore) pointed out the genetic overlaps between different ethnoracial groups:

> Malays [are] actually some[where] between Chinese and Indians. When you plot their genetic information. So, they have sort of mixtures of contributions from the both the Chinese ancestry and the Indian ancestry.

For these interviewees, rather than being mutually exclusive groups, different ethnoracial population groups are perceived as sharing similarities in their genetic profiles. As Dr.41 (Singapore) put it, "Across the board genomically, it looks to be more similar than different."

Contemporary trends of intermarriages and globalization/migration can further blur the boundaries between ethnoracial population groups. Dr.15 (USA), for example, pointed out how "everybody in the U.S. is a mix of something." Likewise, Dr.1 (Canada) said, "Think about the [genetic] heterogeneity of the population that we have, the third and fourth generation[s] of mixed ethnicities." With regards to globalization/migration:

> Frankly speaking, with the very globalized world [in which] people move left and right, the geographical boundary may not correlate with the political boundary, the political boundary may not correlate with the genomic boundary.
> (Dr.33, Singapore)

> Genetic predisposition wash[es] out with migration pretty quickly . . . [and over] subsequent generations . . . that dissipates even further, and assumes the risk profile of this environment.
> (Dr.15, USA)

Migration has an impact on predisposition to diseases because disease risk is often a result of gene-environment interaction, and migration changes the environment that an individual is exposed to:

> You don't just get the genes that you are born with, things happen to them as you grow. And so, people's live[d] experiences are different and the environmental exposure they have is different.
> (Dr.19, USA)

In other words, for these interviewees, the argument that different ethnoracial population groups are distinct is problematic on three fronts: firstly, while the frequencies of some genetic alleles may differ between ethnoracial population groups, there is no genetic allele that occurs only in a particular ethnoracial population group; secondly, existing ethnoracial categories are becoming increasingly irrelevant as the rising trend of intermarriages results in a growing proportion of people who do not clearly belong in any one ethnoracial population group, and, thirdly, individuals from the same ethnoracial population group can have different disease predispositions when they are in different environments.

Genetic heterogeneity within an ethnoracial population group

Interviewees also emphasized that genetic heterogeneity existed within an ethnoracial population group. Using the so-called "Asian race" as an example:

> Asian is very heterogeneous. So, we know that the Middle East is very different from the South Asian, which is the Indian population, than the North Asian or the Northeast Asian and the Southeast Asia. Even within Southeast Asia it's very diverse.
> (Dr.25, Singapore)

> So, for breast cancers, there's a higher incidence in the Philippines. . . . [T]hey are still Asian, you see, but they are different from somebody from mainland [China].
> (Dr.4, Canada)

> Asians are complicated because when you look at just Asian-American, there [are] so many groups, and there are big differences across the different Asian ethnic groups.
>
> (Dr.21, USA)

While the concept of "Asian" is commonly deemed a race (e.g., Goodman et al., 2012), it is far from being a uniform group, with genetic frequencies varying across different subgroups of Asians.

Race as a social construct

Many interviewees also pointed to race/ethnicity as a social construct. Using Asians as an example, firstly, there is no standard meaning of a particular racial/ethnic category:

> "Asians" in Singapore probably describe Chinese, "Asians" in UK describe Indians, and so it's really relative to the reference point of individuals.
>
> (Dr.31, Singapore)

The definition of a particular racial/ethnic group is fluid and varies depending on context. Dr.19 (USA) provided another example:

> From here what we see, all the Malays are Malay. But in . . . Malaysia, not all Malays are Malay. You know, there is . . . this kind of Malay or this ethnic group, or that ethnic group, or Chinese in Malaysia, how do you count those people? You know, it gets kind of tricky, right?

He surmised that:

> The general principle is . . . when you are outside looking in, everybody inside that group is the same, but when you are in that group, they are all looking different, right? . . . [I]f you are a Malay in this country . . . you are not anything but a Malay, right? . . . But in Malaysia, there are different relations of Malaysians. . . . I'm Vietnamese, okay? There's North Vietnamese, South Vietnamese; if I go back to Vietnam, they won't buy the fact that I am Vietnamese, they will be like "Oh you are Vietnamese-American, oh no you are Vietnamese from the South, Vietnamese from the North, from the Central."

While a group may come across as homogeneous from an outsider's perspective, insiders of that group are more attuned and sensitive to the heterogeneity that exists within the group and therefore able to have a more granular perspective. Thus, what makes sense to an outsider may seem incredulous for insiders. As Dr.18 (USA) exclaimed, "They lump the Philippines, for example, with Thailand, which is just crazy."

Overall, based on our interviews, we find that those who believe in race as a biological concept is a minority, with most interviewees supporting the idea that race is socially constructed. Regardless of whether they believe that race is biological or a social construct, interviewees were able to cite evidence to support their stance. On the one hand, those who believe that race is biological pointed to how genetic differences have been found between different ethnoracial population groups. On the other hand, interviewees who believe that race is socially constructed raised various counterarguments against this. Firstly, they pointed out that instead of being unique, different ethnoracial population groups actually bear similarities and overlaps in their genetic profiles and disease risk. Intermarriages and migration can further dilute any apparent genetic differences between different ethnoracial population groups. Secondly, interviewees who believe that race is socially constructed pointed to the differences in genetic profiles between individuals of the same ethnoracial population groups. All of these points from either camp have been raised in existing literature noted in the introduction section of this chapter, but we contribute by adding the perspectives of geneticists, clinicians, and clinician-scientists. It has mostly been anthropologists, social scientists, historians, legal scholars, and philosophers of science who have cited these reasons to argue that race is socially constructed and oppose the use of race in medicine, but we show that many in the biomedical community also recognize that race is not biological.

Interviewees in support of the idea that race is socially constructed also pointed to the lack of standardization of racial categories. Indeed, various scholars have shown that national population categories are racialized and dynamic across time and space. In the next paragraphs, we briefly discuss how race categories are formed in the three countries – the USA, Canada, and Singapore – where our interviewees are from.

Omi and Winant (2015: 114) described racial formation in the USA as a "*longue durée* . . . from religion to science to politics." They attributed its beginning to the European conquest of the Americas and the "discovery" of the indigenous people who "looked and acted differently" (Omi and Winant, 2015: 113). This, coupled with "the conquerors' determination to appropriate labor, land, and goods, and . . . the presence of an axiomatic and unquestioned Christianity among them" led to the "ferocious division of society into Europeans and 'others'" (Omi and Winant, 2015: 113). Subsequently, with the "rise of [scientific] knowledge, and an attempt to provide a more subtle and nuanced account of human complexity in the new, 'enlightened' age," racial formation in the eighteenth century was driven by the "invocation of scientific criteria" (Omi and Winant, 2015: 115), such as phrenology, craniometry, and even genomics (as discussed previously). However, race is "a pre-eminently political phenomenon" (Omi and Winant, 2015: 120). The US Census is the key reference for racial categories across many domains in USA, but depending on the preexisting "political and social agenda" (Omi and Winant, 2015: 121), the types and definitions of racial categories available have continually evolved, with one of the most recent changes being the option of selecting multiple races.

Thompson (2013) provided a succinct overview of racial formation in Canada. In Canada, racial categories can be broadly divided into three main groups. The first is British and French, the majority population in Canada who are recognized as members of the founding nations of Canada but differentiated on the language grounds. The second is aboriginal peoples, namely, the American Indians, Inuit, and Métis, who are differentiated from other racial minorities as they have "unique rights and constitutional status" due to their "sui generis relationship with the British Crown" (Thompson, 2013: 370). The third is "visible minorities," who are defined under the Employment Equity Act as "persons, other than aboriginal peoples, who are non-Caucasian in race and non-White in color" and include "Chinese, South Asian, Black, Korean, Japanese, Southeast Asian, Filipino, West Asian, Arab, and Latin American" (Thompson, 2013: 372). These tend to be first- or second-generation immigrants. Visible minorities became more prominent in Canada only after Canada's immigration policy became more open to non-White immigration in the twentieth century, but they are becoming an increasingly large population in contemporary Canada.

In Singapore, racial formation is influenced by the nation's history as a British colony and a nation of immigrants (Purushotam, 1998). Racial categories were shaped by the colonial powers, who not only sought to differentiate the European from the Other but also within the Other. Races were differentiated based on three aspects: place of origin, which is determined by Britain's "peculiar map of the globe" that divided the world into "six main blocs"; the dominant language in the part of the bloc that an individual hailed from; and the "essential characters" of each race, which were determined based on their respective "occupational niches" (Purushotam, 1998: 30). There were two kinds of race names – "nationalities," which corresponded with the six blocs on the global map, and "races," which were subsets of nationalities that provided more granular groupings of people (Purushotam, 1998: 32). For the purposes of "census simplification," four umbrella categories ("Europeans and Americans," "Malays and Other Natives of the Archipelago," "Chinese," and "Tamils and other natives of India") were used by combining some nationalities. These umbrella categories were further simplified over time into the current CMIO ("Chinese," "Malay," "Indian," and "Others") system, which has been argued to reflect "[t]he Europeans' loss of hegemony" due to their "absorption . . . into the ubiquitous 'Others'" (Purushotam, 1998: 33).

If race is socially constructed, why are there differences in frequencies of genetic alleles between racial/ethnic groups?

Interviewees holding the view that race is socially constructed explained that observations of differences in the frequencies of genetic alleles between racial/ethnic groups do not necessarily mean that race/ethnicity is genetically determined or, by extension, that one's race/ethnicity dictates his/her genetic composition. In the words of Dr.27 (Singapore):

> If you start off with one size fits all, where everybody is the same, then the next step is [that] not everybody is the same, and . . . one of [the] categories [that they differ by] is by ethnicity. But if you believe that the logical trend is even within the same ethnic group, no two individuals [are] the same . . . the logical endpoint is every patient being treated according to his or her personal makeup.

That is, it is always possible to find differences when two (or more) entities are compared, regardless of the criteria upon which these entities were delineated. What is important to note, though, is that correlation does not always equate to causation. While differences in allele frequencies can be found between racial/ethnic groups, this does not mean that racial/ethnic groups are genetically determined or that racial/ethnic identity determines one's genetic composition. Confusing correlation for causation can lead to the molecular reinscription of race (Duster, 2006).

Scholars have also suggested that the attribution of genetic differences between population groups to biological differences between racial/ethnic groups can be viewed as confirmation bias. As Morning (2014: 190) summarized:

> There are myriad ways in which "facts" about human genetic variation are shaped by analysts' assumptions and decisions. . . . Moreover, they leave many openings for our widely shared beliefs about racial difference to filter in.

One way through which researchers' assumptions and decisions result in confirmation bias is in their selection of samples used in genetic studies. As elucidated by Rajagopalan and Fujimura (2018), although initiatives like the single nucleotide polymorphism (SNP) map and the International Haplotype Mapping Project (HapMap) have uncovered differences in genetics from different populations, the genetic maps upon which these differences were found were built using donor DNA from small numbers of individuals from each continent. These small numbers were unlikely to have captured the genotypic diversity of each continent, yet they were "operationalize[d] . . . as if they were representative of continental genotypes," which is what allowed these apparent "racial" genetic differences to surface (Rajagopalan and Fujimura, 2018: 858). A similar problem exists for genetic clustering studies, which also tend to rely on samples from small numbers of individuals from limited numbers of geographical areas. This is exacerbated by samples being unevenly distributed to "the extremes of continental land masses" (Serre and Pääbo, 2004: 1680, as cited by Morning, 2014: 196). As Morning (2014: 196) explained, this "maximizes the geographic and therefore genetic distance between individuals presumed to belong to distinct continental clusters." Hence, it is not surprising that "racial" genetic differences were discovered. In other words, because of the ways in which DNA samples were selected, findings of genetic differences could be read as "racial" genetic differences (Fujimura and Rajagopalan, 2011; Fujimura et al., 2008, 2014).

Another way through which researchers' assumptions and decisions can result in confirmation bias is via design of genomic technologies and tools. One example is microarrays (also known as chips). Each chip contains an array of short DNA sequences, for example, SNPs, that probe for particular genetic sequences. However, due to the limited space available on a chip, researchers have to decide which types of SNPs are to be included (Rajagopalan and Fujimura, 2018). Decisions have been based on understandings of apparent continental genetic differences as revealed by HapMap, and this has resulted in the development of race-specific (based on continental-level ancestry) SNP chips (Rajagopalan and Fujimura, 2018). It should be noted that "these new chips were also *generative* for HapMap (Rajagopalan and Fujimura, 2018: 864; emphasis original), suggesting a positive feedback loop between race-based findings and the tools used to discover them. Another example is ancestry informative markers (AIMs), which have been criticized as "tautological constructs" that "have been cherry-picked precisely for their power to yield the groupings that their users have already decided are clusters" (Morning, 2014: 197). That is, the AIMs used to assess the genetic profiles of present-day individuals were selected based on researchers' "own understandings of race in their larger social contexts" (Fullwiley, 2008: 706). Since these tools were selectively built based on what researchers understood as different races, it is not surprising that genetic differences were found between races using these tools.

Researchers' assumptions and decisions in the analysis of genetic data also contribute to confirmation bias. In genetic clustering studies, results of statistical analyses are amenable to different input data and user-specified boundaries, and these can be influenced by researchers' preexisting notions of racial categories (Fujimura and Rajagopalan, 2011; Fujimura et al., 2014; Morning, 2014). One example is the *a priori* specification of the number of clusters to be found through an analytical program. As Morning (2014: 199) noted:

> It is common for scientists to test the model fit of only a few possible options for the number of clusters (K), ranging in the single digits (e.g., $K = 2$ through 6 in Rosenberg et al., 2005), which is consistent with contemporary notions of the number of races in our species.

Some researchers may also

> check whether [the statistical software] grouped individuals as *expected*. That is, they checked whether these plots group samples according to

the researchers' information and assumptions about sampled individuals' ethnic or geographic backgrounds . . . to see whether their program was working correctly.

(Fujimura and Rajagopalan, 2011: 12, emphasis original)

These two examples once again illustrate the idea of a confirmation bias. That is, what are supposedly more "objective" methods of analyzing population genetic differences were limited by researchers' preexisting notions of race to produce "racial" genetic differences.

In sum, much in the way that race is socially constructed, findings of "racial" genetic differences are also constructed, whether by intentional seeking of differences between racial groups, or by a confirmation bias that results in the racialization of samples and analytical methods. Even when contemporary genomic science researchers make conscious efforts to avoid the use of race (Fujimura and Rajagopalan, 2011; Fujimura et al., 2014; Rajagopalan and Fujimura, 2018), preexisting notions of race can continue to color genomic research in subtle ways.

If not race, what drives human genomic diversity?

Instead of racial/ethnic diversity, some interviewees suggested that "most of the genetic diversity is *driven by [some] sort of geography*" (Dr.12, USA). Dr.28 (Singapore), for example, argued that "[Allele frequency] only varies by geography because people from different geographies have different genetic profiles." Dr.3 (Canada) further illustrated this point using the Chinese ethnoracial population group as an example:

> You look at Chinese people, we're quite a heterogeneous group. You have the Northern Chinese population, [who would] probably mix with the Mongolians and the Russians, and the Southern Chinese people [– they] are very different, you know what I mean?

This example showcases the argument that genetic diversity varies by geographical proximity rather than racial/ethnic categories, as people in Northern China are more similar to people from other ethnoracial population groups (i.e., non-Chinese) who are located nearby than people from the same ethnoracial population group (i.e., Chinese) who are located more distantly.

Similar ideas have been raised, for example, by Livingstone (1962), who, as noted in the introduction section of this chapter, argued that genetic variability occurs clinally. More recently, Maglo et al. (2016: 4) also posited that it is the concept of cline rather than the concept of cluster that "best accounts for human evolutionary diversity." In other words, in genomic science, perhaps genetic diversity should be evaluated on the basis of geography rather than race.

Conclusion

This chapter examines the involvement of race in genomic science, and we contribute to the debate of whether race is a biological or social construct in three primary ways. Firstly, we identify the different (and some new) ways in which racialization occurs in genomic science. In addition, drawing on the interview data, we discuss the problems with each way of racialization, as well as the inconsistencies between different ways of racialization. As such, when "race" is used in genomic science and medicine, the questions that should immediately come to mind are: Are we talking about name/surname-race? Appearance-race? NRIC-race? Self-reported race? Parental or grandparental race? Country of family origin/nativity race? Geographical race? AIMs race? The specific material used for racialization has implications for how we should understand the study and the generalizability and applicability of its findings.

Secondly, we show that among our interviewees, the majority understand that racial categories are arbitrary and change over time, and the meaning of a particular category varies depending on the context. In other words, they understand that racial and ethnic diversity is not the same as genetic diversity. There are two main arguments that can be identified in the interview data in support of their view that racial/ethnic diversity is not genetic diversity: the genetic similarities between ethnoracial population groups and the genetic heterogeneity within each ethnoracial population group. Similar arguments have been made in the existing literature, but we contribute by adding voices from the biomedical community (geneticists, clinicians, and clinician-scientists), whose perspectives have been underrepresented. As such, this chapter presents empirical data pointing to the dubious nature of calling for equitable racial and ethnic representation among participants in precision medicine research. Indeed, some scholars have suggested that gender, race, and ethnicity need to be reevaluated in their roles as disease risk modifiers and perhaps replaced (or at least considered jointly) with environmental or social determinants of health (Prosperi et al., 2018; Shah and Gaedigk, 2018; Edwards et al., 2020). For example, the risk for disease susceptibility may be better determined through one's zip code (Mensah et al., 2019).

Thirdly, our findings indicate that the "molecular reinscription of race" (Duster, 2006) is a real threat. That is, the "molecularization of race" (Fullwiley, 2007) is happening, and the threat of race and ethnicity being seen as biological is real, even though it is a minority view in our study. Some of our interviewees wanted to find out if there were genetic differences between ethnic/racial groups or whether genetics explained racial and ethnic differences in health outcomes, and they did, which led them to believe that race and ethnicity were genetically determined. However, we would like to reiterate that the finding of genetic differences between ethnoracial population groups should not surprise us, because one can always find differences between any two groups. As Duster (2006: 434) stated, "It is possible to make arbitrary groupings of populations defined by geography, language, self-identified faiths, other identified physiognomy and so on and still find statistically significant allelic variations between these groupings." This is seen in Takezawa et al.'s (2014: 3) genomic study of the seemingly homogeneous Japanese population, wherein the authors found that "even among mainland Japanese, statistically meaningful genetic differentiation was found among individuals in different regions, such as Tohoku, Kanto, Kinki, and Kyushu." Hence, it is inaccurate and unreliable to infer that allelic frequency variations represent intrinsic biological distinctions across racial or ethnic populations.

Finally, our arguments build upon the concept of differential racialization as proposed by Baluran (2023). While his conceptualization of differential racialization centers on how definitions of race can vary across different levels (the national/"official" versus the individual/localized level), we demonstrate that definitions of race can also vary within the same level, for example, between different scientists. In other words, our findings suggest that differential racialization not only occurs vertically across different levels, but also occurs horizontally within the same level.

For example, in this chapter, we show the various materials used by scientists, clinician-scientists, and medical doctors for race-making in precision medicine. These can be broadly divided into self-identification based on self-reporting by the DNA donor/patient and external identification, whereby precision medicine stakeholders assign a racial/ethnic identity to the DNA sample/patient. The latter ranges from methods such as determining race/ethnicity based on name/surname and visual appearance, to family history-based methods such as asking about parents' and/or grandparents' ancestry or (family) country of origin, to technology/genetics-based methods like AIMs. As we note, these different methods of racialization may not always yield the same outcomes. Likewise, later in Chapter 5, we show that scientists and clinicians and health economists can all discuss "Caucasian" or "Asian" genetic susceptibility to drug toxicity, but the categories of "Caucasian" or "Asian" have no standard scientific definition and are constructed very differently by different social actors.

In addition, among the different materials for race-making mentioned previously, some may be more relevant to particular group(s) of stakeholders, while others can be used more generally. For instance, racialization based on visual assessment is less likely to be implemented by scientists, who, unlike medical doctors, may not come into direct contact with donors of DNA samples, whereas racialization based on name/surname can easily be utilized by all three groups of stakeholders as scientists, clinician-scientists, and medical doctors are all likely to have access to this data.

It is also important to note that even within different groups of stakeholders, perceptions of racial/ethnic boundaries can differ. This can be attributed in part to colonial (and local) history, which influences the racial/ethnic categories available in different countries and, therefore, the ways in which precision medicine stakeholders may approach population stratification (see Chapter 1). In parallel, in-group/out-group differences can also contribute to differences in the drawing of racial/ethnic boundaries, whereby someone belonging to the in-group tends to provide a more granular delineation of the population than someone from an out-group.

In sum, we suggest that differential racialization is not just about how an individual or a patient's self-identified race may be different from how institutions identify the individual racially/ethnically, but also about how different groups of elites and different individuals within each group of elites may operationalize race.

References

Andreasen R (1998) A new perspective on the race debate. *British Journal for the Philosophy of Science* 44: 199–225.
Andreasen R (2000) Race: Biological reality or social construct? *Philosophy of Science* 47: S653–S666.
Andreasen R (2005) The meaning of 'race': Folk conceptions and the new biology of race. *Journal of Philosophy* 102: 95–106
Bach PB, Guadagnoli E, Schrag D, et al. (2002) Patient demographic and socioeconomic characteristics in the SEER-Medicare database: Applications and limitations. *Medical Care* 40(8): IV19–IV25.
Baluran DA (2023) Differential racialization and police interactions among young adults of Asian descent. *Sociology of Race and Ethnicity* 9(2): 220–234. DOI: 10/1177/23326492221125121.
Blumer H (1958) Race prejudice as a sense of group position. *Pacific Sociological Review* 1(1): 3–7.
Boaz F (1912) Changes in the bodily form of descendants of immigrants. *American Anthropologist* 14(3): 530–562.
California Cancer Registry (2018). Definitions. Available at: https://explorer.ccrcal.org/definitions.html (accessed 22 December 2023)
Canedo JR, Miller ST, Myers HF, et al. (2018) Racial and ethnic differences in knowledge and attitudes about genetic testing in the US: Systematic review. *Journal of Genetic Counselors* 28: 587–601. DOI: 10.1002/jgc4.1078.
Dobzhansky T (1937) *Genetics and the Origins of the Species*. New York: Columbia University Press.
Du Bois WEB (1940) *Dusk of Dawn: An Essay toward an Autobiography of a Race Concept*. New York: Harkhort, Brace.
Duster T (1990) *Backdoor to Eugenics*. New York and London: Routledge.
Duster T (2006) The molecular reinscription of race: Unanticipated issues in biotechnology and forensic science. *Patterns of Prejudice* 40(4–5): 427–441.
Edwards TL, Breeyear J, Piekos JA, et al. (2020) Equity in health: Consideration of race and ethnicity in precision medicine. *Trends in Genetics* 36(11): 807–809.
Fujimura JH, Bolnick DA, Rajagopalan R, et al. (2014) Clines without classes: How to make sense of human variation. *Sociological Theory* 32(3): 208–227. DOI: 10.1177/0735275114551611.
Fujimura JH, Duster T and Rajagopalan R (2008) Race, genetics, and disease: Questions of evidence, matters of consequence. *Social Studies of Science* 38(5): 643–656. DOI: 10.1177/0306312708091926.
Fujimura JH and Rajagopalan R (2011) Different differences: The use of "genetic ancestry" versus race in biomedical human genetic research. *Social Studies of Science* 41(1): 5–30. DOI: 10.1177/0306312710379170.
Fullwiley D (2007) The molecularization of race: Institutionalizing human difference in pharmacogenetics practice. *Science as Culture* 16(1): 1–30.

Fullwiley D (2008) The biologistical construction of race: "Admixture" technology and the new genetic medicine. *Social Studies of Science* 38(5): 695–735. DOI: 10.1177/0306312708090796.

Gallagher C (2021) Lack of diversity in genomic databases may affect therapy selection for minority groups. *Mayo Clinic News Network*. Available at: https://newsnetwork.mayoclinic.org/discussion/lack-of-diversity-in-genomic-databases-may-affect-therapy-selection-for-minority-groups/ (accessed 5 October 2023).

Goodman AH, Moses YT and Jones JL (2012) *Race: Are We So Different?* West Sussex: Wiley-Blackwell.

Gould SJ (1996) *The Mismeasure of Man*. New York: W. W. Norton.

Griffith DM (2020) Preface: Precision medicine approaches to health disparities research. *Ethnicity & Disease* 30(1): 129–134. DOI: 10.18865/ed.30S1.129.

Hacking I (2005) Why race still matters. *Daedalus* 134(1): 102–116.

Haraway D (1997) *Modest_Witness@Second_Millenium.FemaleMan_Meets_OncoMouse: Feminism Meets Technoscience*. Hove: Psychology Press.

Hardimon MO (2013) Race concepts in medicine. *The Journal of Medicine and Philosophy* 38(1): 6–31. DOI: 10.1093/jmp/jhs059.

Hartigan J Jr (2008) Is race still socially constructed? The recent controversy over race and medical genetics. *Science as Culture* 17(2): 163–193.

Hindorff LA, Bonham VL, Brody LC, et al. (2018) Prioritizing diversity in human genomics research. *Nature Reviews Genetics* 19: 175–185.

Hulsen T, Jamuar SS, Moody AR, et al. (2019) From big data to precision medicine. *Frontiers in Medicine* 6(34): 1–14.

Kraft SA, Cho MK, Gillespie K, et al. (2018) Beyond consent: Building trusting relationships with diverse populations in precision medicine research. *The American Journal of Bioethics* 18(4): 3–20.

Krieger N (2001) Theories for social epidemiology in the 21st century: An ecosocial perspective. *International Journal of Epidemiology* 30(4): 668–677.

Landry LG, Ali N, Williams DR, et al. (2018) Lack of diversity in genomic databases is a barrier to translating precision medicine research into practice. *Health Affairs (Millwood)* 37(5): 780–785. DOI: 10.1377/hlthaff.2017.1595.

Lewontin RC (1972) The apportionment of human diversity. In: Dobzhansky T, Hecht MK and Steere WC (eds) *Evolutionary Biology*. New York: Springer, pp. 381–398.

Livingstone FB (1962) On the non-existence of human races. *Current Anthropology* 3(3): 279–281.

Mackley M (2017) How the genomics health revolution is failing ethnic minorities. *The Conversation*, 13 November. Available at: https://theconversation.com/how-the-genomics-health-revolution-is-failing-ethnic-minorities-86385 (accessed 5 October 2023).

Maglo KN, Mersha TB and Martin LJ (2016) Population genomics and the statistical values of race: An interdisciplinary perspective on the biological classification of human populations and implications for clinical genetic epidemiological research. *Frontiers in Genetics* 7: 22. DOI: 10.3389/fgene.2016.00022.

Mensah GA, Jaquish C, Srinivas P, et al. (2019) Emerging concepts in precision medicine and cardiovascular diseases in racial and ethnic minority populations. *American Heart Association* 125(1): 7–13. DOI: 10.1161/CIRCRESAHA.119.314970.

Montagu A (1942) *Man's Most Dangerous Myth: The Fallacy of Race*. New York: Harper.

Morning A (2014) Does genomics challenge the social construction of race? *Sociological Theory* 32(3): 189–207. DOI: 10.1177/0735275114550881.

Omi M and Winant H (2015) *Racial Formation in the United States*. New York and Oxfordshire: Routledge.

Paul DB and Brosco JP (2013) *The PKU Paradox: A Short History of a Genetic Disease*. Baltimore: John Hopkins University Press.

Prosperi M, Min JS, Bian J and Modave F (2018) Big data hurdles in precision medicine and precision public health. *BMC Medical Informatics and Decision Making* 18(139).

Purushotam NS (1998) *Negotiating Language, Constructing Race: Disciplining Difference in Singapore.* Berlin and New York: Mouton De Gruyter.

Rajagopalan RM and Fujimura JH (2012) Making history via DNA, making DNA from history: Deconstructing the race-disease connection in admixture mapping. In: Wailoo K, Lee C and Nelson A (eds) *Genetics and the Unsettled Past: The Collision between DNA, Race and History.* New Brunswick: Rutgers University Press.

Rajagopalan RM and Fujimura JH (2018) Variations on a chip: Technologies of difference in human genetics research. *Journal of the History of Biology* 51: 841–873. DOI: 10.1007/s10739-018-9543-x.

Rajagopalan RM, Nelson A and Fujimura JH (2016) Race and science in the twenty-first century. In: Felt U, Fouché R, Miller CA and Smith-Doerr L (eds) *The Handbook of Science and Technology Studies.* Cambridge and London: The MIT Press, pp. 349–378.

Reardon J (2005) Chapter 2. Post – World War II expert discourses on race. In: *Race to the Finish: Identity and Governance in an Age of Genomics.* Princeton: Princeton University Press, pp. 17–44.

Root M (2003) The use of race in medicine as a proxy for genetic differences. *Philosophy of Science* 70(5): 1173–1183.

Rosenberg NA, Mahajan S, Ramachandran S, et al. (2005) Clines, clusters, and the effect of study design on the inference of human population structure. *PLoS Genetics* 1(6): 660–667.

Rosenberg NA, Pritchard JK, Weber JL, et al. (2002) Genetic structure of human populations. *Science* 298(5602): 2381–2385. DOI: 10.1126/science.1078311.

Ross LF (2012) A re-examination of the use of ethnicity in prenatal carrier testing. *American Journal of Medical Genetics* 158A(1): 19–23. DOI: 10.1002/ajmg.a.34361.

Schaefer GO, Tai E and Sun S (2019) Precision medicine and big data. *Asian Bioethics Review* 11(3): 275–288.

Serre D and Pääbo S (2004) Evidence for gradients of human genetic diversity within and among continents. *Genome Research* 14: 1679–1685.

Shah RR and Gaedigk A (2018) Precision medicine: Does ethnicity information complement genotype-based prescribing decisions? *Therapeutic Advances in Drug Safety* 9(1): 45–62.

Sirugo G, Williams SM and Tishkoff SA (2019) The missing diversity in human genetic studies. *Cell* 177(1): 26–31.

Skinner D (2007) Groundhog day? The strange case of sociology, race and "science". *Sociology* 41(5): 931–943. DOI: 10.1177/0038038507080446.

Smedley A (2007) *Race in North America: Origin and Evolution of a Worldview.* Boulder, CO: Westview Press.

Stephan NC (1986) Race and gender: The role of analogy in science. *Isis* 77(2): 261–277.

Takezawa Y, Kato K, Oota H, et al. (2014) Human genetics research, race, ethnicity and the labeling of populations: Recommendations based on an interdisciplinary workshop in Japan. *BMC Biomedical Ethics* 15: 33.

Thompson D (2013) Racial formations: Canada. In: Mason PL (ed) *Encyclopedia of Race and Racism.* New York: MacMillan Reference USA, pp. 370–373.

University Communications (2019) Lack of diversity in genomic research hinders precision medicine for nonwhite Americans. *University of North Carolina at Chapel Hill University Communications*, 19 June. Available at: https://uncnews.unc.edu/2019/06/19/lack-of-diversity-in-genomic-research-hinders-precision-medicine-for-nonwhite-americans/ (accessed 5 October 2023).

Wailoo K and Pemberton SG (2006) *The Troubled Dream of Genetic Medicine: Ethnicity and Innovation in Tay-Sachs, Cystic Fibrosis, and Sickle Cell Disease.* Baltimore: John Hopkins University Press.

4 The "relative resources" model

Heterogeneity of resources and the racialization of precision medicine[1]

"Race is really the poor man's genomic test."

– Interviewee Dr.3 (Canada)

Introduction

In Chapter 2, we demonstrated an inherent contradiction in the use of race as a proxy for genetics along the precision medicine trajectory from the scientific research domain to the clinical application domain. In this chapter, we provide suggestions to resolve the contradiction. We propose a relative resources model to predict and explain when genetics (as opposed to race/ethnicity) is used in medical decision-making and whether personalized precision medicine or racialized precision medicine will dominate in a particular setting.

As suggested by its name, the relative resources perspective proposes that whether an individual patient experiences personalized precision medicine or racialized precision medicine is relative to the amount of resources he/she has access to. The implementation of personalized precision medicine requires certain types of resources, but such resources are not always distributed evenly across the population. Some patients may have access to all the necessary resources and are thus able to enjoy personalized precision medicine, whereas other patients may not have access to all the necessary resources and may therefore be unwilling or unable to pursue personalized precision medicine. In the latter cases, healthcare providers can only fall back on racialized precision medicine as the alternative, albeit a suboptimal one. To illustrate this relative resources model, we first discuss the possible futures of medicine, before delving into how different types of resources can influence which type of medicine dominates.

The "personalized medicine" versus "racialized medicine" debate

The current practice of medicine is predominantly race/ethnicity-based, but recent developments in genetics/genomic research and medicine present an alternative pathway for the future of medicine – personalized precision

DOI: 10.4324/9781003436102-4

medicine. Instead of using population-based categories like race/ethnicity to guide clinical decisions, personalized precision medicine "utilize[s] genomic, epigenomic and environmental factors to determine the biological characteristics of a disease and subsequently provide specific individualized treatment to the patient" (U.S. Food and Drug Administration, 2013).

The emergence of personalized precision medicine is exciting because "the concept of individualized medicine . . . is a fundamental change in medicine that has long relied on the idea of a typological patient" (Chakravarti, 2015: 12). The conventional use of racial/ethnic categories in medicine may be driven by how "race is a complex but empirically demonstrable stratifying practice" (Ossorio and Duster, 2005: 119; Omi and Winant, 2015). Being able to split the population up into subgroups provides hints about disease occurrence and therefore an individual's susceptibility to the disease based on his/her group membership. However, the classification of patients based on race/ethnicity is problematic because "it is possible to make arbitrary groupings of populations defined by geography, language, self-identified faiths, other identified physiognomy and so on and still find statistically significant allelic variations between these groupings" (Duster, 2006: 434). Takezawa et al. (2014: 3), for example, was able to uncover "statistically meaningful genetic differentiation" between people from different regions of Japan even though they all belong to the same racial/ethnic group of mainland Japanese. The assumption that there are innate biological differences between racial/ethnic groups based on the observation that allelic frequencies differ between these groups is therefore flawed. Personalized precision medicine is also preferable to racialized precision medicine because it addresses the issue of genotypic/phenotypic variations within racial/ethnic groups. By focusing directly on an individual's actual genetic status (rather than an individual's probabilistic risk of having an allele), personalized precision medicine can provide more accurate predictions of one's disease susceptibility and drug response to guide medical decision-making (Chan et al., 2012; Fullwiley, 2007). Chan et al. (2012: 317), for example, concluded in their study of warfarin pharmacogenomics in Asia that "information from genetic testing is superior to clinical biomarkers and self-reported population/ethnic membership for predicting warfarin dose requirements." Given these advantages of personalized precision medicine over racialized precision medicine, some scholars believe that personalized precision medicine will eventually completely replace race-based medicine (Chaussabel and Pulendran, 2015; Dancey, 2012; Fullwiley, 2007; Hunt and Kreiner, 2013; Tutton et al., 2008).

In sharp contrast, other scholars take the view that race-based medicine will persist despite the emergence of personalized precision medicine (Hunt and Kreiner, 2013; Kahn, 2004, 2012; Lee et al., 2001; Prainsack, 2015; Roberts, 2011; Root, 2003; Tate and Goldstein, 2004; Weigmann, 2006; Wolinsky, 2011). This is supported by empirical observations that the actual rates of adopting personalized precision medicine are low, and some clinicians continue to rely on race/ethnicity for clinical decision-making (Bonham et al., 2009; Collier, 2012; Hunt and Kreiner, 2013; Petersen et al., 2014). This may in part be a legacy of medical school training, where the frequent usage of racial/ethnic categories in study materials cultivates the mindset that using race/ethnicity as a diagnostic shortcut is an acceptable norm (Brooks, 2015; Swetlitz, 2016). The continued use of racial/ethnic categories by clinicians may also be influenced by the use of these categories by other stakeholders, who continue to generate racialized statistics that can be used in clinical decision-making (Root, 2003). For example, genetic scientists and researchers have been found to continue using racial/ethnic categories in their work even when they are aware of its limitations (Fullwiley, 2007; Montoya, 2007). They may organize their results based on race/ethnicity even when it is a genome-based study (Prainsack, 2015; Weigmann, 2006), or use race/ethnicity as a convenient "residual category" (Kahn, 2004, 2012, 2013: 158) to address observed differences between populations that cannot be explained by genetics (Kahn, 2004, 2012; Roberts, 2011). The framing of these results in racial/ethnic terms means that clinicians, who rely on these results to inform their clinical decision-making, are led to view their patients through this racial/ethnic lens. In other words, the use of race/ethnicity as a proxy for genetics by different stakeholders involved in precision medicine provides the opportunity for race/ethnicity to reenter the sphere of medicine as biological categories "through the backdoor" (Fullwiley, 2007; Prainsack, 2015; Rajagopalan and Fujimura, 2012). Furthermore, from a practical perspective, various barriers stand in the way of greater uptake of personalized precision medicine. Broadly, this includes its higher financial burden (Bonham et al., 2016; Jensen and Murray, 2005; Kahn, 2012; Kohane, 2015; Petersen et al., 2014; Root, 2003; Rothstein, 2016; Sun, 2017), insufficient evidence of its benefits, and lack of skilled manpower and infrastructure to support the implementation of genomics in medical practice (Bonham et al., 2016; Cyranoski, 2016; Dzau and Ginsberg, 2016; Kahn, 2012; Kohane, 2015; Mirnezami et al., 2012; Rothstein, 2016; Satel, 2002), as well as concerns about the risks of genetic discrimination (Mirnezami et al., 2012; Rothstein, 2016).

There are also other factors fueling the racialization of precision medicine. From a business perspective, for example, medicine marketed based on race/ethnicity may have a higher chance of success. This was exemplified in the case of BiDil, which was marketed as a drug for African Americans and endorsed by African American medical practitioners (Caulfield, 2011; Kahn, 2004). Rather than using biology to get at the individual patient, pharmaceutical companies may benefit more from using biology to "get at race in drug marketing" (Kahn, 2004), because the social traction it brings along may make the drug more profitable. From a political perspective, sustaining the narrative that racial/ethnic-based differences in health outcomes occur because of differences in biology could serve political agendas by diverting attention away from class or societal factors that need to be addressed (Prainsack, 2015). Other movements, such as activism for the mandatory inclusion of women and minorities in genetic research for the sake of fair representation and the resultant introduction of policies like the NIH Policy and Guidelines on the Inclusion of Women and Minorities as Subjects in Clinical Research (Duster, 2006; Epstein, 2007; Fullwiley, 2007; Knerr et al., 2011; National Institutes of Health, 2017; Roberts, 2008), as well as the increasing number of countries claiming sovereignty over their populations' DNA in the name of protection against "possible bio-piracy from the pharmaceutical industry" (Benjamin, 2009; Duster, 2015), have also contributed to reinforcing the idea that there are inherent biological differences between racial/ethnic groups and the reinscription of race at the molecular level (Duster, 2006).

In short, the existing literature seems to paint a rather dichotomous future for medicine, where either personalized precision medicine or racialized precision medicine will predominate across the board. However, we seek to provide a more nuanced view by suggesting that whether personalized precision medicine or racialized precision medicine dominates is context-dependent. Drawing from our interview data, we propose that the key determinant of whether a patient will experience personalized precision medicine or racialized precision medicine is the amount of resources crucial for the implementation of personalized precision medicine that he/she has access to.

"Race is really the poor man's genomic test": The relative resources model

All interviewees in our study had no issue agreeing with the idea that personalized precision medicine is superior to racialized precision medicine in managing an actionable genetic disease because the treatment in such cases is molecular-based. What is it then that stops personalized precision medicine from being used all the time? Interviewees revealed that it is the availability of resources that determine whether personalized precision medicine is clinically practiced:

> They [physicians who use race/ethnicity to decide on medical treatment] just don't have the *resources* to go and look for the genomic signature. So they've been using race instead [be]cause it's easy, race is cheap, you just tick it off on a box, versus trying to sequence everybody, for an extra thirty to fifty thousand dollars per patient . . . that's going to add hundreds of million dollars to your cost. So if you just do it this way, this is just the cheap version of figuring out your genomics, to be quite honest, right? . . . [T]hat's why I say *race is really the poor man's genomic test*.
>
> (Dr.3, Canada)

> That's a pragmatic decision, it's not actually based upon racial things, rather that it's a hint, and you're doing that because of . . . a cost model, because it's more prevalent in that population . . . if I were to tell you that you were to screen 10,000 Chinese to benefit one, and you

screen 100 [Indians] to benefit seven, *and you only have that amount of resource[s]*, then you would choose to screen only the Indians, and that would be sensible and pragmatic.

(Dr.39, Singapore)

In an ideal situation, screening recommendations and medical treatment for an individual are guided by his/her unique genetic information (i.e., personalized precision medicine). However, clinical realities may not be so straightforward. Several studies have pointed out the need for a variety of resources at the level of the individual patient in the context of genomic medicine (Cooke-Hubley and Maddalena, 2011; Hall and Olopade, 2005; Markens, 2017; Senier et al., 2015; Sleeboom-Faulkner, 2009).

Here, we suggest that the availability of resources also facilitate or undermine physicians' ability to practice personalized precision medicine. Sometimes, physicians may not be in a position to use a patient's genetic information for more precise medical care. Racialized precision medicine sometimes becomes the alternative because information about one's race/ethnicity is easily obtainable and racialized probability statements are readily available to guide medical decisions:

> They [race/ethnicity-based data] are helpful in the sense that if we have no information, and we have these characteristics . . . it gives us an *a priori* probability that the treatment will work . . . if we . . . cannot get a result from [a] biopsy, or [if] a patient is not able to undergo [a] biopsy, somebody who's really sick. . . . These [data] are very helpful to make decisions.
>
> (Dr.20, USA)

That said, interview data suggested that race- or ethnicity-based estimates are less convincing than family-history-based estimates for disease susceptibility and drug responsiveness. Having shown that the availability of resources is a key determinant for the realization of personalized precision medicine, one other question remains: what are the resources important for realizing personalized precision medicine, and what can public health policymakers do to enable the physicians to practice personalized precision medicine? Drawing from our interviewees' responses, we identified three main categories of resources: financial resources, human and informatics resources, as well as legal and infrastructural resources.

Financial resources

One of the resources required to realize personalized precision medicine is financial resources. Personalized precision medicine can be a huge financial burden on patients, and there are various factors contributing to this. Firstly, the need to identify one's genetic status means additional expenses required to conduct genomic/genetic sequencing (Jensen and Murray, 2005; Kahn, 2012; Kohane, 2015; Petersen et al., 2014; Root, 2003; Sun, 2017). This was also highlighted by Dr.3 (Canada) in the quote previously, where he pointed out that "trying to sequence everybody, for an extra thirty to fifty thousand dollars per patient . . . that's going to add hundreds of million dollars to your cost." These cost estimations are clearly quite daunting, regardless of whether they are considered at the individual or systemic level. As such, whether in a multi-payer health system like the USA and Singapore, where healthcare costs are borne by the patient if they are not covered by insurance, or a single-payer public health system like Canada, where healthcare costs are mostly borne by the government, the financial burden of genomic/genetic testing can be challenging.

Secondly, molecular-based drugs are more expensive. Because molecular-based drugs are deemed to have smaller target groups, they are often priced higher to ensure their profitability (Bonham et al., 2016; Kohane, 2015; Petersen et al., 2014; Rothstein, 2016; Sun, 2017). Despite the high costs of molecular-based drugs, some physicians remained optimistic about personalized precision medicine:

> I think it is good, it keeps the hospital functioning, patients can go back to work and they feel good. . . . So, for example, gefitinib (i.e., Iressa), there's a small population of patients [who have] a very high chance of getting a response to . . . a very easy non-toxic drug that do not actually cost the medical system anything in terms of nurses, chemo time or any of that stuff. They feel great and they live longer and contribute back to society with $2600 a month.
>
> (Dr.1, Canada)

For these physicians, even though molecular-based drugs are expensive, the overall cost-benefit ratio of molecular-based drugs is positive because of their greater efficacy. However, as some interviewees lamented, even if molecular-based drugs do offer greater benefits, their exorbitant prices are often beyond one's means, and compromises may have to be made:

> [E]ven though the benefits of target drugs are really impressive . . . the cost of the target drugs is prohibitive. These drugs are coming to the marketplace now at . . . astronomical prices, prices that the vast majority of patients would not be able to afford even with a co-pay. . . . [T]hese drug prices are . . . not sustainable.
>
> (Dr.13, USA)

> Even if the patient has got a[n] EGFR mutation, and you say that "Look, you've got to spend $3000 . . . a month to pay for this drug, and you got 18 months of [expected survival]" . . . the guy might say, "so for the extra year . . . I'm gonna spend a heck of a lot of money for something

[i.e. cancer] that is ultimately going to kill me. So why don't I save the money and give it to my kids for their education?"

(Dr.44, Singapore)

The cost of molecular-based drugs is not just a concern in multi-payer public health systems where individuals have to pay out of pocket for their medical treatment, but also in single-payer public health systems like Canada:

In the US, the cost [of targeted therapy] may be higher than in Canada. Even if you cut down the price by half . . . gefinitib (i.e. Iressa) costs about $20,000 Canadian dollars here; Tarceva is about $3000, and Crizotinib is about $50,000. . . . [E]verything is out of our control. Look at all the drugs, who is going to pay for it? . . . I have some patients who sell their house and buy this drug to live for two months.

(Dr.7, Canada)

In other words, personalized precision medicine may have a good cost-benefit ratio in theory, but in practice, it is difficult to access the drug in the first place (much less enjoy the benefits it offers) because the high prices are too inhibitive.

Given the exorbitant price of targeted therapies, clinicians may sometimes be forced to make treatment recommendations based on their own assessments of a patient's financial situation, as the following interviewee suggested:

If I say this in front of [the] patient's children, "Here are three drugs for your mother, SGD $10,000, SGD $5000, SGD $1000, which one do you want?" How do you . . . expect [them] to answer this question? . . . So here, we roughly assess and look at the patient's and family's financial background . . . and we make our own decision, "Look, I think that six months' extra life is not worth putting in all this money." . . . If I think using this drug is good enough, I will treat this patient with this drug and I will not escalate.

(Dr.34, Singapore)

Dr.34's (Singapore) comments are significant because it is indicative of a mechanism of stratification of healthcare services less discussed in the literature. Specifically, medical sociology has long recognized that treatment options stratify by social-economic class through the mechanism of insurance access. Here, in addition to such insurance-stratified healthcare services, we've found that physicians in a co-pay system may be forced to decide on the treatment based what they think their patients can afford to pay.

Thirdly, personalized precision medicine may not be covered by insurance policies, so patients who choose to take this route often must fork out money from their own pockets (Bonham et al., 2016; Rothstein, 2016; Sun, 2017). This is especially relevant for patients in multi-payer public health systems.

Dr.12 (USA) illustrated this by comparing two genetic tests, but the same logic applies to molecular-based drugs:

> Provided you have insurance, [genetic testing is pretty much] covered without much question. . . . I don't think [EGFR mutation testing is] a major barrier now, especially because it's approved. . . . [T]here are more expensive type tests, like . . . [the] Oncotype Dx test . . . and I think in [the] US, it is about $4000 for the test . . . and patients will have to pay out of pocket for that, so that's more challenging.

Insurance policies can be a source of financial support for patients, but insurance coverage with respect to personalized precision medicine is inadequate. This lack of insurance coverage could be due to how personalized precision medicine is not yet mature, but as we point out later, insurers may also limit coverage to protect their own interests. Without insurance coverage, a patient will have to shoulder the financial burden of personalized precision medicine himself/herself, and this may not be viable if he/she does not have sufficient financial resources on an individual level.

In sum, to implement personalized precision medicine, the availability of financial resources is crucial. Moreover, one needs to consider financial resources at both the systemic level and individual level (i.e., an individual's financial capability). Therefore, policymakers can assist in facilitating personalized precision medicine by providing state subsidies and public insurance coverage. Without sufficient financial resources, the substantial burden of financing the necessary genomic/genetic testing and molecular-based drugs prevents personalized precision medicine from being realized, even if it is available.

Human and informatics resources

The second type of resources necessary for the realization of personalized precision medicine is human and informatics resources. Existing literature has highlighted a precision medicine skills and knowledge gap amongst healthcare professionals (Bonham et al., 2016; Cyranoski, 2016; Mirnezami et al., 2012; Rothstein, 2016). Indeed, there appears to be a differential rate of diffusion in terms of the adoption of personalized precision medicine across healthcare institutions:

> [W]ith any technology, there is a diffusion and . . . rates of testing are just a lot higher around academic medical centers . . . where you . . . have . . . a lot more updates and . . . advanced choices.
>
> (Dr.12, USA)

Academic or university medical centers (vis-à-vis, for example, community hospitals) are more likely to implement personalized precision medicine. This

The "relative resources" model 79

is unsurprising as academic medical centers, with their access to cutting-edge technologies, manpower, and knowledge, have historically also been at the forefront of adopting new technologies in patient care. But this has implications for the realization of personalized precision medicine at an individual level. As Dr.12 (USA) also pointed out, "If the provider doesn't offer testing, the patient would never have probably known of it." Physicians are gatekeepers between patients (generally, the untrained lay public) and personalized precision medicine. Given the current situation, patients without access to academic medical centers are more likely to miss out on opportunities to enjoy personalized precision medicine even if the other required resources are in place, simply because the healthcare institution they visit lack the necessary skills and knowledge. Policymakers can support the implementation of personalized precision medicine by facilitating the knowledge transfer and arranging for the sharing of medical specialists and equipment.

However, acquiring the necessary skills and knowledge to apply personalized precision medicine is not an easy feat. Dr.29 (Singapore) admitted that it "becomes more and more difficult for the doctor to have that amount of knowledge with them." As a form of translational medicine, personalized precision medicine is an interdisciplinary endeavor that requires knowledge and skills from many different fields, including medicine, genetics, epidemiology, and informatics. It is therefore unrealistic to expect a single individual to master all of these. Rather, the implementation of personalized precision medicine requires the assembly of multidisciplinary teams that can come together to provide the different types of knowledge required:

> I think there need[s] to be ideally experts in the field to come together. . . . We're talking about medical geneticists, ethicists, sometimes lawyers. . . . you need to put together all the minds, in order to figure out how to safely and most effectively use this tool. . . . So, for example, my unit [of] thinking [is] patients, but then there are some people whose units of thinking are genes, proteins, cells.
>
> (Dr.4, Canada)

Moreover, as there are limitations to human capabilities, another important resource is the development of informatic tools that can help to support the implementation of personalized precision medicine. Currently, the lack of computational capabilities, effective diagnostic and clinical support tools to help identify, measure, and interpret the impact of genomic/genetic factors, as well as the long turnaround time for genetic tests are impeding the implementation of personalized precision medicine (Bonham et al., 2009, 2016; Kohane, 2015; Mirnezami et al., 2012; Satel, 2002). Dr.5 (Canada) brought up some of these issues and highlighted the ways better informatic tools can help:

> You have attended some of the meetings and you can see there are many people physically in the room and a lot of them are involved in

the analysis of tumor[s] and also there's [a] two to three month gap between the time you do the biopsy and the time you get the read out. The tim[ing] of it . . . and the manpower required at the moment is impractical. When it becomes more automated, there [will be] this kind of electronic library of searchable treatments. . . . Where a computer does most of that work then the time will [be] cut down and it may become more practical.

Although multidisciplinary knowledge is crucial, frequently pulling together many experts in one place may not be viable in the long run. The long waiting time for genetic testing results that are critical for the implementation of personalized precision medicine may also not be feasible for patients in urgent need of medical care. Better informatics tools – particularly with algorithms which do not have automatic "race corrections" (Roberts, 2021) – can help to streamline these processes by shortening the time required to obtain genetic testing results and compiling multidisciplinary knowledge to support healthcare professionals in making decisions based on the genetic testing results more efficiently.

Personalized precision medicine cannot be realized without the accurate and timely identification of an individual's genetic profile and understanding of what it means. Human and informatics resources are thus another important resource required for the implementation of precision medicine as they carry out or facilitate the processes required to ascertain and interpret an individual's genetic profile. Patients in health systems with stronger financial support on a systemic level, such as that in Canada, may have easier and more equal access to these human and informatics resources as they are likely to be less reliant on their personal financial resources to access medical care from more advanced healthcare institutions.

Legal and infrastructural resources

Another barrier to the realization of personalized precision medicine that is often cited in literature is the lack of adequate regulatory frameworks to protect the interests of patients (Mirnezami et al., 2012; Rothstein, 2016). This was also raised by Dr.38 (Singapore) during the interview:

> In Singapore, we have no law to prevent . . . discrimination for patients with germline mutations. Say, you are found with [a] BRCA mutation . . . and you go for a job interview, if somehow you have blogged about it on your Facebook, and your . . . employers see it; and he . . . chooses not to employ you because he is worried about you taking sick leave if you do get breast cancer, there is nothing to protect [you].
>
> (Dr.38, Singapore)

In Singapore, although there are existing legislations to govern medical data in general ("Private Hospitals and Medical Clinics Act" and the "Human

Biomedical Research Act"; Chong et al., 2018; Ministry of Health, Singapore, 2023) and a code of practice detailing standards that should be upheld for the provision of genetic/genomic testing ("Code of Practice Standards for the Provision of Clinical Genetic/Genomic Testing Services"; Ministry of Health, Singapore, 2018), there is no specific legislation to safeguard genetic data privacy. This is in contrast to the USA and Canada, where there are laws to specifically prevent genetic discrimination, namely, the Genetic Information Nondiscrimination Act (GINA) in the USA and the Genetic Non-Discrimination Act (GNDA) in Canada.

As Dr.38 (Singapore) suggested, the lack of adequate regulatory frameworks to protect patients against genetic discrimination, such as in the context of Singapore, is worrying because misappropriation of one's genetic profile can happen, with serious consequences for the patient and their families. Beyond employment opportunities, another area where knowledge of one's genetic profile can have an impact is health insurance:

> It's very clear to me that, if you have a genetic risk, it can affect your job, it can affect your health insurance, it can affect what kind of medical care you get.
>
> (Dr.19, USA)

> Genetic germline testing . . . or . . . even acquired mutations [i.e. somatic mutations] . . . which could predispose people to certain diseases . . . could be used as a basis for denying employment, denying . . . medical healthcare coverage, all those things. So, of course that's . . . more tricky, because that data, used in the wrong way . . . could be harmful to the individual.
>
> (Dr.40, Singapore)

Acquired somatic mutation is nonhereditary, and hence, there is no concern about how the genetic information would implicate a patient's biological descendants. By contrast, genetic testing for germline mutations could pose concerns as germline mutations could be passed on to descendants. They could thus be affected by the genetic testing results even if they did not undergo the test themselves.

From the perspective of employers and insurers, hiring or insuring individuals with high disease susceptibility goes against their interest because these companies run the risk of suffering monetary losses should the individuals really fall ill (Billings et al., 1992; Gostin, 1991; Hall and Rich, 2000; Levin, 2013; Miller, 1998; Roberts et al., 2011; Taylor, 2001). Knowledge about an individual's genetic profile can therefore also be useful for employers and insurers even though its intended purpose was for medical treatment. Being able to identify individuals with high genetic risk of disease allows employers and insurers to take measures to minimize their losses, for example, by shunning such individuals in employment, charging higher insurance premiums or even excluding insurance coverage for the diseases that an individual has higher genetic risks for.

As such, knowing one's genetic profile can be a double-edged sword. On the one hand, it allows an individual to receive more tailored medical care, for example, in terms of more accurate screening recommendations, or more efficacious and/or less toxic treatment options. On the other hand, it exposes the individual to greater risks of experiencing discrimination, especially in terms of employment and health insurance. Public policymakers can facilitate in providing sufficient legal protection so that patients are not forced to choose between the risk of not having the most optimal medical treatment and the risk of being subject to employment or insurance discrimination. Such regulatory or legal protection is even more important when we take into account potential socioeconomic impact of the genetic testing results on both the patients and their biological family members. This can then cause individuals to reject personalized precision medicine even when it is available. Policymakers can facilitate the implementation of personalized precision medicine by providing the right legal and infrastructural resources to address the issue of fear of genetic discrimination.

Implications of the relative resources model

In demonstrating our proposed relative resources perspective, we identified the heterogeneity of resources (i.e., financial resources and human and informatics resources respectively) necessary to enable physicians to practice personalized precision medicine in their clinics. Importantly, besides financial resources, other resources such as the introduction of the necessary legislative frameworks must also be in place for the implementation of personalized precision medicine. Moreover, given that our interviewees hail from three different countries with different public healthcare systems and legislative contexts, the fact that they reflected similar views about the barriers of personalized precision medicine suggests that these barriers are shared concerns across different contexts.

This proposed relative resources model also implies the practical impact that a heterogeneous distribution of resources can have on the future of medicine. It is similar to the knowledge gap hypothesis proposed by Tichenor et al. (1970), which posits that knowledge is also unevenly distributed, such that information tends to reach those of a higher socioeconomic status more quickly than those of a lower socioeconomic status. In the current context of heterogeneity of resources in medicine, those who are resource-rich are more likely to enjoy better health outcomes than those who are resource-poor. This could in turn lead to worse health inequalities in a precision medicine era. Our interview data provides a comparative view of the experiences of different public health systems (Canada's single-payer public health system versus the multi-payer health system in the USA and Singapore) and suggests that investments in the necessary resources at a systemic level are more likely to reduce such inequalities as access to such resources become more equal and evenly spread amongst individuals.

Conclusion

In this chapter, we consider what the future of medicine will look like given the emergence of personalized precision medicine as a better alternative to the race-based practice that has predominated in the clinical sphere so far. Contrary to existing literature that seem to paint a dichotomous future where either personalized precision medicine or racialized precision medicine will predominate, we put forth the argument that the future of medicine will be a mix of personalized precision medicine and racialized precision medicine.

Moreover, we delineate the various kinds of solutions required to implement personalized precision medicine in the clinic to achieve its fullest promise. These solutions target the different types of resources that we suggest are required for the shift from racialized precision medicine to personalized precision medicine. We organize these resources into three categories: (i) financial resources, (ii) human and informatics resources, as well as (iii) legal and infrastructural resources.

Because personalized precision medicine hinges upon genetics, it requires more financial and human and informatics resources to not only uncover and interpret each individual patient's unique genetic profile but also address the increased pricing of drugs by pharmaceutical companies to counter the companies' possibility of reduced profitability. Hoskins et al. (2015) discussed how the drug Bevacizumab was disapproved by Canada and the United Kingdom, but approved in European Union, because of its excessive cost. They argued that the

> so-called cost of a drug can be changed either directly by the manufacturers of their own accord or, more likely, secondary to funding bodies refusing to pay the asking price, or by physicians using the drug more effectively. NICE's rejection of a drug on the basis of its excessive cost, although correct in principle, does preclude the possibility of subsequent price renegotiation.
>
> (Hoskins et al., 2015: 1540)

In other words, the costs of precision medicine drugs are often not inherently high and can be adjusted with the right support.

The existing legal framework also needs to be able to protect patients specifically from genetic discrimination. These three types of resources thus contribute to creating a conducive environment for the realization of personalized precision medicine and making personalized precision medicine a feasible alternative.

We have empirically demonstrated our argument that resource-relativity exacerbates a trade-off between personalized and racialized precision medicine.

Since resources are finite and tend to be unevenly distributed (Cazap, 2014; Chong et al., 2018; Gray et al., 2017), access to these three types of resources can differ from individual to individual depending on, for example, the public healthcare system he/she is in and his/her personal financial capabilities. To ensure that more people are able to enjoy the benefits of personalized precision medicine and avoid worsening existing health inequalities, sufficient investments need to be injected into all of the identified resources, especially on a systemic level, to ensure a wider reach and a more level playing field for all patients.

Note

1 This chapter has been adapted from the journal article in *International Sociology* "Between personalized and racialized precision medicine: A relative resources perspective" (Sun, 2020), and the permission to quote from published materials has been sought from *Sage Publications*.

References

Benjamin R (2009) A lab of their own: Genomic sovereignty as postcolonial science policy. *Policy and Society* 28(4): 341–355.

Billings PR, Kohn MA, de Cuevas M, et al. (1992) Discrimination as a consequence of genetic testing. *American Journal of Human Genetics* 50(3): 476–482.

Bonham VL, Callier SL and Royal CD (2016) Will precision medicine move us beyond race? *New England Journal of Medicine* 374(21): 2003–2005.

Bonham VL, Sellers SL, Gallagher TH, et al. (2009) Physicians' attitudes toward race, genetics, and clinical medicine. *Genetics in Medicine* 11(4): 279–286.

Brooks K (2015) A silent curriculum. *Journal of American Medical Association* 313(19): 1909–1910.

Caulfield T (2011) Public representation of genetics: Reifying race. In: Maheu L and Macdonald RA (eds) *Challenging Genetic Determinism: New Perspectives on the Gene in Its Multiple Environments*. Montreal: McGill-Queen's University Press, pp. 158–181.

Cazap E (2014) Personalised cancer care – a global perspective. *European Oncology & Haematology* 10(2): 104–106.

Chakravarti A (2015) Perspectives on human variation through the lens of diversity and race. *Cold Spring Harbor Perspectives in Biology* 7(9): a023358.

Chan S, Suo C, Lee S, et al. (2012) Translational aspects of genetic factors in the prediction of drug response variability: A case study of warfarin pharmacogenomics in a multi-ethnic cohort from Asia. *The Pharmacogenomics Journal* 12(4): 312–318.

Chaussabel D and Pulendran B (2015) A vision and a prescription for big data-enabled medicine. *Nature Immunology* 16(5): 435–439.

Chong HY, Allotey PA and Chaiyakunapruk N (2018) Current landscape of personalized medicine adoption and implementation in Southeast Asia. *BMC Medical Genomics* 11(1): 94. DOI: 10.1186/s12920-018-0420-4.

Collier R (2012) A race-based detour to personalized medicine. *Canadian Medical Association Journal* 184: E351–E353.

Cooke-Hubley S and Maddalena V (2011) Access to genetic testing and genetic counseling in vulnerable populations: The d/Deaf and hard of hearing population. *Journal of Community Genetics* 2(3): 117–125.

Cyranoski D (2016) China embraces precision medicine on a massive scale. *Nature* 529(7584): 9–10.
Dancey J (2012) Genomics, personalized medicine and cancer practice. *Clinical Biochemistry* 45(6): 379–381.
Duster T (2006) The molecular reinscription of race: Unanticipated issues in biotechnology and forensic science. *Patterns of Prejudice* 40(4–5): 427–441.
Duster T (2015) A post-genomic surprise: The molecular reinscription of race in science, law and medicine. *The British Journal of Sociology* 66(1): 1–27.
Dzau VJ and Ginsberg GS (2016) Realizing the full potential of precision medicine in health and healthcare. *Journal of the American Medical Association* 316(16): 1659–1660.
Epstein S (2007) *Inclusion: The Politics of Difference in Medical Research.* Chicago and London: University of Chicago Press.
Fullwiley D (2007) The molecularization of race: Institutionalizing human difference in pharmacogenetics practice. *Science as Culture* 16(1): 1–30.
Gostin L (1991) Genetic discrimination: The use of genetically based diagnostic and prognostic tests by employers and insurers. *American Journal of Law and Medicine* 17(1–2): 109–144.
Gray M, Lagerberg T and Dombrádi V (2017) Equity and value in 'precision medicine'. *The New Bioethics* 23: 87–94. DOI: 10.1080/20502877.2017.1314891.
Hall M and Olopade OI (2005) Confronting genetic testing disparities: Knowledge is power. *Journal of the American Medical Association* 293(14): 1783–1785.
Hall MA and Rich SS (2000) Patients' fear of genetic discrimination by health insurers: The impact of legal protections. *Genetics in Medicine* 2(4): 214–221.
Hoskins, PJ, Fung M, Miller D, et. al. 2015. Time for a level playing field: Inequalities in regulatory/approval processes – the example of Bevacizumab in Epithelial Ovarian Cancer. *Journal of Clinical Oncology* 33(14): 1539–1542.
Hunt LM and Kreiner MJ (2013) Pharmacogenetics in primary care: The promise of personalized medicine and the reality of racial profiling. *Culture, Medicine, and Psychiatry* 37(1): 226–235.
Jensen K and Murray F (2005) Intellectual property landscape of the human genome. *Science* 310(5746): 239–240.
Kahn J (2004) How a drug becomes "ethnic": Law, commerce, and the production of racial categories in medicine. *Yale Journal of Health Policy, Law, and Ethics* 4(1): 1–46.
Kahn J (2012) The troubling persistance of race in pharmacogenomics. *Journal of Law, Medicine and Ethics* 40(4): 873–885.
Kahn J (2013) *Race in a Bottle: The Story of BiDil and Racialized Medicine in a Post-Genomic Age.* New York and West Sussex: Columbia University Press.
Knerr S, Wayman D and Bonham VL (2011) Inclusion of racial and ethnic minorities in genetic research: Advance the spirit by changing the rules? *Journal of Law, Medicine and Ethics* 39(3): 502–512.
Kohane IS (2015) Ten things we have to do to achieve precision medicine. *Science* 349(6243): 37–38.
Lee SS-J, Mountain J and Koenig BA (2001) Meanings of race in the new genomics: Implications for health disparities research. *Yale Journal of Health Policy, Law and Ethics* 1(1): 33–76.
Levin N (2013) A defense of genetic discrimination. *Hastings Center Report* 43: 33–42. DOI: 10.1002/hast.193.
Markens S (2017) 'I'm not sure if they speak to everyone about this option': Analysing disparate access to and use of genetic health services in the US from the perspective of genetic counselors. *Critical Public Health* 27(1): 111–124.

Miller PS (1998) Genetic discrimination in the workplace. *Journal of Law Medicine, and Ethics* 26(3): 189–197.

Ministry of Health, Singapore (2018) Code of practice on the standards for the provision of clinical genetic/genomic testing services. Available at: www.moh.gov.sg/docs/librariesprovider5/licensing-terms-and-conditions/genetictestingstandards.pdf (accessed 28 September 2023).

Ministry of Health, Singapore (2023) Human Biomedical Research Act. Available at: www.moh.gov.sg/policies-and-legislation/human-biomedical-research-act (accessed 6 October 2023).

Mirnezami R, Nicholson J and Darzi A (2012) Preparing for precision medicine. *New England Journal of Medicine* 366(6): 489–491.

Montoya MJ (2007) Bioethnic conscription: Genes, race, and Mexicana/o ethnicity in diabetes research. *American Anthropological Association* 22(1): 94–128.

National Institutes of Health (2017) NIH policy and guidelines on the inclusion of women and minorities as subjects in clinical research. Available at: https://grants.nih.gov/grants/funding/women_min/guidelines.htm (accessed December 2018).

Omi M and Winant H (2015) *Racial Formation in the United States*. New York and Oxfordshire: Routledge.

Ossorio P and Duster T (2005) Race and genetics: Controversies in biomedical, behavioral, and forensic sciences. *American Psychologist* 60(1): 115–128.

Petersen K, Prows C, Martin L and Maglo K (2014) Personalized medicine, availability, and group disparity: An inquiry into how physicians perceive and rate the elements and barriers of personalized medicine. *Public Health Genomics* 17(4): 209–220.

Prainsack B (2015) Is personalized medicine different? (Reinscription: The sequel) a response to Troy Duster. *The British Journal of Sociology* 66(1): 28–35.

Rajagopalan R and Fujimura JH (2012) Will personalized medicine challenge or reify categories of race and ethnicity? *American Medical Association Journal of Ethics Virtual Mentor* 14(8): 657–663.

Roberts DE (2008) Is race-based medicine good for us?: African American approaches to race, biomedicine, and equality. *Journal of Law, Medicine & Ethics* 36(3): 537–545.

Roberts DE (2011) *Fatal Invention: How Science, Politics, and Big Business Re-Create Race in the Twenty-First Century*. New York: New Press.

Roberts DE (2021) Abolish race correction. *The Lancet* 367(10268): 17–18. DOI: 10.1016/S0140-6736(20)32716-1.

Roberts LW, Barry LK and Warner TD (2011) Potential workplace discrimination based on genetic predisposition: Views of workers. *American Journal of Bioethics Primary Research* 2(3): 1–12. DOI: 10.1080/21507716.2011.617717.

Root M (2003) The use of race in medicine as a proxy for genetic differences. *Philosophy of Science* 70(5): 1173–1183.

Rothstein MA (2016) Some lingering concerns about the Precision Medicine Initiative. *Journal of Law, Medicine & Ethics* 44(3): 520–525.

Satel S (2002) I am a racially profiling doctor. *The New York Times*, 5 May. Available at: www.nytimes.com/2002/05/05/magazine/i-am-a-racially-profiling-doctor.html (accessed November 2016).

Senier L, Kearney M and Orne J (2015) Using public-private partnerships to mitigate disparities in access to genetic services: Lessons from Wisconsin. *Genetics, Health and Society* 16: 269–305.

Sleeboom-Faulkner M (2009) *Human Genetic Biobanks in Asia: Politics of Trust and Scientific Advancement*. London and New York: Routledge.

Swetlitz I (2016) Teaching medical students to challenge 'unscientific' racial categories. Available at: www.statnews.com/2016/03/10/medical-schools-teaching-race/ (accessed November 2016).

Sun S (2017) *Socio-Economics of Personalized Medicine in Asia*. London and New York: Routledge.

Sun S (2020) Between personalized and racialized precision medicine: A relative resources perspective. *International Sociology* 35(1): 90–110.
Takezawa Y, Kato K, Oota H, et al. (2014) Human genetic research, race, ethnicity and the labeling of populations: Recommendations based on an interdisciplinary workshop in Japan. *BMC Med Ethics* 15: 33.
Tate SK and Goldstein DB (2004) Will tomorrow's medicines work for everyone? *Nature Genetics* 36: S34–S42.
Taylor JR (2001) Mixing the gene pool and the labor pool: Protecting workers from genetic discrimination in employment. *Temple Environmental Law & Technology Journal* 20(1): 51–71.
Tichenor PJ, Donohue GA and Olien CN (1970) Mass media flow and differential growth in knowledge. *Public Opinion Quarterly* 34(2): 159–170.
Tutton R, Smart A, Martin PA, et al. (2008) Genotyping the future: Scientists' expectations about race/ethnicity after BiDil. *Journal of Law, Medicine and Ethics* 36(3): 464–470.
U.S. Food and Drug Administration (2013) Paving the way for personalized medicine: FDA's role in a new era of medical product development. Available at: www.fdanews.com/ext/resources/files/10/10-28-13-Personalized-Medicine.pdf (accessed November 2016).
Weigmann K (2006) Racial medicine: Here to stay? *EMBO Reports* 7: 246–249.
Wolinsky H (2011) Genomes, race and health. *EMBO Reports* 12(2): 107–109.

5 Pharmacogenetic/pharmacogenomic drug toxicity studies, race/ethnicity, and managing adverse drug reactions in the clinic
Ongoing tensions

> If you are using SNP to say that "oh this person because of their SNP profile is going to get a bad toxicity [reaction] to a drug," that I might believe. I don't think you can short cut to say SNP shows that toxicity is more common in this ethnicity and therefore you can use ethnicity. . . . I don't think it is un-interesting but I think it is a dangerous pattern to use ethnicity to make medical decisions.
> – Interviewee Dr.1 (Canada)

Introduction

Existing studies on drug efficacy and race have shown that population groups can be strategically appropriated by interested parties to the detriment of the health care of individuals designated as members of said groups (Kahn, 2013; Roberts, 2011). We explore an emergent but less-studied phenomenon in this chapter: pharmacogenetic/pharmacogenomics drug toxicity studies and race. It is important to understand this development concerning drug safety, not least because scholars have warned that prescribing medications on the basis of race/ethnicity oversimplifies the complexities and interplay of ancestry, health, disease, and drug response (Tishkoff and Kidd, 2004). Moreover, the conflation of race with genetics could open the door to prejudice, racial stereotyping, and ultimately, poor health care (Bliss, 2011; Bonham et al., 2016; Ventura Santos et al., 2015). Indeed, as Bowser (2001: 119) pointed out,

> physicians may miss clinically relevant information or assume the presence or absence of genetic or cultural factors that, in fact, may or may not be present . . . racial profiling leads to errors in diagnosis, distorted judgments about the appropriate course of treatment, and, ultimately, to different and inferior medical treatment.

Furthermore, the genetic mutations shaping drug toxicity effects are germline mutations (not somatic mutations) that can be passed down across generations. As such, the testing of such germline mutations has implications for the larger familial and racial/ethnic groups.

In addition, predictive pharmacogenetic testing further complicates the pharmaceutical firms' profit-making agenda, which relies on producing effective and safe drugs for the masses, not on segmenting the population and catering to them differently and specifically in accordance with drug toxicity findings (Surendiran et al., 2008). Racialization of pharmacogenomic drug toxicity studies adds another layer of complexity to the practice of medicine, which has legal implications.

This chapter has three sections: first, we provide documentary evidence, including a review of published studies on two cancer drug prescriptions, allopurinol and 5-fluorouracil (5-FU), used in the US, Canada, and Singapore, as well as a systematic review of journal articles on cost-effectiveness studies for precision medicine/targeted therapies/stratified medicine drugs and race/ethnicity, in order to reveal the racialization and ethnicization of pharmacogenetics/pharmacogenomics toxicity studies. Second, drawing on interview data with 46 scientists and clinician-scientists in three places, we attempt to identify the social, political, and historical nature and character of racial/ethnic population categories. Third, we end by highlighting clinicians' stated reservations concerning the use of such information in clinical decision-making.

Examples of racialized pharmacogenomic studies in the US, Canada, and Singapore

In studying the clinical utility of genome-based toxicity studies in the US, Canada, and Singapore, we found evidence to suggest that there is racialization in pharmacogenomics. This is true in the case of a number of drugs prescribed in these countries, including but not limited to cancer drugs allopurinol and 5-fluorouracil (5-FU).

Allopurinol

Allopurinol is a widely prescribed drug used to manage high serum and uric acid levels in patients suffering from chronic gout or undergoing cancer therapy for leukemia or lymphoma (FDA, 2018; Health Canada, 2018). Allopurinol has been seen as a frequent cause of a variety of delayed severe cutaneous adverse drug reactions (SCARs), including Stevens-Johnson syndrome (SJS) and toxic epidermal necrolysis (TEN) (FDA, 2018; Jarjour et al., 2015). A strong association has been observed between allopurinol-induced SCARs and the HLAB*5801 allele, and genotyping prior to therapy is encouraged by a number of agencies, including the Canadian Medical Association (Fernando and Broadfoot, 2010), the Clinical Pharmacogenomics Implementation Consortium (Hershfield et al., 2013), the FDA (FDA, 2018), and Singapore's Health Sciences Authority (HSA) (HSA, 2016).

Studies of allopurinol side effects have been racialized. Hung et al. (2005) was the first to describe a strong association between HLA genomic markers and the risk of developing SJS/TEN in Han Chinese patients. Since then, a number of studies have explored this association in other populations: in addition to the Han Chinese, the Korean and Thai populations had higher propensities for developing allopurinol-induced SCARs (Hung et al., 2005; Jarjour et al., 2015; Lee et al., 2008; Lonjou et al., 2008; Ramasamy et al., 2013; Tohkin et al., 2013; Yang et al., 2015).

In 2014, Singapore's HSA conducted a study involving four public healthcare institutions. It found a strong association between the HLA-B*5801 allele and allopurinol-induced SCARs, as well as inter-ethnic differences in frequency distribution of the allele. In a letter to healthcare professionals in 2016, the HSA indicated that, in the case of Singapore, this was estimated to be "1 in 5 Chinese, 1 in 15 Malays and 1 in 25 Indians" (HSA, 2016), and that "while genotyping is not required as [the] standard of care for new patients starting allopurinol . . . doctors may consider genotyping patients to identify the patients who are at a greater risk of [an] allopurinol-induced SCAR" (HSA, 2016).

In September 2016, the HSA sent an updated advisory to healthcare professionals, reporting that it had "received nine allopurinol-induced SCAR reports between March and August 2016. . . . A majority of these cases reported the use of allopurinol for gout in Chinese patients" (HSA, 2016). This finding appeared to be consistent with an earlier study conducted in Singapore which concluded that "the decision to initiate allopurinol in the following patient populations: elderly, Chinese race, patients with underlying renal disease, should not be taken lightly" (Lee et al., 2008: 387). In the same vein, the Canadian Medical Association informed healthcare professionals that "to minimize the high morbidity and mortality associated with severe cutaneous adverse drug reactions, genetic screening is advisable for at-risk groups (. . . for HLA-B*5801 before allopurinol therapy in patients of Southeast Asian, Japanese and European ethnicities)" (Fernando and Broadfoot, 2010: 480).

Nonetheless, the mechanism by which HLA-B*5801 is specifically involved has yet to be established (Tohkin et al., 2013). Indeed, Jarjour et al. (2015: 3) pointed out:

> although HLA-B*5801 is a major risk factor of CADRs [Cutaneous Adverse Drug Reactions], it is not necessary nor sufficient to develop these hypersensitivity reactions in patients taking allopurinol. Indeed, other non-genetic factors could also contribute to increasing the risk of allopurinol-induced hypersensitivity reactions, such as the dosage of allopurinol, chronic renal insufficiency and concomitant use of thiazide diuretics, ampicillin or amoxicillin.

Similarly, based on data from their own study, Stamp and Barclay (2018: i37) contended that "additional factors must be involved in development of allopurinol-related SCAR in at least some individuals, and . . . allopurinol may not need to be avoided in certain HLA-B*5801-positive individuals."

5-Fluorouracil (5-FU)

We also observe a pattern of racialization of 5-Fluorouracil drug safety studies. Flouoroucil (5-FU) is an antimetabolite chemotherapeutic used as a part of the standard therapy for a variety of malignancies, including gastrointestinal, head and neck, and breast cancers (FDA, 2016). It is widely prescribed either alone or in combination with other chemotherapeutic drugs (Diasio and Johnson, 2000). Despite its widespread use, approximately 40 to 60% of cancer patients develop severe 5-FU related toxicities (Milano et al., 1999; Saif et al., 2006; Matsusaka and Lenz, 2015).

The toxicity profile of 5-FU is schedule-dependent (Matsusaka and Lenz, 2015). Myelotoxicity is the major toxic effect in patients receiving bolus doses (FDA, 2016; BC Cancer Agency, 2019; Matsusaka and Lenz, 2015). Hand-foot syndrome (palmar-plantar erythrodysesthesia), stomatitis, and neuro- and cardiotoxicities are associated with continuous infusions (FDA, 2016; BC Cancer Agency, 2019; Matsusaka and Lenz, 2015). Other adverse effects associated with both bolus-dose and continuous-infusion regimens include nausea and vomiting, diarrhea, alopecia, and dermatitis (FDA, 2016; BC Cancer Agency, 2019; Matsusaka and Lenz, 2015).

The etiology of 5-FU related toxicities has been linked to reduced activity in the dihydropyrimidine dehydrogenase (DPD) enzyme caused by various functional dihydropyrimidine dehydrogenase (DPYD) gene variants (Milano et al., 1999; Liem et al., 2002; Ma et al., 2010; Saif et al., 2006, 2008; van Staveren et al., 2013).

Over the past 20 years, several studies have suggested that there is a pattern of toxicities associated with 5-FU that varies in patients with different ethnic backgrounds, including African, Asian, and European Caucasian populations (Caudle et al., 2013; Etienne et al., 1994; Liem et al., 2002; Ma et al., 2010; Mattison et al., 2006; Saif et al., 2006, 2008; Yamaguchi et al., 2001). For instance, according to Caudle et al. (2013), the frequency of the *6 rs1801160 A risk allele, associated with DPD deficiency, seemed comparable in Caucasian, Middle Eastern, and African American populations but was less frequent in Asian populations. In another example, a study of germline mutations among 107 Japanese cancer patients and healthy volunteers only detected an incidence of homozygous mutations in the DPD gene of 0.2% of the study population (Yamaguchi et al., 2001). Following this, in a study comprising subjects of Indian, Malay, and Chinese origin in Singapore, the authors reported a statistically significant decrease in DPD activity among the Chinese population (0.06 nmol/min/mg) compared to the Indian cohort (0.66 nmol/min/mg), but not when compared to the Malay cohort (0.31 nmol/min/mg) (Liem et al., 2002).

However, we find that such attempts by scientists to characterize the clinical impact of risk alleles and claim that certain ethnoracial groups are genetically predisposed to decreased DPD activity and, by extension, drug-induced toxicity, problematic. As van Staveren et al. (2013: 389) suggested, the reported distribution of DPD deficiency may be disputed

> as there is still no consensus on the definition of DPD deficiency, and therefore the incidence of DPD deficiency reported in numerous studies is strongly dependent on the method used to assess DPD deficiency and the cutoff level chosen to define DPD deficiency.

In addition, van Staveren et al. (2013: 392) noted that "some patients who suffer from severe side effects caused by 5-FU show normal 5-FU pharmacokinetics or wild-type DPYD genotype, and therefore it is important to realize that prospective testing for DPD deficiency will not exclude all 5-FU-related toxicity."

Cost-effectiveness studies, race/ethnicity, and precision medicine

In order to further understand the relationship between pharmacogenomic drug toxicity studies and racialization, we conducted a systematic review of journal articles published from January 2000 to July 2021 to answer this question, "How has race/ethnicity been used to conduct cost-effectiveness studies for precision medicine/targeted therapies/stratified medicine drugs?" A comprehensive literature search was conducted on the following databases: Medline, CINAHL, Embase, PsychINFO, PubMed, Global Health (via EBSCOhost). It was performed independently by two research assistants using identical key terms accompanied with Boolean operators: "AND," "OR," and brackets for each database. A combination of the following MeSH terms was used: "genetics," "genomics," "precision medicine," "personalized medicine." All searches were limited to studies written and published in English. Although the studies included a variety of precision medicine fields across different countries, they all directly or indirectly mentioned the use of race and/or ethnicity when determining the population to be studied.

Our analysis of the resulting 73 journal articles (see Appendix B) that met the inclusion criteria reveals four themes, namely: (1) The term "Caucasians" was undefined; specifically, the systematic review identified 15 population-based precision medicine studies that used the term "Caucasians" without clear definitions. (2) The usage of race/ethnicity was often not justified; specifically, 38 of the 67 studies did not attempt to justify why specific races or ethnicities were used for that specific clinical trial or test. (3) It was common to use social-politically constructed populations (such as the "national" populations of Japanese, Latinos, Canadians) as if such populations were genetically homogeneous, and (4) there was a pattern of exporting numbers, figures, and models in scientific studies from developed to less-developed countries; specifically, for studies conducted in less-advanced countries, 14 studies framed themselves by referencing numbers from US-based clinical trials.

Taken together, the examples cited previously show the phenomenon of racialization and ethnicization of pharmacogenetic/pharmacogenomics toxicity studies, on the pretext of advancing personalized precision medicine.

Who is Asian and who is Caucasian?

A fundamental problem with these racialized pharmacogenetic/pharmacogenomics studies is the fluid and arbitrary definitions of the ethnic and racial population groups. These ethnoracial categories are not biologically determined but are produced relationally and processually, as explained in the introductory chapter. For instance, the definition of "Caucasian" can sometimes be geographically defined, but at other times it is based on preconceived racial thinking that originated in eighteenth-century Europe (Goodman et al., 2012), or even on "word-of-mouth." Dr.36 (Singapore), for instance, said that he identified who was "Caucasian" based on what his colleagues told him: "Because one of my colleagues is from Germany . . . and he gave us samples. Normal German, Caucasians . . . they tell us."

Alternatively, if a pharmacogenetic/pharmacogenomics study was done in Singapore, "Caucasian" could be defined based on the Singapore government's National Registration Identity Card (NRIC), as garnered from interview data with clinician-scientists:

INTERVIEWER: The question is, what's the definition of Caucasian?

DR.31 (Singapore): Well, I think in this sort of study done in Asia . . . I think it's just basically anybody from European heritage or American heritage.

INTERVIEWER: What about Europeans?

DR.35 (Singapore): Those that are in Europe. Australians are considered to be of European descent . . . [U]sually, it's more of the racial thing rather than the geography.

INTERVIEWER: How [are] Western European[s] different?

DR.35 (Singapore): Caucasian appearance.

INTERVIEWER: Not location based?

DR.35 (Singapore): No. Like Chinese migrants who migrate to Europe or US will not be considered . . . Western European. They will still be called East Asian in [terms of] their ethnicity.

INTERVIEWER: So for this paper, the first paper, that's the latest, can you share with us how you identify a healthy individual as a Chinese, Indian, Malay, or Caucasian[?]

DR.37 (Singapore): By verbal. Verbally asking them, and by their IC [i.e., NRIC]. Because that is their national identification. So that's the only proof we have.

While it may appear to scientists and physicians that using the patient or human subject's Singaporean National Registration Identity Card is "scientific," such census racial categories are demonstrably a function of the shifting agendas of the political-economic elites who do the categorizing. In the case of Singapore, it is also obviously a British-colonial legacy. Leong (1997: 86) explained the official labeling and simplification of ethnic categories in this way:

> The CMIO [Chinese-Malay-Indian-Others] categories were convenient labels for bureaucratic functions of form-filling and rational administration, but the British recognised much finer distinctions in census surveys. In the census of 1881, forty-seven ethnic groups were named; these increased to fifty-six in the 1921 census (Purushotam, 1995). The reduction of ethnicity to four categories and the use of these narrow classifications in official policy began when Singapore was granted sovereign and independent status on 9 August 1965.

The "Others" category in the census includes the "Caucasian" category. Until recently, a Singaporean citizen's race followed that of his or her father. However, it can now be registered differently if he or she is of mixed parentage (e.g., a child of Chinese and European descent can be registered "Chinese," "European," or "Eurasian"). In January 2010, it was announced in Parliament that registration of overlapping and mixed-race options for Singaporean children born to parents of different races would be implemented. For couples of inter-ethnic marriages, in addition to existing options of choosing only one of the two different races for their children, they would now be able to choose to reflect both. For instance, if a child is of Chinese and Indian descent, his or her race can be recorded as "Chinese," "Indian," "Chinese-Indian," or "Indian-Chinese." This policy subsequently came into effect in January 2011. The government has explained that such added flexibility in registering race is consistent with a continual review of policies in order to recognize and respond to the evolving social landscape in Singapore.

Turning our attention to the category of "Asian" in racialized drug toxicity studies, geographically, Asia (if it can be unambiguously defined at all) is such a broad region that it would be difficult, if not prohibitive, for a research project to take a randomized sample that would be truly representative. Asia is also sometimes conveniently delineated by political boundaries (i.e., identifying an entire state to be in Asia or otherwise). Even so, the category can become ambiguous and debatable when it comes to states at the edges of the region. In practice, researchers may simply use the prevailing ethnic classification in their societies to make a claim about "Asians." For example, Singapore-based researchers placed Chinese, Malays, and migrants from the Indian subcontinent in the Asian category.

We have highlighted the socially determined definitions and identifications of "Asians" and "Caucasians." As such, it is problematic when physicians use such categories as if they were biomedical entities. That is, if a particular drug is found to be less toxic to a patient perceived to be Caucasian and more toxic to a patient perceived to be Asian, a doctor might be tempted to adjust the dosage of the drug to be prescribed accordingly, even if he or she is not entirely sure of why and how its toxicity would affect the particular patient.

Debating race/ethnicity-based pharmacogenetic toxicity data in the clinic

Some of the clinicians interviewed for our study felt that racial/ethnicity-based toxicity studies were valuable in highlighting the probable risk for each individual so that adjustments could be made to decrease the risk of toxicity (e.g., change dosage or increase surveillance) and to shape testing guidelines. This appears to be true in the case of drugs such as abacavir, allopurinol, and 5-FU:

> You know recognizing that there are differences . . . can actually [be] harnessed for good. So we can say that we are doing this because you are Asians because I think there is a higher probability among Asians than Caucasians that [they will] respond to this drug because of this toxicity [so that] we have to avoid it. That's harnessing a racial difference for good, for [the] good of the individual not for the harm of the individual.
> (Dr.5, Canada)

> It's an attempt to begin to differentiate the fact that there are people of certain backgrounds that seem to have a higher risk. If you have an East Asian mother, and a Persian father, and you have a child . . . the question is, does this East Asian risk variant exist in that child? I don't know, it depends upon the inheritance patterns, right? . . . [B]ut because of the East Asian background, knowing the ancestral background, this is an opportunity to check for those variants in that child, because we know that the potential for toxicity exists before we begin. So we wouldn't begin on the same dose, or the same way.
> (Dr. 11, Canada)

> None of these drugs benefit everybody. . . . So, to me it seems perfectly reasonable that if you identify that African Americans were at a higher risk for toxicity from this particular drug, maybe that's the subpopulation that you do a broad testing in.
> (Dr.15, USA)

In sharp contrast, other respondents warned against simply using race/ethnicity as a basis for making medical decisions, for several reasons. First, this appears to emanate from a shared appreciation that there is genetic variation within populations (prevalence of mutation; not 100% penetrance) and that intermarriage complicates the calculation of race-and-ethnicity-based toxicity risk estimates:

> I think ultimately it is simplistic to say that Asians may get more toxicity. . . . Asians are not a homogenous group of people and it may be also true that Pol[ish] Caucasians are at a higher risk of neutropenia. But then if you have someone Polish . . . marry someone Irish, you dilute that effect. So ultimately I think [these] studies are of interest, but I think they have limited value in terms of applicability to individuals. Because individuals are very unique.
>
> (Dr.5, Canada)

Importantly, it was not that clinicians did not see the value of incorporating pharmacogenetic testing into patient care; rather, they disputed the practice of integrating perceptions of ethnic identification and assumptions of biological difference into medical decision-making:

> If you are using SNP to say that this person because of their SNP profile is going to get a bad toxicity to a drug, that I might believe. I don't think you can short cut to say SNP shows that toxicity is more common in this ethnicity and therefore you can use ethnicity. . . . I don't think it is un-interesting but I think it is a dangerous pattern to use ethnicity to make medical decisions.
>
> (Dr.1, Canada)

> I think if you can show . . . with almost 100% certainty that certain genetic variations are present based on ethnic grouping, then you can kind of assume that you don't need to do the test and treat people differently based on what their ethnicity is. But I think that is unlikely to happen. . . . Even if it is 99% or 95%, would you be willing to accept [a] lower dose of chemotherapy not knowing for certain that you have that gene and you are going to get a less effective treatment[?] . . . So I don't think that will work really, by basing dosing on ethnicity.
>
> (Dr.8, Canada)

Evidently, while some clinicians supported using race in deciding who should be screened, others pointed out that race is an imprecise proxy for ascertaining drug responsiveness and for guiding patient management.

Subjective interpretation of drug toxicity risks

Another argument often cited against the usage of racialized/ethnicized risks of drug toxicity revolves around the notion that the value judgment of toxicity risk estimates and accompanied course of action is subjective, in that there is interpersonal variability in the definition of acceptable/unacceptable levels of risk, as well as differences in the way figures are presented. Interviewees elaborated here:

> It's a subjective decision; it's not a scientific decision. It's completely subjective. . . . [It] doesn't matter whether you're scientists or labourers, and those are just risk estimates, and it's how you personally feel about risk.
>
> (Dr.10, Canada)

> I was trying to develop these risk-prediction models and I couldn't figure out how to do it. . . . [W]hen I say, your baby is at high risk of cardiomyopathy, I'm talking twenty percent chance. When you say high risk, you mean ninety percent chance. You can't use high risk, it doesn't mean anything to people, it means different things.
>
> (Dr.11, Canada)

> So, two percent of Asians will have an adverse reaction to this drug, and only 0.1% of Caucasians will have an adverse effect, right? So you could say, there's a twenty-fold increased risk, if Asians hav[e] adverse [reactions], so we should not give them this drug. Well . . . obviously I don't agree with that, because two percent is still a pretty small risk, right? Because ninety-eight percent of Asians are still gonna respond to the drug.
>
> (Dr. 10, Canada)

Together, these observations suggest that racialization and ethnicization of the probability estimate for the drug toxicity risk can also lead to erroneous and potentially harmful conclusions and clinical outcomes for patients.

Toxicity is a multifactor phenomenon and is not just about genetics

The interviewees also emphasized that toxicity tests (which normally test for only one genetic factor) alone were not entirely useful in determining toxicity risks, because drug-related toxicity is influenced by a complex interplay between genetic and non-genetic factors. Citing the example of 5-FU, this clinician from the US shared that diet was more likely to impact an individual's drug metabolism than genetic composition:

> Our foods are all enriched with folate, and so, for instance, toxicity for 5-FU is different in the population that's eating folate enriched food, like bread . . . if you're getting the 5-FU. I think actually it's higher here with the enrichment than in other parts of the world, where it's not enriched. But presumably, someone who came here from another part of the world and started you know, eating what's available in our grocery stores, would then have the same toxicity. It's not something that's

necessarily genetic, although there may be some components, but it's really thought to be a dietary thing.

(Dr.17, USA)

Corroborating this view, Dr.34 (Singapore) pointed out that because adverse reactions (i.e., bleeding) to drugs such as warfarin could be caused by many non-genetic factors, it would make more sense for doctors to monitor and manage their patients through other diagnostics, instead of relying solely on toxicity data:

> For example, a certain kind of herbal tea, even [something] simple like chamomile tea, will affect the coagulation of warfarin. So we can't tell patients that you must not eat this and that . . . there are thousands of things [to avoid]. . . . So one way is to do that [genetic] test and use it to assess how much warfarin to give. But even with that test . . . we still have to monitor the warfarin, titrate the dose by looking at the clotting duration or the clotting time. . . . Anybody who is on warfarin will do the clotting test and make sure that their blood clot[s] within 24 seconds. . . . If it is too fast, we increase the dose. Now you have this genetic test, does that mean that you don't have to do the clotting test? You still need to! So with or without this genetic test, we still need to do the observation test.

Thus, while toxicity studies may show the presence of a certain gene, this finding alone cannot determine a patient's drug response. Toxicity is polygenic and is determined by a complex interplay of factors, including underlying genotypic variation and the complex nature of drug metabolism, as well as environmental factors.

In *Effect of Mushroom Diet on Pharmacokinetics of Gabapentin in Healthy Chinese Subjects*, Toh et al. (2014) found that there may be diet-drug pharmacokinetic interactions during co-exposure to gabapentin and mushroom constituents. While the authors concluded that there may be only limited or no clinically important consequences, it showed how environmental factors play a part in shaping our toxicity levels to certain drugs.

In addition, existing studies have emphasized on the lack of clear guidelines for translating germline genetic variation into actionable clinical recommendations for managing adverse drug reactions. For instance, Relling and Evans (2015: 347) lamented that "professional societies and other guideline-generating groups sometimes disagree on whether to proceed with pharmacogenetic testing and if so, how." The polygenic nature of drug toxicity may have contributed to the difficulties of creating clinical guidelines based on the genetic data.

Pharmacogenetics/pharmacogenomics studies and pharmaceutical companies are at odds

Finally, in sharp contrast to pharmacogenetics/pharmacogenomics studies of drug efficacy, studies of pharmacogenetics/pharmacogenomics drug toxicity are not necessarily welcomed by pharmaceutical companies. A pharmacogenetic scientist from Canada who had observed firsthand the inclinations of pharmaceutical companies shared his experience as follows:

> I went to Pfizer in New York, and I said, I want you to fund this work, you know, identify genetic variance, um, of drug risk, you know, to reduce your liability because people who will end up with terrible reactions won't sue you because they won't get the drug. . . . [They said] "that's great . . . thank you . . . don't call us, we'll call you" . . . They're not interested . . . why would they not be interested? . . . [B]ecause your liability reduction model isn't the model they use. They have a liability plan already. . . . [T]he best product liability lawyers on the planet work for pharma. It's called out of court settlements. They have legal teams; this is their model of managing risk. You're talking about a different risk management paradigm. . . . [T]hese guys are not altruistic in the same way that we are in the academic medical context; these guys are focused on earning a profit, as quickly as possible. So after that meeting in Pfizer . . . they went to meet the senior legal counsel of Health Canada, our FDA. . . . [H]e told me, [be]cause I know him well . . . [h]e said . . . that I scared the crap out of them, because I was gonna be able to identify genetic variance that people . . . would be able to use to sue the company successfully. . . . They think I'm increasing their liability.
>
> (Dr.11, Canada)

Obviously, the advent of a new science – predictive pharmacogenomic testing – has complicated the pharmaceutical firms' profit-making agendas. Pharmaceutical firms in general share the goal of "marketing drugs for as broad a patient group as possible," thereby rejecting the findings of predictive pharmacogenomic testing that inevitably segregates the market or limits the market size as it would identify certain groups as at-risk for drug toxicity (Aspinall and Hamermesh, 2007). From the point of view of major pharmaceutical companies, utilizing racialized pharmacogenomics is counterintuitive as it goes against their premise of "providing miracle drugs" to everyone, if possible (Sun, 2017). Some of the reasons underpinning this rejection of pharmacogenomics include the high costs associated with developing and manufacturing drugs for different segments of the patient population and the ensuing need to cater to arising legal or ethical questions (Meurer, 2003; Robertson et al., 2002).

A unique case study showcasing this inherent contradiction between pharmaceutical companies' chase for the "opportunistic one-size-fits-all" solution vis-à-vis the customized approach of pharmacogenomic testing is the lawsuit against Bristol-Myers Squibb and Sanofi-Aventis (pharmaceutical companies that manufacture the blood-thinning drug clopidogrel – Plavix). At the crux of the lawsuit was the fact that Hawaiian citizens found themselves paying "100-times more than aspirin for an ineffective drug" (Wu et al., 2015).

The Department of the Attorney General (2014) reported that Plavix was considered largely ineffective for Hawaiians due to a high percentage of the population who may have had poor metabolization of the drug, at 38 to 79% of Pacific-Islanders and 40 to 50% of "East Asians." East Asians and Pacific Islanders make up an estimated 52% of the total Hawaiian population (Wu et al., 2015). The poor metabolization of the drug can be attributed to the population distribution of genetic polymorphism of CYP2C19, a gene coding for liver enzyme required to metabolize clopidogrel, which has three variants of which two, 2C19*2 and 2C19*3, are poor metabolizers with no CYP2C19 function (Price et al., 2012). Price et al. (2012) referred to previous clinical studies and stated that neither the standard 75 mg dose of clopidogrel nor an increased dosage is effective for Hawaiians. Taking these into consideration, the eventual ruling was that Sanofiy and Bristol-Myers Squibb each had to pay $417 million to Hawaii for their failure to disclose that Plavix may be less effective or yield no effect for certain segments of the population, specifically those of the East Asian or Pacific Island ancestry (Bellon and Raymond, 2021). This example shows how pharmacogenomic testing in the 21st century can reveal the gaps in treatment previously touted as unequivocally effective, thereby leading to possible lawsuits.

Conclusion

This chapter focuses on the issue of racialization and ethnicization of pharmacogenetics/pharmacogenomics drug toxicity studies. We draw attention to the racialization and ethnicization of germline mutations that can be passed down across generations. As Lee (2012) noted,

> the central challenge in pharmacogenomics is how to identify the illusive SNPs that influence drug response – the metaphoric needles in the haystack of clinical significance. Understanding the relative frequencies of SNPs in different populations is one strategy for decreasing the size of the haystacks one would be required to inspect.

The problem, in our view, is that such "populations" are routinely racialized/ethnicized. We draw on interview data to indicate the changing definitions of "Caucasian" and "Asian" to oppose the view that such race/ethnic categories are innately biological in nature. Indeed, as Bhopal and Donaldson (1998: 1303) argued in their article titled "White, European, Western, Caucasian, or What? Inappropriate Labeling in Research on Race, Ethnicity and Health":

> Given that scientific use of a social category can be interpreted as an endorsement of its validity, avoidance of loose terminology in research might . . . counter the predominance of color as a means of grouping populations.

Moreover, while some scientists and clinician-scientists have uncritically accepted the framing of risks of drug toxicity along racial and ethnic lines, others have elaborated on the reasons why such framing is fundamentally problematic in clinical settings. While there may be different frequencies of a genetic allele across different racial/ethnic populations, these population-based comparisons are but averages derived from actually genetically heterogeneous populations, which are not applicable to the unique patient sitting in front of the physician. We also note that the phenomenon of drug toxicity is multifactorial and that the interpretation of risks and judgement of the accompanying course of action are subjective and specific to the patient's wishes and the treating physician's professional advice. Further complicating the relationship between the pharmaceutical industry and pharmacogenomic testing is the fact that their goals are not aligned; the former seeks to manufacture for the masses, while the latter segregates the population based on drug toxicity results. In short, this chapter challenges genetic determinism in adverse drug reactions and problematizes the clinical application of race/ethnicity-based pharmacogenetic/pharmacogenomics drug toxicity studies.

References

Aspinall MG and Hamermesh R (2007) Realizing the promise of personalized medicine. *Harvard Business Review* 85(10): 108–117, 165.

BC Cancer Agency (2019) Drug monograph: Fluorouracil. Available at: www.bccancer. bc.ca/drug-database-site/Drug%20Index/Fluorouracil_monograph.pdf (accessed 24 February 2021).

Bellon T and Raymond N (2021) Bristol-Myers, Sanofi ordered to pay Hawaii $834 million over Plavix warning label. *Reuters*, 16 February. Available at: www.reuters. com/article/us-bristol-myers-sanofi-plavix/bristol-myers-sanofi-ordered-to-pay-hawaii-834-million-over-plavix-warning-label-idUSKBN2AF1YI (accessed 6 October 2023).

Bhopal R and Donaldson L (1998) White, European, Western, Caucasian, or what? Inappropriate labeling in research on race, ethnicity, and health, American Journal of Public Health 88(9): 1303–1307. DOI: 10.2105/AJPH.88.9.1303.

Bliss C (2011) Racial taxonomy in genomics. *Social Science & Medicine* 73(7): 1019–1027. DOI: 10.1016/j.socscimed.2011.07.003.

Bonham VL, Callier SL and Royal, CD (2016) Will precision medicine move us beyond race? *New England Journal of Medicine* 374(21): 2003–2005.

Bowser R (2001) Racial profiling in health care: An institutional analysis of medical treatment disparities. *Michigan Journal of Race and Law* 7(1): 78–133.

Caudle KE, Thorn CF, Klein TE, et al. (2013) Clinical Pharmacogenetics Implementation Consortium guidelines for dihydropyrimidine dehydrogenase genotype and fluoropyrimidine dosing. *Clinical Pharmacology & Therapeutics* 94(6): 640–645. DOI: 10.1038/clpt.2013.172.

The Department of the Attorney General (2014) Attorney General files suit against manufacturers and distributors of the prescription drug Plavix. Available at: https:// ag.hawaii.gov/wp-content/uploads/2014/01/News-Release-2014-09.pdf (accessed 23 October 2023).

Diasio R and Johnson R (2000) The role of pharmacogenetics and pharmacogenomics in cancer chemotherapy with 5-fluorouracil. *Pharmacology* 61(3): 199–203. DOI: 10.1159/000028401.

Etienne MC, Lagrange JL, Dassonville O, et al. (1994) Population study of dihydropyrimidine dehydrogenase in cancer patients. *Journal of Clinical Oncology* 12(11): 2248–2253. DOI: 10.1200/JCO.1994.12.11.2248.

Fernando SL and Broadfoot AJ (2010) Prevention of severe cutaneous adverse drug reactions: The emerging value of pharmacogenetic screening. *Canadian Medical Association Journal* 182(5): 476–480. DOI: 10.1503/cmaj.090401.

Food and Drug Administration (FDA), US (2016) Approved medication guide for fluorouracil. Available at: www.accessdata.fda.gov/drugsatfda_docs/label/2016/012209s040lbl.pdf (accessed 24 February 2021).

Food and Drug Administration (FDA), US (2018) Approved medication guide for Zyloprim (allopurinol). Available at: www.accessdata.fda.gov/drugsatfda_docs/label/2018/016084s044lbl.pdf (accessed 24 February 2021).

Goodman AH, Moses YT and Jones JL (2012) *Race: Are We So Different?* West Sussex: Wiley-Blackwell.

Health Canada (2018) Product monograph: Pms-allopurinol. Available at: https://pdf.hres.ca/dpd_pm/00043198.PDF.

Health Sciences Authority (HSA), Singapore (2016) Safety alerts: Allopurinol-induced serious cutaneous adverse reactions and the role of genotyping. Available at: www.hsa.gov.sg/announcements/safety-alert/allopurinol-induced-serious-cutaneous-adverse-reactions-and-the-role-of-genotyping (accessed 26 February 2021).

Hershfield MS, Callaghan JT, Tassaneeyakul W, et al. (2013) Clinical Pharmacogenetics Implementation Consortium Guidelines for human leukocyte antigen-B genotype and allopurinol dosing. *Clinical Pharmacology & Therapeutics* 93(2): 153–158. DOI: 10.1038/clpt.2012.209.

Hung SI, Chung WH, Liou LB, et al. (2005) HLA-B*5801 allele as a genetic marker for severe cutaneous adverse reactions caused by allopurinol. *Proceedings of the National Academy of Sciences USA* 102(11): 4134–4139. DOI: 10.1073/pnas.0409500102.

Jarjour S, Barrette M, Normand V, et al. (2015) Genetic markers associated with cutaneous adverse drug reactions to allopurinol: A systematic review. *Pharmacogenomics* 16(7): 755–767. DOI: 10.2217/pgs.15.21.

Kahn J (2013) *Race in a Bottle: The Story of BiDil and Racialized Medicine in a Post-Genomic Age*. New York and West Sussex: Columbia University Press.

Lee HY, Ariyasinghe TN and Thirumoorthy T (2008) Allopurinol hypersensitivity syndrome: A preventable severe cutaneous adverse reaction? *Singapore Medical Journal* 49(5): 384–387.

Lee S (2012) Waiting on the promise of prescribing precision: Race in the era of pharmacogenomics. In: *Genetics and the Unsettled Past*. New Brunswick, NJ: Rutgers University Press.

Leong LW-T (1997) Commodifying ethnicity: State and ethnic tourism in Singapore. In: Picard M and Wood RE (eds) *Tourism, Ethnicity and the State in Asian and Pacific Societies*. Honolulu: University of Hawaii Press, pp. 71–98.

Liem LK, Choong LH and Woo KT (2002) Porous graphitic carbon shows promise for the rapid screening partial DPD deficiency in lymphocyte dihydropyrimidine dehydrogenase in Chinese, Indian and Malay in Singapore by using semi-automated HPLC-radioassay. *Clinical Biochemistry* 35(3): 181–187. DOI: 10.1016/s0009-9120(02)00303-x.

Lonjou C, Borot N, Sekula P, et al. (2008) A European study of HLA-B in Stevens-Johnson Syndrome and toxic epidermal necrolysis related to five high-risk drugs. *Pharmacogenetics and Genomics* 18(2): 99–107. DOI: 10.1097/FPC.0b013e3282f3ef9c.

Ma JD, Lee KC and Kuo GM (2010) HLA-B*5701 testing to predict abacavir hypersensitivity. *PLoS Currents* 2: RRN1203. DOI: 10.1371/currents.RRN1203.

Matsusaka S and Lenz H-J (2015) Pharmacogenomics of fluorouracil-based chemotherapy toxicity. *Expert Opinion on Drug Metabolism & Toxicology* 11(5): 811–821. DOI: 10.1517/17425255.2015.1027684.

Mattison LK, Fourie J, Desmond RA, et al. (2006) Increased prevalence of dihydropyrimidine dehydrogenase deficiency in African-Americans compared with Caucasians. *Clinical Cancer Research* 12(18): 5491–6595. DOI: 10.1158/1078-0432.CCR-06-0747.

Meurer MJ (2003) Pharmacogenomics, genetic tests, and patent-based incentives. *Advanced Genetics* 50: 399–426. DOI: 10.1016/s0065-2660(03)50021-9.

Milano G, Etienne MC, Pierrefite V, et al. (1999) Dihydropyrimidine dehydrogenase deficiency and fluorouracil-related toxicity. *British Journal of Cancer* 79(3–4): 627–630. DOI: 10.1038/sj.bjc.6690098.

Price MJ, Murray SS, Angiolillo DJ, et al. (2012) Influence of genetic polymorphisms on the effect of high- and standard-dose clopidogrel after percutaneous coronary intervention: The GIFT (Genotype Information and Functional Testing) study. *Journal of the American College of Cardiology* 59(22): 1928–1937. DOI: 10.1016/j.jacc.2011.11.068.

Purushotam, N (1995) *Disciplining differences: "Race in Singapore"*. National University of Singapore: Department of Sociology Working Paper no. 126.

Ramasamy SN, Korb-Wells CS, Kannangara DR, et al. (2013) Allopurinol hypersensitivity: A systematic review of all published cases, 1950–2012. *Drug Safety* 36(10): 953–980. DOI: 10.1007/s40264-013-0084-0.

Relling MV and Evans WE (2015) Pharmacogenomics in the clinic. *Nature* 526: 343–350. DOI: 10.1038/nature15817

Roberts DE (2011) *Fatal Invention: How Science, Politics, and Big Business Re-Create Race in the Twenty-First Century*. New York: New Press.

Robertson JA, Brody B, Buchanan A, et al. (2002) Pharmacogenetic challenges for the health care system. *Health Affairs (Millwood)* 21(4): 155–167. DOI: 10.1377/hlthaff.21.4.155.

Saif MW, Mattison L, Carollo T, et al. (2006) Dihydropyrimidine dehydrogenase deficiency in an Indian population. *Cancer Chemotherapy and Pharmacology* 58(3): 396–401. DOI: 10.1007/s00280-005-0174-5.

Saif MW, Seller S and Diasio RB (2008) Atypical toxicity associated with 5-fluorouracil in a DPD-deficient patient with pancreatic cancer. Is ethnicity a risk factor? *Journal of Oncology Practice* 9(2): 226–229.

Stamp L and Barclay M (2018) How to prevent allopurinol hypersensitivity reactions? *Rheumatology* 57(suppl_1): i35–i41. DOI: 10.1093/rheumatology/kex422.

Sun S (2017) *Socio-Economics of Personalized Medicine in Asia*. London and New York: Routledge.

Surendiran A, Pradhan SC and Adithan C (2008) Role of pharmacogenomics in drug discovery and development. *Indian Journal of Pharmacology* 40(4): 137–143. DOI: 10.4103/0253-7613.43158.

Tishkoff SA and Kidd KK (2004) Implications of biogeography of human populations for 'race' and medicine. *Nature Genetics* 36(11 Suppl): S21–S27. DOI: 10.1038/ng1438.

Toh DSL, Limenta LMG and Yee JY, et al. (2014) Effect of mushroom diet on pharmacokinetics of gabapentin in health Chinese subjects. *British Journal of Clinical Pharmacology* 78(1): 129–134. DOI: 10.1111/bcp.12273.

Tohkin M, Kaniwa N, Saito Y, et al. (2013) A whole-genome association study of major determinants for allopurinol-related Stevens-Johnson syndrome and toxic epidermal necrolysis in Japanese patients. *The Pharmacogenomics Journal* 13(1): 60–69. DOI: 10.1038/tpj.2011.41.

van Staveren MC, Guchelaar HJ, Kuilenburg ABP, et al. (2013) Evaluation of predictive tests for screening for dihydropyrimidine dehydrogenase deficiency. *The Pharmacogenomics Journal* 13(5): 389–395. DOI: 10.1038/tpj.2013.25.

Ventura Santos R, da Silva G and Gibbon S (2015) Pharmacogenomics, human genetic diversity and the incorporation and rejection of color/race in Brazil. *BioSocieties* 10: 48–69. DOI: 10.1057/biosoc.2014.21.

Wu AH, White MJ, Oh S, et al. (2015) The Hawaii clopidogrel lawsuit: The possible effect on clinical laboratory testing. *Personalized Medicine* 12(3): 179–181. DOI: 10.2217/pme.15.4.

Yamaguchi K, Arai Y, Kanda Y, et al. (2001) Germline mutation of dihydropyrimidine dehydrogenese gene among a Japanese population in relation to toxicity to 5-fluorouracil. *Japanese Journal of Cancer Research* 92(3): 337–342. DOI: 10.1111/j.1349-7006.2001.tb01100.x.

Yang CY, Chen CH, Deng ST, et al. (2015) Allopurinol use and risk of fatal hypersensitivity reactions: A nationwide population-based study in Taiwan. *JAMA Internal Medicine* 175(9): 1550–1557. DOI: 10.1001/jamainternmed.2015.3536.

6 Conclusion

In this chapter, we first provide a summary of the state of knowledge concerning the problem of race-based medicine, precision medicine, and the phenomenon of the "molecular reinscription of race," before we elaborate on the new insights contained in the book, as well as the implications of our findings and arguments.

What is known on the topics of race-based medicine, precision medicine, and the molecularization of race?

In part a legacy of colonial history, the current practice of medicine often relies on the use of racial/ethnic categories to guide medical decision-making, a phenomenon known as race-based medicine. Race-based medicine is problematic in numerous ways, many of which are related to the arbitrariness and imprecision of the definitions of race and ethnicity. Racial/ethnic boundaries have been shown to vary across different contexts (Braun, 2006; Travassos and Williams, 2004), and do not correspond neatly with patterns of the presence or absence of particular genetic alleles (Schwartz, 2001; Tsai et al., 2016). Basing medicine on such arbitrary and imprecise racial/ethnic terms can lead to substandard health care, including errors in diagnosis and treatment (Acquaviva and Mintz, 2010; Braun et al., 2007; Bowser, 2001; Root, 2003; Tsai et al., 2016). Differential treatment among patients of different racial/ethnic groups can also occur due to physicians' implicit racial/ethnic biases (Hoberman, 2012). In the longer term, the pathologizing of race through race-based medicine can culminate in stigmatization and discrimination against particular racial groups and worsen health disparities (Braun, 2006; Brower, 2002; Jenkins, 2015; Kahn, 2003; Tsai et al., 2016).

Advances in genomic science have led to the rise of precision medicine, which has been lauded as the cure for race-based medicine and is broadly defined as an approach to health that "takes into account individual variability in genes, environment, and lifestyle for each person" (US National Library of Medicine, n.d). It is seen as "a fundamental change in medicine" as it moves away from the idea of a "typological patient" (Chakravarti, 2015: 12). Precision medicine seeks to avoid the problem of genotypic/phenotypic ambiguity that occurs with a race/ethnicity-based approach to medicine, as it enables physicians to make decisions based on the individual patient's actual genetic information. Indeed, the superiority of genomic/genetic-based information over race-based information has been demonstrated (Chan et al., 2012), leading some scholars to believe that race-based medicine will be replaced (Chaussabel and Pulendran, 2015; Dancey, 2012; Fullwiley, 2007; Hunt and Kreiner, 2013; Tutton et al., 2008). However, the reliance on racial/ethnic categories lingers. Racialized precision medicine, which is differentiated from personalized precision medicine, can be attributed to several factors, including the perception of some scientists/clinician-scientists that race/ethnicity is a useful stepping stone to eventually reaching individualized care (Wolinsky, 2011), the financial, logistical, and legal barriers (Bonham et al., 2016; Kahn, 2012; Rothstein, 2016), as well as market forces that favor racialized drugs (Kahn, 2004). As such, the debate about the place of race in the era of precision medicine continues.

Moreover, existing studies have shown that the use of racial/ethnic categories has remained pervasive in the genomic era (Epstein, 2007; Fullwiley, 2008). Indeed, some geneticists believe that race/ethnicity is a good measure of human genetic diversity in research (Bliss, 2012, 2015). However, when scientific studies examining the genetic basis of differences use racial/ethnic categories to stratify members of a population, such studies tend to be (mis)interpreted as studies examining the "genetics of race" (Fujimura et al., 2008: 644). This has led to the conflation of race with genetics, which scholars have termed the molecular reinscription of race (Duster, 2006) and the molecularization of race (Reardon, 2004; Koenig et al., 2008; Bliss, 2012; Fullwiley, 2007, 2008; TallBear, 2013; Nelson, 2016). Contrary to this worrying phenomenon, some researchers have attempted to disprove the idea that race is genetically defined by showing that racial/ethnic disparities in health are a result of social forces such as racial discrimination and the political forces that define the research environment and influence research practices (Hardimon, 2013: 16; Krieger, 2001; Root, 2003; Shim, 2014). Other scholars, such as Lee et al. (2001), have suggested that "holding scientists accountable for their use of racial categories and racialized populations in their research is a promising intervention" that will help to counter the biological reification of race. Yet some stakeholders in precision medicine have been found to stand by the use of race/ethnicity even when they recognize that it is an arbitrary social construct. They argued that race/ethnicity as a proxy can still "[yield] reliable inferences or sound probabilistic reasoning in some specifically well-defined biomedical contexts" (Maglo, 2010: 362), and that it is precisely the "classificatory ambiguity" of racial/ethnic categories that helps to overcome some of the challenges in research (Panofsky and Bliss, 2017: 59). Such perceptions, thus, help to sustain the molecularization of race/ethnicity in genomic science.

What does this book add to the existing state of the art?

In this book we examine the phenomenon of racialization along the trajectory of precision medicine from genomic science to medical decision-making. We analyze precision medicine as it moves from the bench to the bedside using a sociological concept, namely, "racialization," and make the case against the use of race as a proxy for genetics in the context of precision medicine. While there has been an extensive discussion about the relationship between race and science, particularly in terms of the "molecular reinscription of race" and the "molecularization of race" (e.g., Duster, [1990]2003, 2006, 2015; Hammonds and Herzig, 2009; Reardon, 2004; Koenig et al., 2008; Bliss, 2012; Fullwiley, 2007, 2008; TallBear, 2013; Nelson, 2016), we extend this discussion by highlighting the relationship between race, science, and medicine and elucidating the racialization of precision medicine in the genomic era. Through utilizing firsthand accounts of practicing clinicians and researchers, we not only explain how racialization unfolds in genomic science and precision medicine (Chapter 3) but reveal the inherent contradiction in the use of race as a proxy for genetics in precision medicine (Chapter 2). The focus on the concept of racialization makes the book analytical, thus setting it apart from more descriptive books in the field. Examples of these include Jain's (2015) *Textbook of Personalized Medicine*, which provided an overview of how precision medicine has evolved and the different roles it plays in day-to-day treatment of diseases; McCarthy and Mendelsohn's (2016) *Precision Medicine: A Guide to Genomics in Clinical Practice*, which took readers through how genomic medicine can and should be practiced and Pothier's (2017) *Personalizing Precision Medicine: A Global Voyage from Vision to Reality*, which presented a historical account of precision medicine and charts the future trajectory in the field.

In particular, we answer several questions that are key to the field of racialization (Gans, 2017), namely: who are the racializers in precision medicine, what do they do, and how and why do they do it? Where can we see deracialization? Under what conditions do clinicians racialize, instead of personalize, medical treatment in the context of cancer precision medicine? We suggest that, in additon to scientists, clinician-scientists, and physicians who are directly involved in precision medicine research and practice, public policy-makers and health economists can also contribute to racialization in precision medicine (Chapters 5). We also show that different groups of racializers can racialize in different ways (Chapter 3) and for different reasons depending in part on the nature of their work, which leads to an inherent contradiction in precision medicine as the focus shifts from populations in the scientific research domain to the individual patient in medical practice (Chapter 2). Furthermore, in Chapter 4, we demonstrate that given the right amount, type, and level of resources, it is possible to deracialize and personalize precision medicine in the clinic.

While many existing studies have provided interesting and extensive insights into genomics and health, they have tended to draw from either only the developed (e.g., Bliss, 2012; Duster, [1990]2003) or developing worlds (e.g., Kumar, 2012; Nelson and Jones-Nelson, 2012). Aihwa Ong's *Fungible Life: Experiment in the Asian City of Life* (2016) has also provided an ethnographic account of the development of genomic science, but in the singular context of Singapore. In contrast, this book is based on interviews with participants from three different countries – the USA, Canada, and Singapore. While these are all developed economies, they differ in terms of stages of precision medicine development as well as their public health systems and legislative environments – the USA and Canada are more advanced than Singapore in both their states of precision medicine development and legislative environments surrounding genomics. At the same time, while the USA and Singapore have adopted multi-payer public health systems, Canada has a single payer public health system. Findings in this book will thus be relevant for a wider group of scholars and precision medicine stakeholders from the developing to developed precision medicine worlds and from different public health and legislative environments. Of note, this comparative lens is crucial in allowing us to realize that there are various types of resources – namely, financial resources, human and informatics resources, as well as legal and infrastructural resources – required for the implementation of personalized precision medicine that are shared across different contexts. Although access to such resources is necessarily heterogeneous across individuals, certain contexts (e.g., single payer public health systems) may be more conducive in facilitating access to these resources than others (Chapter 4).

We also add to the discussion about the future of medicine. Ginsburg and Huntington's (2013: ix) *Genomic and Personalized Medicine*, for instance, looked at the opportunities and potential of genomic science and medicine and presented an optimistic view that "genomics will usher in improved approaches for practicing medicine." In sharp contrast, our study shows that there is real potential harm in recent developments in precision medicine – particularly in terms of the racialization of precision medicine, which hinders the realization of personalized precision medicine. Another book that discusses the future of precision medicine is Prainsack's (2017) *Personalized Medicine: Empowered Patients in the 21st Century*. Focusing on the issue of empowering the individual patient, Prainsack suggested that the future of health care may either be centered on "evidence produced by technical devices and algorithms" or "shared decision making, dialogue, and 'subjective' values of patients." We extend this discussion by adding another layer of consideration: personalized versus racialized precision medicine. Existing literature seems to suggest a dichotomous future where either personalized precision medicine will replace race-based medicine or race-based medicine will persist despite advancements in genomics (e.g., Fullwiley, 2007; Prainsack, 2015). However, we provide a more nuanced perspective by suggesting that the degree to which personalized precision medicine is realized is relative to the availability of resources to which an individual patient or a physician has access (Chapter 4).

Given our focus on the phenomenon of racialization in precision medicine, we also engage with the existing body of knowledge on race and genetics. We argue against the use of race as a proxy for genetics (e.g., Wade, 2014) and add to the existing literature by highlighting problems with the racialization of science and medicine (e.g., Hoberman, 2012; Kahn, 2012), in part by presenting empirical data pointing to the dubious nature of calling for equitable racial and ethnic representation among human subjects/participants in precision medicine research. We also build upon Koenig et al.'s (2008) interdisciplinary endeavor examining the social, political, and ethical concerns of genomic technology by going beyond drug development and race-based therapeutics to look at the less well-studied aspect of genetic testing for drug toxicity (Chapter 5). With a few exceptions (Bliss, 2012; Verma and Barh, 2017; Reardon, 2022), as noted in Chapter 1, while anthropologists, social scientists, historians, legal scholars, and philosophers of science have provided cogent criticism of the use of race in science, voices from the biomedical community have received comparatively less scholarly attention. We find that while scientists use ethnicity and race in human genomic studies, physicians opine that using the patient's race/ethnicity as a proxy for genetics in medical decision-making is problematic. Indeed, the use of racial and ethnic categories can blind clinicians to patients' real health risks. Physicians are also concerned that using race/ethnicity as a proxy will lead to racial/ethnic discrimination and violation of patients' privacy. By engaging with 45 genetic scientists and clinicians and one health economist, this book corrects the misperception that criticisms of the usage of race/ethnicity as genetic variation come mostly from non-geneticists.

What are the arguments and findings in each chapter?

To recap, Chapter 1 provides a definition of genome-based precision medicine, describes it on a global scale, and explains why it has been seen as a solution to race-based medicine. It also explains what the problems are with race-based medicine and racial profiling in medicine in both contemporary and historical times. It then goes on to highlight an ongoing debate regarding whether medicine in the genomic era will really move beyond race. We propose the usage of the concept of racialization to examine what happens in precision medicine. In particular, this book addresses the following questions: Who are the racializers in precision medicine, what do they do, and how and why do they do it? Where can we see de-racialization? Under what conditions do clinicians racialize (instead of personalize) medical treatment in the context of precision medicine for cancer?

Chapter 2 examines the process of racialization by addressing questions of when and why race may be used in translational precision medicine, which consists of three empirical domains: genomic research, clinical trials, and medical decision-making. We find that the use of race is more accepted in the scientific research domain but becomes less relevant and even problematized by the interviewees when knowledge moves to clinical trials and, subsequently, sites of clinical application. In other words, the acceptable degree of racialization of precision medicine is, at least in part, a function of specific domain logic – the population/collective is more prominent in research, and the individual is more central in the clinic. The individual genetic characteristic cannot be inferred from the population, as each person is genetically unique. At the same time, we find that there is little categorical acceptance of the usage of race in any of the three domains. For example, even if interviewees are supportive of using race/ethnicity in scientific research or clinical trials, most emphasize the need to eventually move beyond using it towards using the potential genetic driver as the basis for recruiting human subjects. Overall, there is an inherent contradiction regarding the use of race in precision medicine. Geneticists are using race in their research, but physicians treating patients think that usage of the racial identity of the patient is something to be overcome.

In Chapter 3, we aim to understand where and how racialization occurs in genomic science. As already noted in Chapter 2, genetic/genomic scientists tend to support the usage of race/ethnicity when they conduct human genome variation research. In Chapter 3, we provide further nuances. Specifically, among our interviewees, those who support the usage of race/ethnicity often want to find out if there are genetic differences between ethnic/racial groups, and when they do, it leads them to believe that race and ethnicity are genetically determined. Those who oppose the call for increasing racial/ethnic diversity in human subjects often point out that there are greater genetic similarities between ethnoracial population groups, and there is greater genetic heterogeneity within each ethnoracial population group.

While we believe that including greater human genetic diversity may be good for medical genetics, we argue against the usage of race/ethnicity to measure it or to use race/ethnicity as a proxy for it. It is already well-known that there is no universally agreed upon definition of race/ethnicity. Similarly, in our study, we found the different ways in which race/ethnicity is defined, identified, and assigned. While it is valid to ask "does having databases biased towards people with lots of 'European' ancestry lead to bad consequences for people with less of such ancestry in terms of improving health in the long run?", our findings suggest that when "race"/"European"/"Caucasian"/"Asian"/ "African/Black" etc. is mentioned in the context of genomic science and precision medicine, we should immediately raise some questions: Are we talking about self-reported race? Name/surname race? Appearance race? National Registration Identity Card (NRIC) race? Parental or grandparental race? Country of family origin/nativity race? Geographical race? Ancestry informative markers (AIMs) race? The specific ways that racialization is carried out by scientists have implications for the generalizability of a particular genomic study and the applicability of research findings.

We also highlight in Chapter 3 that the debate about whether race is biological or a social construct is still not settled – a minority of the scientists we interviewed believed that racial/ethnic populations are not only genetically different, but genetically determined. In other words, the use of racial and ethnic categories in genomic science encourages perceptions among scientists that racial and ethnic population groups are genetically determined; this is a phenomenon known as the "molecular reinscription of race" (Duster, 2003; Phelan et al., 2013). However, the majority of the scientists we interviewed were of the view that there is no clear genetic distinction between different racial/ethnic population groups and that there is genetic heterogeneity within a racial/ethnic group.

Chapter 4 addresses the question of "under what conditions would precision medicine most likely become racialized in the clinic?" We report that physicians understand that genomic data categorized by race and ethnicity is inherently faulty. One clinician-scientist called using race/ethnicity "the poor man's genetic testing." At the same time, data is delivered to these healthcare providers in a racialized format, and they are then tasked to utilize this data to make treatment decisions for their patients. For example, data categorized along ethnic and racial lines provides shorthand devices to help patients understand their disease probability. We propose the "relative resources" theoretical model to argue that precision medicine is most likely to become racialized (as opposed to personalized) for individuals and populations that do not have access to resources at the individual and/or systemic level. "Resources" refers not only to financial resources but also human and computational resources and legal and infrastructural resources. Lack of relevant resources to receive personalized medical treatment may contribute to further health inequality among already vulnerable populations, which are likely to be ethnic and racial minority groups.

Does genome-based precision medicine live up to its promise of fixing the problems of race-based medicine? In Chapter 5, we suggest that it is important to distinguish between pharmacogenomic drug efficacy studies/testing versus pharmacogenomic toxicity studies/testing in answering this question. The majority of clinicians and clinician-scientists we interviewed highlighted the limitations of pharmacogenomic drug toxicity testing in diagnosis, management, and prevention of ADRs, partly because drug-related toxicity is mostly a function of the interaction between genetic and environmental factors. Moreover, we found evidence of racialization of pharmacogenomic drug toxicity studies. Such racialization of genetic variants shaping drug toxicities merits our attention as such genetic variants are germline variants (as opposed to somatic variants) that can be transmitted across generations. Some interviewees highlighted the issues with using racially/ethnically framed probability statements about possible drug toxicities in clinical care. Furthermore, instead of fixing the problem of race-based medicine, public health officials' or health economists' cost-effectiveness studies sometimes contribute to such racialization, and we present findings that show that national populations have also been used as if they were genetically homogeneous.

112 *Conclusion*

How might this study affect research, practice, or policy?

Research

To prevent the molecular reinscription of race and to allow personalized precision medicine to be delivered in the clinic, it is important to stop using racial/ethnic diversity as a proxy for genetic diversity. While the existing social science literature on the molecularization of race/ethnicity shows that geneticists' usage of racial categories encourages genetic determinism among the lay public, we demonstrate that the perception of race/ethnicity as being genetically determined also exists among some scientists and clinicians. To counter this, better research practices addressing the problematic use of racial/ethnic categories in science can be established and disseminated among the scientific community. The best research practices can include ways to approach diversity and representation in scientific research, guidance on what scientists should do if they cannot avoid labelling samples by race/ethnicity in their studies, and how they should respond to manuscript submissions using racial/ethnic categories (Lee et al., 2001; Khan et al., 2022).

Additionally, there has been a recent increase in a type of studies done known as the N-of-1 trials – where studies focus on a single person as compared to aggregates. Schork (2015) stated that

> if enough data are collected over a sufficiently long time, and appropriate control interventions are used, the trial participant can be confidently identified as a responder or non-responder to a treatment. Aggregated results of many N-of-1 trials will offer information about how to better treat subsets of the population or even the population at large.

We think the N-of-1 clinical trials can be a way to avoid race/ethnicity-based clinical trials.

Our study also highlights the importance of simultaneously involving both geneticists and medical doctors in translational precision medicine research projects. Such interdisciplinary endeavors will help to address the inherent contradictions in precision medicine (see Chapter 2). That is, as the function and nature of the job of different domains varies, what works for one group of experts may not make sense for another. In the current context of precision medicine, scientists may find the use of race/ethnicity to be a practical way of eventually approaching the causative factor of genetics-based diseases, but for medical doctors whose job is to ensure the best possible treatment for the patients sitting in front of them, such race-based findings are "dangerous," as one interviewee put it. Similarly, Reardon (2022: 193) also noted that there exist "collective concerns about the rise of corporate-backed, informatic and individualistic approaches to medicine" between ethnographers and biomedical experts, and such concerns can form an important new basis for collaboration. In short, interdisciplinary projects can help facilitate communication of shared concerns and different perspectives between different groups of stakeholders in precision medicine.

Practice

A key argument of our study is that race-based clinical practice is problematic and its use in the presence of better alternatives is unacceptable. As seen in Chapter 2, one of the issues with racialized precision medicine is that racialized probabilities reflect racial/ethnic population averages, which may or may not apply to the individual patient sitting in the clinic. Relying on race/ethnicity to advise, diagnose, or even treat patients for genetically based diseases when uncertainty can be avoided via the adoption of personalized precision medicine thus runs the risk of unnecessarily harming them. Another limitation of racialized precision medicine is its growing lack of relevance due to the rising trend in interracial/interethnic marriages (Chapter 2). Information organized based on racial/ethnic categories is difficult to apply to children of interracial/interethnic relationships, who do not fall neatly into any one racial/ethnic category. Moreover, as we have noted in Chapter 3, racialization is an ongoing process. There are a number of methods via which medical doctors can racialize a patient, but each of these different methods is problematic, and different methods can yield different results. Therefore, to maintain a high quality of clinical practice, medical doctors should endeavor to offer personalized precision medicine as a first line of treatment whenever possible.

In cases wherein personalized precision medicine cannot be implemented, medical doctors can seek to use family history as a proxy for genetics instead of immediately falling back on race (Chapter 2 and 4).

Our study also demonstrated an interesting difference between stakeholders' stances towards genetic testing for drug efficacy and genetic testing for drug toxicity (Chapter 5). While it is generally agreed upon that genetic tests for drug efficacy are clinically useful, the clinical value of genetic tests for toxicity is debatable. This is in part because genetics is but one of the many factors influencing whether a patient will have an adverse drug reaction. There are other non-genetic factors (e.g., environmental factors) at play. Moreover, evaluation of drug toxicity risks is also subjective. A patient may find a 20% risk of adverse drug reactions to be too high and choose to take another drug, which is less effective but also less likely to cause adverse drug reactions, while another patient may feel willing to bear the risk of adverse drug reactions regardless of drug toxicity testing results. In the latter case, genetic testing for toxicity becomes redundant. As such, unlike genetic testing for drug efficacy, where the general consensus is that every patient should undergo such testing when available, the impetus for predictive genetic testing for toxicity is less clear.

114 *Conclusion*

Policy

As we see in Chapter 4, whether precision medicine can be realized for a patient is relative to the amount of resources available to him/her; availability of these resources tends to be unequally distributed across individuals and systems, leading to unequal access to personalized precision medicine. Public policies should therefore aim to overcome this resource heterogeneity so that patients can have equal access to all three categories of resources that must be present for the realization of personalized precision medicine: financial, human and informatics, as well as legal infrastructural, resources. Our findings point to three ways in which this can occur.

Firstly, our findings reveal that since genetics is the keystone of personalized precision medicine, one of the most important types of policy that needs to be in place is legislation against genetic discrimination. Two of the most common ways in which genetic discrimination can happen are in employment, wherein individuals are denied job opportunities on the basis of predisposition towards diseases, and in health insurance, wherein they are denied coverage or charged higher premiums due to higher disease risk. Moreover, as disease susceptibility stems from germline genetic mutations, other biological family members are also at risk of facing genetic discrimination even if they did not undergo genetic testing themselves. Fear of these potentially far-reaching negative implications can thus hold one back from undergoing genetic testing even if it is available. As such, passing legislation against genetic discrimination, such as the Genetic Information Nondiscrimination Act (GINA) in the USA and the Genetic Non-Discrimination Act (GNDA) in Canada, should be viewed as a key priority for countries like Singapore, where such regulatory frameworks to specifically safeguard genetic data privacy are missing despite precision medicine being a key healthcare strategy.

Another area wherein public policy is required is in terms of healthcare costs. While personalized precision medicine promises more tailored treatment, it comes at a price; genomic/genetic sequencing and molecular-based drugs, both critical components of personalized precision medicine, are at present very costly. Our study, which involves interviewees from both multi-payer and single-payer public health systems, indicates that this is a bigger hurdle for patients in multi-payer public health systems, wherein most costs are often borne out of pocket by patients themselves, rendering precision medicine prohibitively expensive to a large proportion of patients. In contrast, cost is less of a concern for patients in single-payer public health systems (although the financial burden borne by the patient is still significant). Thus, we suggest that for the benefit of patients, there should be state subsidies and/or policies ensuring extensive and sufficient coverage to ensure equal access to personalized precision medicine.

Lastly, findings from this study indicate a need for public policy addressing the knowledge and equipment gap between academic and non-academic medical institutions. Academic medical institutions tend to be at the forefront of medical advancements as they have both the manpower and equipment required to implement advanced medical technologies. In contrast, non-academic medical institutions tend to trail behind in their adoption of new medical technologies. This can affect patients' access to personalized precision medicine because whether they even have the opportunity to think about taking it up depends on the type of medical institution they attend. To level the playing field and ensure equal access to personalized precision medicine, public policy can be introduced to reduce the knowledge and equipment gap between medical institutions. This can be through making sure that critical informatic tools are made available or the sharing of medical specialists and equipment between medical institutions.

Science communication by scientists and journalists

As noted in the previous section, existing literature has shown that geneticists' use of racial categories can encourage genetically deterministic thinking along racialized lines among the lay public. When race is implicated in genetic studies, it inadvertently creates an impression of association, however unintentional or misplaced it may be, between race and genetics. This needs to be addressed as it can result in misconceptions about disease susceptibility and drug response to the detriment of individuals' access to proper preventive measures and medical treatments. To address this, we suggest that both scientists and journalists need to be more mindful of the ways in which they frame and present scientific findings (Tsai, 2022; Bin Khidzer, 2023).

Scientists, as the creators of these studies and findings, should resist the temptation to organize their study populations and/or results based on race/ethnicity, particularly in the case of a genetics/genome-based study. This is one of the most direct ways to avoid having associations drawn between race and genetics. However, we recognize that scientific work does not occur in a vacuum; there are other external factors that can shape scientific research, and it may take time before these external forces relinquish their emphasis on racial/ethnic categories. If scientists have to organize sample populations by race/ethnicity due to, for example, pragmatic reasons (Sun, 2020), they need to at least clearly describe how such racial/ethnic labels were derived and determined. On what basis did this racialization occur? Using Asian/Caucasian/Chinese as an example, how was a sample determined to be "Asian," "Caucasian," or "Chinese," according to whom? Contextualizing their race-based findings as such will enable others to interpret their work more accurately. Similarly, in reviewing journal submissions, scientists should scrutinize any use of racial/ethnic categories and carefully consider whether such racial/ethnic framing is necessary and, if so, ensure that sufficient details about the way race/ethnicity is used are provided. This type of "self-governance" within the scientific community can help to ensure that racial/ethnic categories are not being used indiscriminately, and that any such usage is being communicated properly.

The propagation of genetically deterministic thinking along racialized lines occurs in part through journalists, who serve as a bridge between the "elites" (in this case, geneticists and clinicians) and the lay public when they report on scientific findings concerning precision medicine. The way journalists present scientific findings can influence how the lay public perceives and understands the findings. What may be obvious to elite professionals may not be immediately obvious to the lay public. To avoid cultivating genetically deterministic thinking along racialized lines among the lay public, when reporting on studies that present findings in racial/ethnic terms, what needs to be made clear is that (1) race/ethnicity is not the biological basis for the disease/drug response; (2) not everyone from a particular racial/ethnic group will share the genetic characteristic of the racial/ethnic population average as it still depends on the individual's genetic makeup, which can be different from the typical person in that racial/ethnic group; and (3) the racial/ethnic labels used in the studies may not correspond with the racial/ethnic categories as understood by the lay person: Thus, the specific details of how the racial/ethnicities were defined in that scientific study should be clarified to help the lay person appreciate the differences and the social processes involved in the construction of those differences.

Medical education

The actual rates of adopting personalized precision medicine are low, and some clinicians continue to rely on race/ethnicity for clinical decision-making (Bonham et al., 2016; Collier, 2012; Hunt and Kreiner, 2013; Petersen et al., 2014). This may in part be a legacy of medical school training, where medical students are socialized to see race/ethnicity as biologically meaningful and the usage of racial/ethnic categories as a diagnostic shortcut as an acceptable norm (Anderson, 2008; Brooks, 2015; Swetlitz, 2016). Given the findings of our study, we suggest that medical education should be modified to include courses on topics such as racial essentialism and racial discrimination, the social sciences perspectives of race/ethnicity, racism, and social determinants of health, to raise awareness among medical students about the controversial and problematic nature of relying on race/ethnicity for medical decision-making.

What should different stakeholders take away from this book?

This book was written with the intent of reaching out to four main groups of stakeholders in the precision medicine movement (scientists, medical doctors, public policymakers, and health economists), among others, and the key takeaways for each group are as follows:

Scientists

Scientists have a critical role to play in influencing whether race- or genetics-based precision medicine will prevail, as their research findings are the foundation upon which medical practice and policies are built. If research is framed in racial/ethnic terms, medical doctors and public policymakers have no choice but to apply the same racial framing in practice. Our study emphasizes that race is a social construct that does not accurately capture genetic differences between populations, and this is a view with which many of our scientist interviewees concur. Responsible scientists should therefore critically reflect on what may seem to be the norm in research practices. Is identifying sample populations by race/ethnicity necessary when it can be misinterpreted to drive racialization of precision medicine? While encompassing more human diversity in genetic science would be helpful in identifying actual causes of diseases, using race/ethnicity as the basis for assessing diversity is controversial at best and harmful at worst. Scientists should thus refrain from organizing their data or framing their study in racial/ethnic terms or, at the very least, be aware of the social construction of race/ethnicity and be transparent about how such racial/ethnic labels were derived and determined in their studies. In addition, scientists need to think around their own work. On the one hand, their research can have downstream impact on medical practice. On the other hand, scientists should consider the upstream history of their research, for example, how the technology they are using came to be and the potential biases and assumptions embedded within it and acknowledge these as limitations in their own studies. Moreover, as many scientist interviewees in this study qualified, race/ethnicity is often used just as a stepping stone to find the actual causative factor. The scientific community should, thus, commit to pursuing the actual causative factor instead of just stopping at race/ethnicity as an explanatory factor.

Physicians/medical doctors

The use of race in medical practice might be a reflex as a result of medical school training and the current environment wherein race-based medicine is predominant. But as many physician interviewees have acknowledged, the use of race in diagnosing and treating a patient is problematic. While race is undeniably a cheaper and quicker way of identifying probabilities of disease susceptibilities and drug response (efficacy and toxicity) for a patient, and there may be anecdotal evidence that points to the usefulness of race-based medicine, the reliance on race is really a function of inadequate resources. But even then, interview data suggest that race- or ethnicity-based estimates are less convincing than family history-based estimates for disease susceptibility and drug responsiveness. Using race-based medicine when genetics-based precision medicine is feasible would be akin to taking unnecessary risks with the patient's health/life. Relatedly, in reading academic publications, if one finds that racial/ethnic categories are being used in a study, one should immediately ask himself/herself: how was race-making done?

Public policymakers

Public policymakers should also recognize the impact they have in shaping precision medicine research and practice. Public policy can contribute to the realization of personalized precision medicine by creating a conducive environment for personalized precision medicine to flourish. As can be seen in the example of the US's NIH Policy and Guidelines on the Inclusion of Women and Minorities as Subjects in Clinical Research, which was introduced with the intent of bettering scientific research by ensuring fair representation but unexpectedly contributed to the molecular reinscription of race, public policies can sometimes have unintended effects. Knerr et al. (2011) investigated how NIH's mandate for the inclusion of minority groups in research further perpetuated the entrenchment of the usage of race/ethnicity in genomic studies. Public policymakers, thus, need to carefully consider such possibilities, and be ready to quickly remedy any negative outcomes; in other words, representation of genetic diversity cannot be based on race/ethnicity. In addition, since resources tend to be unevenly distributed, intervention at a systemic level through public policymaking is more likely to secure equal access to personalized precision medicine across individuals. This will help to prevent further worsening of health inequalities as a result of the persistence of racialized precision medicine. What is important to note, however, is that public policymakers need to ensure that all three categories of resources – financial, human, and informatics, as well as legal and infrastructural resources – are accounted for, as the lack of any of these categories of resources will prevent genetics-based personalized precision medicine from being realized.

Health economists

Health economists should recognize that they also have a role to play in the racialization (and deracialization) of precision medicine. The framing of cost-effectiveness studies using racial/ethnic categories contributes to the racialization of precision medicine. As such, health economists should avoid using racial/ethnic categories in framing the population in cost-effectiveness studies.

What are the theoretical and empirical contributions of this book?

On "racialization"

Genome-based precision medicine is often said to provide the solution to the problem of race-based medicine and/or racial profiling in medicine. We examine such claims in the context of precision medicine for cancer and contribute theoretically by arguing that, in the genomic era, the "molecular reinscription of race" (Duster, [1990]2003) is only half the story; the other half is the racialization of precision medicine. We define racialization of precision medicine as the social processes by which racial/ethnic categories are incorporated into the development, interpretation, and implementation of precision medicine research and practice (Chapter 1). While we recognize that race and ethnicity are technically different concepts, we have used them interchangeably in this book, as our interviewees tend to do so (Chapter 1). Drawing from interviews with scientists and clinicians in precision medicine, we also show the phenomenon of racialization of precision medicine in the different domains of scientific research, clinical trials, and medical practice (Chapter 2) as well as in the different contexts of disease susceptibility, drug efficacy (Chapter 2), and drug toxicity (Chapter 5).

Moreover, our analysis of the data reveals that although the usage of race/ethnicity is embraced by interviewees in the genome scientific research domain, it becomes less relevant and even problematized by them when knowledge translates and moves to clinical trials and subsequently to sites of clinical application (Chapter 2). We argue that this shows an inherent contradiction in precision medicine, in that race is being used to develop precision medicine when precision medicine is supposed to provide a solution for race-based medicine (i.e., race is being used to overcome race).

This inherent contradiction can be attributed to how scientists and clinicians think differently about the usage of race. Scientists are more open to using race/ethnicity in human genome variation research as their research focuses more on the idea of populations (race). We suggest that confirmation bias is also at play in driving the notion that race is a useful tool in scientific research (Chapter 3). In contrast, physicians think that the usage of race in medical decision-making is something to be overcome because their priority is the particular individual sitting in front of them, who can behave differently from the average individual from the (racial) population he/she is from. In other words, scientists may be committing the "fallacy of racialism," the mistaken belief "that the human species is naturally divisible into a reasonably small number of reasonably discrete kinds of people, equivalent to the zoologist's subspecies" (Marks, 2012: 1174).

On the nexus of relative resources and racialization of precision medicine

Our argument about the racialization of precision medicine also points to the possibility of "deracializing" precision medicine. As noted previously, although proponents of precision medicine posit that the usage of race in medicine will become obsolete with the integration of an individual's genomic information in clinical decision-making, we show in Chapter 2 that race-based medicine persists in some situations. While Gans (2017: 342) suggested that deracialization occurs when racialized individuals "are no longer viewed as undeserving," we put forward the idea that, in the context of precision medicine, deracialization occurs in the presence of sufficient resources. This argument is elaborated on in Chapter 4, wherein we propose our relative resources theory to explain and predict when individual genome-based clinical decisions are most likely to happen.

Our relative resources theory suggests that whether an individual patient experiences racialized or personalized precision medicine is relative to the amount of resources that he/she has access. Based on our interview data, these resources can be grouped into three main categories – financial, human, and informatics, as well as legal and infrastructural resources. This argument complements the existing literature in noting the different barriers to realization of personalized precision medicine (e.g., Bonham et al., 2016; Kohane, 2015; Mirnezami et al., 2012; Rothstein, 2016), but our study adds empirical evidence from the perspective of scientists and medical doctors and organizes these barriers into types of resources.

According to our relative resources theory, precision medicine can only be deracialized when all three types of resources are available, but this will not always happen in reality because such heterogeneous resources tend to be unevenly distributed. Given the inadequacy of any of these resources, precision medicine becomes racialized. This relative resources theory not only provides countries looking to deracialize precision medicine with a roadmap for the issues that they should tackle, but also, in general, helps to explain why the future of clinical medicine is likely to involve experiences of varying degrees of racialized/deracialized precision medicine, depending on the availability of these three types of resources – financial, human and computer informatics, and legal and infrastructural resources – for each individual.

On differential racialization

In conceptualizing differential racialization, Baluran (2023) made a good point about the contextual dependence of definitions of race/ethnicity, but his definition of differential racialization focused on different levels of definitions of race (the national/"official" versus the individual/localized level). We extend this concept of differential racialization by demonstrating that differential racialization also occurs laterally – different stakeholders in precision medicine can draw boundaries between racial/ethnic groups differently, as well, even if they belong to the same level.

In Chapter 3, for example, we show the various materials used by scientists, clinician-scientists and medical doctors for race-making in precision medicine. These can be broadly divided into self-identification based on self-reporting by the DNA donor/patient and external identification whereby precision medicine stakeholders assign a racial/ethnic identity to the DNA sample/patient. The latter ranges from methods such as determining race/ethnicity based on name/surname and visual appearance, to family history-based methods such as asking about parents' and/or grandparents' ancestry or (family) country of origin, to technology/genetics-based methods like AIMs. As we note, these different methods of racialization may not always yield the same outcomes. Likewise, in Chapter 5, we show that scientists and clinicians and health economists can all discuss "Caucasian" or "Asian" genetic susceptibility to drug toxicity, but the categories of "Caucasian" or "Asian" have no standard scientific definition and are constructed very differently by different social actors.

Differential racialization of precision medicine is in part a function of who is making the call. That is, the way samples or individuals are racialized depends on the group of social actors in question and their roles. Health economists, whose job is to conduct cost-effectiveness studies to support public health policymakers in making policy decisions, tend to draw from given administrative categories (typically census categories) (Chapter 5). In addition, among the different materials for race-making mentioned previously, some may be more relevant to particular group(s) of stakeholders, while others can be used more generally. For instance, racialization based on visual assessment is less likely to be implemented by scientists, who, unlike medical doctors, may not come into direct contact with donors of DNA samples, whereas racialization based on name/surname can easily be utilized by all three groups of stakeholders as scientists, clinician-scientists, and medical doctors are all likely to have access to this data.

It is also important to note that even within the same group of stakeholders, perceptions of racial/ethnic boundaries can differ. This can be attributed in part to colonial (and contemporary) history, which influences the racial/ethnic categories available in different countries and, therefore, the ways in which precision medicine stakeholders may approach population stratification (Chapter 1). In addition, in-group/out-group differences can also contribute to differences in the drawing of racial/ethnic boundaries, whereby someone belonging to the in-group tends to provide a more granular delineation of the population than someone from an out-group (Chapter 3).

In sum, we suggest that differential racialization is not just about how an individual or a patient's self-identified race may be different from how institutions identify the individual racially/ethnically, but also about how different *groups* of elites and different individuals *within* each group of elites may operationalize race.

What are the tensions with the usage of race/ethnicity in genomic science with medical and public health implications?

Conceptually speaking, in the existing literature, it has been established that the usage of race as a proxy for genetics is problematic because the completion of the Human Genome Project has shown that there is no genetic basis to race. Instead, race is a socially constructed concept. The continual usage of race as a proxy for genetics leads to racialization of precision medicine and also reifies race as a biologically determined phenomenon.

Methodologically speaking, the variable "race" in the statistical analysis that is integral to precision medicine is used as a synchronic variable, and this usage misses the truth that "race" is also a diachronic variable. This is why it is important to ask "when are you from," rather than "where are you from". For example, the notion of "Asian" usually is a function of answering the question "where are you from?" People who answer "I am from Singapore" will most likely self-identify or be identified by others as "Asian." But if we ask the question "when are you from?", we start to realize that the notion of "Singapore" did not exist prior to 1965. Similarly, the concept of "Asian" did not exist prior to the eighteenth century. Concepts of "Caucasian," "Asian," "Chinese," etc. emerge in specific historical moments and contexts, and their meanings change over time.

Practically speaking, there is an inherent contradiction in the usage of race manifested in precision medicine. While scientists use race/ethnicity in labelling "populations" in population-based genetic studies, physicians and doctors say that the usage of race/ethnicity is to be overcome in treating the individual patient.

What are some of the limitations of this study?

We used snowball sampling to gain access to scientists and physicians, who are highly respected professionals with very busy schedules and thus hard to reach. Snowball sampling is a non-probability sampling technique routinely used in qualitative research wherein the target population is difficult to access. While such a sampling technique allowed us to build rapport with our interviewees, the findings from our sample, while valid, cannot be easily generalized due to the non-random selection process. It is also possible that a particular viewpoint is more salient in our sample compared to the general population due to the snowball sampling bias due to people's tendency to refer potential participants sharing similar viewpoints. To address these limitations, a quantitative project with probability sampling of scientists and clinicians involved in precision medicine research and clinical practice can be developed to test the hypotheses and arguments presented in this book, which we now turn to.

What are some of the future research projects based on this book?

The arguments advanced in this book are based on qualitative interview data primarily concerning cancer care. Future research can examine the extent to which the theory of relative resources and racialization applies to other contexts, such as cardiovascular diseases (Bayne et al., 2023; Mensah et al., 2019), and/or quantitatively examine the hypotheses using probability sampling. For example, quantitative researchers can test the following two hypotheses using probability sampling: (1) the usage of race becomes less acceptable when one moves from genomic science to clinical trials to medical decision-making, and (2) the more resources available at the individual and systemic level, the greater the likelihood that precision medicine will be personalized (as opposed to racialized) in the clinic. Another hypothesis that is implicit in our study and can be explicitly tested is this: the more an individual believes that race/ethnicity is genetically determined, the more likely that the individual will accept racial profiling in medicine. One can also propose to examine when, how, and why the BIM [B cell lymphoma-2-like11] polymorphism – a germline polymorphism that could be used as a predictor to identify who would benefit from EGFR-TKIs treatment in Non-Small-Cell Lung Cancer (NSCLC) patients, as noted in Chapter 2 – became racialized and how it became part of racialized statistics.

Existing studies have shown that race-based medicine and race-correction and racialized algorithms are harmful. In this book, we aim to make the often-hidden usage of race/ethnicity in (genome-)scientific work explicit and to show how scientists' conceptualization and usage of race/ethnicity structure can impact healthcare provision. However, we are not suggesting that race/ethnicity has no place in science; there is a body of literature on ethnicity and race as predictors in health and illness. Social constructs of race and ethnicity have biological consequences, without themselves being biological in origin. Indeed, while studying how genetics interacts with the environment to shape health outcomes is essential, we agree with scholars working on "race-conscious medicine" (Cerdeña et al., 2020) that it is equally important to have scientific studies to learn more about how social processes of racialization and racism shape the health outcomes of the populations and individuals that genomic scientists and clinician-scientists study and treat. As Collier (2012) suggested, "the scientific community must aim to elucidate the genetic and environmental factors that contribute to drug reactions and not be satisfied with a simple race-based approach." In addition, we can shift the focus from physicians to patients and raise research questions such as "how do healthy individuals and/or patients understand racialized/ethnicized probabilities of disease susceptibility, drug effectiveness and drug toxicity?" "To what extent do sensorial experiences shape the way healthy individuals and/or patients interpret their disease risks based on genomic data (i.e. polygenic score (PGS)/polygenic index (PGI)/polygenic risk score (PRS)?" "In what ways does the source (social media and digital media, traditional news media, physicians, family members and friends, for example) of racialized/ethnicized probabilities shape decision-making about health-related behaviors?" "How do people who identify themselves as mixed-race interpret racialized/ethnicized probabilities of disease risk and drug effectiveness?" In general, future research can examine the interactive effects of relative resources and racialization in various contexts and identify the kinds of resources relevant to specific contexts to reduce the degree of racialization.

In this book, we have demonstrated that the racialization of precision medicine contributes to errors in medical decision-making, as each individual's genetic profile is unique. This has implications beyond the practice of medicine itself. For instance, Marchant and Lindor (2018: 35) found that genomic malpractice litigation suits have a higher success rate for plaintiffs compared to traditional medical malpractice cases, with greater "monetary payouts," reflective of how "errors in genetic testing often have devastating impacts on the patients' health (and perhaps other family members)." Marchant and Lindor (2018: 36) concluded that with the uptake of genomic medicine such cases will "grow steadily even if slowly." We hope the findings and arguments in this book contribute to efforts to deracialize precision medicine, thus avoiding harm and/or potential medical litigation.

References

Acquaviva KD and Mintz M (2010) Perspective: Are we teaching racial profiling? The dangers of subjective determinations of race and ethnicity in case presentations. *Academic Medicine* 85(4): 702–705. DOI: 10.1097/acm.0b013e3181d296c7.

Anderson W (2008) Teaching 'race' at medical school: Social scientists on the margin. *Social Studies of Science* 38(5): 785–800. DOI: 10.1177/0306312708090798.

Baluran DA (2023) Differential racialization and police interactions among young adults of Asian descent. *Sociology of Race and Ethnicity* 9(2): 220–234. DOI: 10.1177/23326492221125121.

Bayne J, Garry J and Albert MA (2023) Brief review: Racial and ethnic disparities in cardiovascular care with a focus on congenital heart disease and precision medicine. *Current Atherosclerosis Reports* 25(5): 189–195. DOI: 10.1007/s11883-023-01093-3.

Bin Khidzer, MK (2023) Asian bio(values): Constructing Asian difference and biovalue in the Singapore Diabetes Discourse. *Science, Technology and Human Values* DOI:10.1177/01622439231182778

Bliss C (2012) *Race Decoded: The Genomic Fight for Social Justice*. Stanford: Stanford University Press.

Bliss C (2015) Science and struggle: Emerging forms of race and activism in the genome era. *The Annals of the American Academy of Political and Social Science* 661(1): 86–108.

Bonham VL, Callier SL and Royal CD (2016) Will precision medicine move us beyond race? *New England Journal of Medicine* 374(21): 2003–2005.

Bowser R (2001) Racial profiling in health care: An institutional analysis of medical treatment disparities. *Michigan Journal of Race and Law* 7(1): 78–133.

Braun L (2006) Reifying human difference: The debate on genetics, race, and health. *International Journal of Health Services* 36(3): 557–573. DOI: 10.2190/8jaf-d8ed-8wpd-j9wh.

Braun L, Fausto-Sterling A, Fullwiley D, et al. (2007) Racial categories in medical practice: How useful are they? *PLoS Medicine* 4(9): 1423–1428. DOI: 10.1371/journal.pmed.0040271.

Brooks KC (2015) A silent curriculum. *Journal of the American Medical Association* 313(19): 1909–1910.

Brower V (2002) Is health only skin-deep?: Do advances in genomics mandate racial profiling in medicine? *EMBO Reports* 3(8): 712–714. DOI: 10.1093/embo-reports/kvf168.

Cerdeña JP, Plaisime MV and Tsai J (2020) From race-based to race-conscious medicine: How anti-racist uprisings call us to act. *The Lancet* 396(10257): 1125–1128. DOI: 10.1016/S0140-6736(20)32076-6

Chakravarti A (2015) Perspectives on human variation through the lens of diversity and race. *Cold Spring Harbor Perspectives in Biology* 7(9): a023358.

Chan S, Suo C, Lee S, et al. (2012) Translational aspects of genetic factors in the prediction of drug response variability: A case study of warfarin pharmacogenomics in a multi-ethnic cohort from Asia. *The Pharmacogenomics Journal* 12(4): 312–318.

Chaussabel D and Pulendran B (2015) A vision and a prescription for big data-enabled medicine. *Nature Immunology* 16(5): 435–439.

Collier R (2012) A race-based detour to personalized medicine. *Canadian Medical Association Journal* 184(7): E351–E353. DOI: 10.1503/cmaj.109-4133.

Dancey J (2012) Genomics, personalized medicine and cancer practice. *Clinical Biochemistry* 45(6): 379–381.

Duster, T ([1990]2003) *Backdoor to Eugenics*. New York: Routledge.

Duster T (2006) The molecular reinscription of race: Unanticipated issues in biotechnology and forensic science. *Patterns of Prejudice* 40(4–5): 427–441.

Duster T (2015) A post-genomic surprise: The molecular reinscription of race in science, law and medicine. *The British Journal of Sociology* 66(1): 1–27.
Epstein S (2007) *Inclusion: The Politics of Difference in Medical Research*. Chicago: University of Chicago Press.
Fujimura JH, Duster T and Rajagopalan R (2008) Race, genetics, and disease: Questions of evidence, matters of consequence. *Social Studies of Science* 38(5): 643–656. DOI: 10.1177/0306312708091926.
Fullwiley D (2007) The molecularization of race: Institutionalizing human difference in pharmacogenetics practice. *Science as Culture* 16(1): 1–30.
Fullwiley D (2008) The biologistical construction of race: "Admixture" technology and the new genetic medicine. *Social Studies of Science* 38(5): 695–735. DOI: 10.1177/0306312708090796.
Gans HJ (2017) Racialization and racialization research. *Ethnic and Racial Studies* 40(3): 341–352. DOI: 10.1080/01419870.2017.1238497.
Ginsburg GS and Huntington FW (2013) *Genomic and Personalized Medicine*. Cambridge, MA: Academic Press.
Hammonds EM and Herzig RM (2009) *The Nature of Difference: Sciences of Race in the United States from Jefferson to Genomics*. Cambridge, MA: MIT Press.
Hardimon MO (2013) Race concepts in medicine. *The Journal of Medicine and Philosophy* 38(1): 6–31.
Hoberman J (2012) *Black and Blue: The Origins and Consequences of Medical Racism*. Oakland, CA: University of California Press.
Hunt LM and Kreiner MJ (2013) Pharmacogenetics in primary care: The promise of personalized medicine and the reality of racial profiling. *Culture, Medicine, and Psychiatry* 37(1): 226–235.
Jain KK (2015) *Textbook of Personalized Medicine*. New York: Humana Press.
Jenkins K (2015) *I think therefore you are: Detecting the social construction of race in medicine*. PhD Thesis, University of Florida, US.
Kahn J (2003) Getting the numbers right: Statistical mischief and racial profiling in heart failure research. *Perspectives in Biology and Medicine* 46(4): 473–483. DOI: 10.1353/pbm.2003.0087.
Kahn J (2004) How a drug becomes "ethnic": Law, commerce, and the production of racial categories in medicine. *Yale Journal of Health Policy, Law, and Ethics* 4(1): 1–46.
Kahn J (2012) The troubling persistance of race in pharmacogenomics. *Journal of Law, Medicine and Ethics* 40(4): 873–885.
Khan AT, Gogarten SM, McHugh CP, et al. (2022) Recommendations on the use and reporting of race, ethnicity, and ancestry in genetic research: Experiences from the NHLBI topmed program. *Cell Genomics* 2(8): 100155.
Knerr S, Wayman D and Bonham VL (2011) Inclusion of racial and ethnic minorities in genetic research: Advance the spirit by changing the rules? *Journal of Law, Medicine & Ethics* 39(3): 502–512. DOI: 10.1111/j.1748-720X.2011.00617.x
Koenig BA, Lee SS-J and Richardson SS (2008) *Revisiting Race in a Genomic Age*. New Brunswick, NJ: Rutgers University Press.
Kohane IS (2015) Ten things we have to do to achieve precision medicine. *Science* 349(6243): 37–38.
Krieger N (2001) Theories for social epidemiology in the 21st century: An ecososial perspective. *International Journal of Epidemiology* 30(4): 668–677.
Kumar D ed. (2012) *Genomics and Health in the Developing World*. New York: Oxford University Press.
Lee SS-J, Mountain J and Koenig BA (2001) Meanings of race in the new genomics: Implications for health disparities research. *Yale Journal of Health Policy, Law and Ethics* 1(1): 33–76.

Maglo KN (2010) Genomics and the conundrum of race: Some epistemic and ethical considerations. *Perspectives in Biology and Medicine* 53(3): 357–372.

Marchant GE and Lindor RA (2018) Genomic malpractice: An emerging tide or gentle ripple? *Food and Drug Law Journal* 73(1): 1–37.

Marks J (2012) Making race without racism. *Science* 337(6099): 1174–1175.

McCarthy J and Mendelsohn B (2016) *Precision Medicine: A Guide to Genomics in Clinical Practice*. New York: McGraw-Hill Education.

Mensah GA, Jaquish C, Srinivas P, et al. (2019) Emerging concepts in precision medicine and cardiovascular diseases in racial and ethnic minority populations. *Circulation Research* 125(1): 7–13.

Mirnezami R, Nicholson J and Darzi A (2012) Preparing for precision medicine. *New England Journal of Medicine* 366(6): 489–491.

Nelson A (2016) *The Social Life of DNA: Race, Reparations, and Reconciliation After the Genome*. Boston, MA: Beacon Press.

Nelson KE and Jones-Nelson B (2012) *Genomics Applications for the Developing World*. New York: Springer.

Ong A (2016) *Fungible Life: Experiment in the Asian City of Life*. Durham, NC: Duke University Press.

Panofsky A and Bliss C (2017) Ambiguity and scientific authority: Population classification in genomic science. *American Sociological Review* 82(1): 59–87. DOI: 10.1177/0003122416685812

Petersen KE, Prows CA, Martin LJ, et al. (2014) Personalized medicine, availability, and group disparity: An inquiry into how physicians perceive and rate the elements and barriers of personalized medicine. *Public Health Genomics* 17(4): 209–220. DOI: 10.1159/000362359.

Phelan JC, Link BG and Feldman NM (2013) The genomic revolution and beliefs about essential racial differences. *American Sociological Review* 78(2): 167–191.

Pothier KC (2017) *Personalizing Precision Medicine: A Global Voyage from Vision to Reality*. Hoboken, NJ: Wiley.

Prainsack B (2015) Is personalized medicine different? *The British Journal of Sociology* 66: 28–35.

Prainsack B (2017) *Personalized Medicine: Empowered Patients in the 21st Century?* New York: New York University Press.

Reardon JE (2004) *Race to the finish: Identity and governance in an age of genomics*. PhD dissertation, Princeton, NJ.

Reardon JE (2022) The pathos of precision. *New Genetics and Society* 41(3): 187–195. DOI: 10.1080/14636778.2022.2115352.

Root M (2003) The use of race in medicine as a proxy for genetic differences. *Philosophy of Science* 70(5): 1173–1183. DOI: 10.1086/377398.

Rothstein MA (2016) Some lingering concerns about the precision medicine initiative. *Journal of Law, Medicine & Ethics* 44(3): 520–525.

Schork NJ (2015) Personalized medicine: Time for one-person trials. *Nature* 520: 609–611.

Schwartz R (2001) Racial profiling in medical research. *The New England Journal of Medicine* 344(18): 1392–1393.

Shim JK (2014) *Heart-Sick: The Politics of Risk, Inequality, and Heart Disease*. New York: NYU Press.

Sun S (2020) Clinical usefulness of genetic testing for drug toxicity in cancer care: Decision-makers' framing, knowledge and perceptions. *New Genetics and Society* 39(4): 359–384.

Swetlitz I (2016) Teaching medical students to challenge 'unscientific' racial categories. *STATNews*, 10 March. Available at: www.statnews.com/2016/03/10/medical-schools-teaching-race/ (Accessed 23 October 2023).

TallBear K (2013). *Native American DNA: Tribal Belonging and the False Promise of Genetic Science*. Minneapolis: University of Minnesota Press.

Travassos C and Williams DR (2004) The concept and measurement of race and their relationship to public health: A review focused on Brazil and the United States. *Cadernos De Saúde Pública* 20(3): 660–678. DOI: 10.1590/s0102-311x2004000300003.

Tsai J (2022) How should educators and publishers eliminate racial essentialism. *American Medical Association Journal of Ethics* 24(3): E201–E211. DOI: 10.1001/amajethics.2022.201.

Tsai J, Ucik L, Baldwin N, et al. (2016) Race matters? Examining and rethinking race portrayal in preclinical medical education. *Academic Medicine* 91(7): 916–920. DOI: 10.1097/acm.0000000000001232.

Tutton R, Smart A, Martin PA, et al. (2008) Genotyping the future: Scientists's expectations about race/ethnicity after BiDil. *Journal of Law, Medicine and Ethics* 36: 464–470.

US National Library of Medicine (n.d.) What is precision medicine? Available at: https://medlineplus.gov/genetics/understanding/precisionmedicine/definition/.

Verma M and Barh D (2017) *Progress and Challenges in Precision Medicine*. Amsterdam: Academic Press.

Wade, N (2014) *A Troublesome Inheritance: Genes, Race and Human History*. New York: Penguin Press.

Wolinsky H (2011) Genomes, race and health. *EMBO Reports* 12(2): 107–109. DOI: 10.1038/embor.2010.218.

Appendix A
Profile of the 46 interviewees

Interviewee No.	Treating patients (yes/no)	Public hospital or private clinic	Clinical specialty	Scientific research interests
Canada (a total of 11 interviewees)				
1	Yes	Public	Head, neck, and lung cancers	Head, neck, and lung cancers, genomic and precision medicine
2	No			Drug resistance in cancers
3	Yes	Public	Gastrointestinal cancer	Clinical trials, ethics, and genomic-based research
4	Yes	Public	Breast and lung cancer	Cancer genetics, oncogenomics, and clinical trials, especially in breast and lung cancer
5	Yes	Public	Breast cancer	Breast cancer
6	No			Cancer in relation to genes and environment, particularly hematologic and breast cancers
7	Yes	Public	Lung cancer	Detection, prevention, and therapy of lung cancer
8	Yes	Public	Gastrointestinal oncology	Developmental therapeutics, genomics, and biomarker development in gastrointestinal cancers
9	No			Cancer biology, genetics/genomics, epigenomics, and bioinformatics
10	No			Myeloid malignancies, immune signaling, and genomics-based clinical diagnostics
11	No			Drug therapies, including effectiveness, surveillance systems, and policy development

Appendix A: Profile of the 46 interviewees 129

Interviewee No.	Treating patients (yes/no)	Public hospital or private clinic	Clinical specialty	Scientific research interests
USA (a total of 10 interviewees)				
12	No			Health economics, biomarker development and implementation
13	Yes	Public	Lung, head, and neck cancers	Outcomes research and pharmacoeconomics of cancer therapies
14	Yes	Public	Hematology/ Oncology	Gastrointestinal cancers, cancer prevention, and genetic epidemiology
15	Yes	Public	Gastrointestinal cancers	Epidemiology and outcomes research in gastrointestinal cancers
16	Yes	Public	Lung cancer	Resistance in lung cancer
17	Yes	Public	Gastrointestinal cancer	Colorectal cancer genetics
18	Yes	Public	Breast cancer	Breast cancer risks
19	Yes	Public	General internal medicine	Health in Asian American populations
20	Yes	Public	Thoracic malignancies and soft tissue sarcomas	Treatments to manage thoracic malignancies
21	No			Social determinants of health
Singapore (a total of 25 interviewees)				
22	Yes	Private	Breast cancer and cancer genetics	Clinical and translational research on cancer, as well as chemotherapy and targeted therapy drugs
23	Yes	Public	Thoracic oncology and pharmacogenomics	Early phase clinical studies in head, neck, and lung cancer
24	Yes	Public	Oncology-hematology	Development of new drugs and new treatment strategies, as well as differences between Asian and Caucasian cancers
25	Yes	Public	Gastrointestinal cancer	Pharmacogenetics and epigenetics in cancer
26	Yes	Public	Head, neck, and lung cancers	Pharmacokinetics/ pharmacogenomics, as well as Phase I and II cancer clinical trials
27	No			Genomic oncology of stomach cancer
28	No			Health economics

(*Continued*)

Appendix A: Profile of the 46 interviewees

(Continued)

Interviewee No.	Treating patients (yes/no)	Public hospital or private clinic	Clinical specialty	Scientific research interests
29	Yes	Public	Geriatric medicine and palliative medicine	End-of-life care in the elderly
30	Yes	Public	Gastrointestinal cancers	Cancer immunology and immunotherapy
31	No			Research interests: Asian cancers (especially colorectal, lung, and gastric cancers) and translational research in precision medicine
32	Yes	Public	General medicine, endocrinology, and diabetology	Various aspects of diabetes, including epidemiology and genomic medicine
33	Yes	Private	Gastrointestinal, liver, breast, and lung cancers	Tumor angiogenesis, anti-angiogenesis, and cancer gene therapy
34	Yes	Public	Colorectal, hepato-pancreato-biliary and upper gastrointestinal cancers	Oncology, medical education, end-of-life care
35	Yes	Public	Head, neck, and thoracic oncology	Head, neck, and thoracic oncology, including phase II and III clinical trials and translational clinical studies
36	Yes	Public	Hematology and medical oncology	Translational research, drug resistance in human cancers, as well as dysregulation of mRNA translations
37	No			Clinical pharmacology (pharmacokinetics/pharmacodynamics/pharmacogenetics) and early-phase clinical trials of anti-cancer agents
38	Yes	Public	Colorectal, hepatobiliary, and upper gastrointestinal tract cancer	Cancer genetics, including clinical care and translational research
39	Yes	Public	Colorectal cancer	Early detection and diagnosis of colorectal cancers, precision medicine for stomach cancer

Appendix A: Profile of the 46 interviewees

Interviewee No.	Treating patients (yes/no)	Public hospital or private clinic	Clinical specialty	Scientific research interests
40	Yes	Private	Lymphomas as well as head and neck cancers	Molecularly targeted cancer therapies and immunotherapy as well as fundamental epigenetic studies
41	Yes	Private	Lung, gynecological, and breast cancers	Lung and women's cancers
42	Yes	Public	Thoracic, head, and neck cancers	Drug resistance in lung cancer, including molecular profiling and drug development in phase I trials
43	Yes	Public	Breast, lung, gastrointestinal, liver, prostate, kidney, and head and neck cancers	Cancer genetics and precision oncology
44	Yes	Public	Ovarian, endometrial, cervical, kidney, prostate, and bladder cancers	Gynecological and genitourinary cancers as well as development of novel anti-cancer therapeutic agents
45	Yes	Private	Breast, lung and colon cancer, lymphoma, sarcoma, and neuro-oncology (brain and spinal cord cancers)	Targeted therapy and novel mutations in rare cancers
46	No			Genetics and genomics of complex diseases and precision medicine

Appendix B
Articles included in the systematic review of cost-effectiveness studies and race/ethnicity

No.	Authors	Year	Journal article title
1	Black et al.	2008	Should asymptomatic men be included in chlamydia screening programs? Cost-effectiveness of chlamydia screening among male and female entrants to a national job training program
2	Ke et al.	2017	Cost-effectiveness Analysis for Genotyping before Allopurinol Treatment to Prevent Severe Cutaneous Adverse Drug Reactions
3	Rubinstein et al.	2009	Cost-effectiveness of population-based BRCA1/2 testing and ovarian cancer prevention for Ashkenazi Jews: a call for dialogue
4	Holland et al.	2009	Cost-effectiveness of testing for breast cancer susceptibility genes
5	Manchanda et al.	2017	Cost-effectiveness of population based BRCA testing with varying Ashkenazi Jewish ancestry
6	Patel et al.	2018	Cost-effectiveness of population based BRCA1 founder mutation testing in Sephardi Jewish women
7	Sun et al.	2019	A cost-effectiveness analysis of multigene testing for all patients with breast cancer
8	Wang et al.	2012	Predictive genetic testing of frst degree relatives of mutation carriers is a cost-efective strategy in preventing hereditary non-polyposis colorectal cancer in Singapore
9	Chen et al.	2007	Cost-effectiveness analysis of prenatal diagnosis intervention for Down's syndrome in China
10	Eckman et al.	2009	Cost-effectiveness of using pharmacogenetic information in warfarin dosing for patients with nonvalvular atrial fibrillation
11	Schackman et al.	2008	The cost-effectiveness of HLA-B*5701 genetic screening to guide initial antiretroviral therapy for HIV

Appendix B: Articles included in the systematic review

No.	Authors	Year	Journal article title
12	Kim et al.	2006	Cost-effectiveness analysis of MTHFR polymorphism screening by polymerase chain reaction in Korean patients with rheumatoid arthritis receiving methotrexate
13	Oh et al.	2004	Pharmacoeconomic analysis of thiopurine methyltransferase polymorphism screening by polymerase chain reaction for treatment with azathioprine in Korea
14	Lehmann et al.	2003	Polymorphisms and the pocketbook: the cost-effectiveness of cytochrome P450 2C19 genotyping in the eradication of helicobacter pylori infection associated with duodenal ulcer
15	Dong et al.	2012	Cost-effectiveness of HLA-B*1502 genotyping in adult patients with newly diagnosed epilepsy in Singapore
16	Kapoor et al.	2015	Reducing hypersensitivity reactions with HLA-B*5701 genotyping before abacavir prescription: clinically useful but is it cost-effective in Singapore?
17	de Lima et al.	2012	Cost-effectiveness of epidermal growth factor receptor mutation testing and first-line treatment with gefitinib for patients with advanced adenocarcinoma of the lung
18	Plumpton et al.	2015	Cost-effectiveness of screening for HLA-A*31:01 prior to initiation of carbamazepine in epilepsy
19	Rattanavipapong et al.	2013	Economic evaluation of HLA-B*15:02 screening for carbamazepine-induced severe adverse drug reactions in Thailand
20	Shiroiwa et al.	2010	Cost-effectiveness analysis of KRAS testing and cetuximab as last-line therapy for colorectal cancer
21	Hagaman et al.	2010	Thiopurine S-methyltransferase [corrected] testing in idiopathic pulmonary fibrosis: a pharmacogenetic cost-effectiveness analysis
22	Goldie et al.	2001	Policy analysis of cervical cancer screening strategies in low-resource settings: clinical benefits and cost-effectiveness
23	Hannouf et al.	2012	Cost-effectiveness of a 21-gene recurrence score assay versus Canadian clinical practice in women with early-stage estrogen- or progesterone-receptor-positive, axillary lymph-node negative breast cancer
24	Teixeira et al.	2020	Cervical cancer screening program based on primary DNA-HPV testing in a Brazilian city: a cost-effectiveness study protocol
25	Somigliana et al.	2019	Cost-effectiveness of preimplantation genetic testing for aneuploidies

(Continued)

Appendix B: Articles included in the systematic review

(Continued)

No.	Authors	Year	Journal article title
26	Howell et al.	2018	A population-based cost-effectiveness study of early genetic testing in severe epilepsies of infancy
27	Stark et al.	2017	Prospective comparison of the cost-effectiveness of clinical whole-exome sequencing with that of usual care overwhelmingly supports early use and reimbursement
28	Seror et al.	2016	PAP assays in newborn screening for cystic fibrosis: a population-based cost-effectiveness study
29	Gausachs et al.	2012	MLH1 promoter hypermethylation in the analytical algorithm of Lynch syndrome: a cost-effectiveness study
30	Geuzinge et al.	2020	Cost-effectiveness of Breast Cancer Screening With Magnetic Resonance Imaging for Women at Familial Risk
31	Aguiar et al.	2018	Cost-effectiveness of Osimertinib in the First-Line Treatment of Patients With EGFR-Mutated Advanced Non-Small Cell Lung Cancer
32	Blank et al.	2011	KRAS and BRAF mutation analysis in metastatic colorectal cancer: a cost-efectiveness analysis from a Swiss perspective
33	Severin et al.	2015	Economic evaluation of genetic screening for Lynch syndrome in Germany
34	Chou et al.	2009	First trimester Down syndrome screening in women younger than 35 years old and cost-effectiveness analysis in Taiwan population
35	Garrouste et al.	2011	The choice of detecting Down syndrome: does money matter?
36	Winter et al.	2004	Cost-effectiveness of thiopurine methyltransferase genotype screening in patients about to commence azathioprine therapy for treatment of inflammatory bowel disease
37	Donnan et al.	2011	A cost-effectiveness analysis of thiopurine methyltransferase testing for guiding 6-mercaptopurine dosing in children with acute lymphoblastic leukemia
38	Hall et al.	2012	Economic evaluation of genomic test-directed chemotherapy for early-stage lymph node-positive breast cancer
39	Thompson et al.	2014	The cost-effectiveness of a pharmacogenetic test: a trial-based evaluation of TPMT genotyping for azathioprine
40	Nieves et al.	2010	Cost-effectiveness analysis of HLA-B*5701 typing in the prevention of hypersensitivity to abacavir in HIV? patients in Spain

Appendix B: Articles included in the systematic review

No.	Authors	Year	Journal article title
41	Mittmann et al.	2009	Prospective cost-effectiveness analysis of cetuximab in metastatic colorectal cancer: evaluation of National Cancer Institute of Canada Clinical Trials Group CO.17 trial
42	Oliva et al.	2009	Cost-effectiveness analysis of a genetic screening program in the close relatives of Spanish patients with familial hypercholesterolemia
43	Debniak et al.	2000	Value of pedigree/clinical data, immunohistochemistry and microsatellite instability analyses in reducing the cost of determining hMLH1 and hMSH2 gene mutations in patients with colorectal cancer
44	Lux et al.	2018	Budget impact analysis of gene expression tests to aid therapy decisions for breast cancer patients in Germany
45	Kondo et al.	2008	Economic evaluation of 21-gene reverse transcriptase-polymerase chain reaction assay in lymph-node-negative, estrogen-receptor-positive, early-stage breast cancer in Japan
46	Tsoi et al.	2010	Cost effectiveness analysis of recurrence score-guided treatment using a 21-gene assay in early breast cancer
47	Kondo et al.	2011	Economic evaluation of the 21-gene signature (Oncotype DX) in lymph node-negative/positive, hormone receptor-positive early-stage breast cancer based on Japanese validation study (JBCRG-TR03)
48	Lamond et al.	2012	Cost-utility of the 21-gene recurrence score assay in node-negative and node-positive breast cancer
49	Blohmer et al.	2013	Using the 21-gene assay to guide adjuvant chemotherapy decision-making in early-stage breast cancer: A cost effectiveness evaluation in the German setting
50	Reed et al.	2013	Cost-effectiveness of the 21-gene recurrence score assay in the context of multifactorial decision making to guide chemotherapy for early-stage breast cancer
51	Holt et al.	2013	A decision impact, decision conflict and economic assessment of routine Oncotype DX testing of 146 women with nodenegative or pNImi, ER-positive breast cancer in the U.K.
52	Paulden et al.	2013	Cost-effectiveness of the 21-gene assay for guiding adjuvant chemotherapy decisions in early breast cancer

(*Continued*)

Appendix B: Articles included in the systematic review

(Continued)

No.	Authors	Year	Journal article title
53	Yamauchi et al.	2014	Societal cost-effectiveness analysis of the 21-gene assay in estrogen-receptor-positive, lymph-node-negative early-stage breast cancer in Japan
54	Kip et al.	2015	Long-term cost-effectiveness of Oncotype DX® versus current clinical practice from a Dutch cost perspective
55	Katz et al.	2015	Economic impact of gene expression profiling in patients with early-stage breast cancer in France
56	Jahn et al.	2015	Cost-effectiveness of personalized treatment in women with early breast cancer: The application of OncotypeDX and Adjuvant! Online to guide adjuvant chemotherapy in Austria
57	El-Serag et al.	2000	Screening for hereditary hemochromatosis in siblings and children of affected patients. A cost-effectiveness analysis
58	Chen et al.	2015	Cost-effectiveness analysis of alternative screening and treatment strategies for heterozygous familial hypercholesterolemia in the United States
59	Le Guellec et al.	2010	Cost-effectiveness of UGT1A1*28 genotyping in preventing severe neutropenia following FOLFIRI therapy in colorectal cancer
60	Gold et al.	2009	Cost-effectiveness of pharmacogenetic testing for uridine diphosphate glucuronosyltransferase 1A1 before irinotecan administration for metastatic colorectal cancer
61	Vegter et al.	2009	Cost-effectiveness of ACE inhibitor therapy to prevent dialysis in nondiabetic nephropathy: influence of the ACE insertion/deletion polymorphism
62	Smith et al.	2008	Should female relatives of factor V leiden carriers be screened prior to oral contraceptive use? A cost-effectiveness analysis
63	Welton et al.	2008	A cost-effectiveness analysis of genetic testing of the DRD2 Taq1A polymorphism to aid treatment choice for smoking cessation
64	Veenstra et al.	2007	Pharmacogenomic testing to prevent aminoglycoside-induced hearing loss in cystic fibrosis patients: potential impact on clinical, patient, and economic outcomes
65	Meckley et al.	2006	Screening for the alpha-adducin Gly460Trp variant in hypertensive patients: a cost-effectiveness analysis

No.	Authors	Year	Journal article title
66	Priest et al.	2006	Pharmacoeconomic analyses of azathioprine, methotrexate and prospective pharmacogenetic testing for the management of inflammatory bowel disease
67	Heitjan et al.	2008	Cost-effectiveness of pharmacogenetic testing to tailor smoking-cessation treatment
68	Obradovic et al.	2008	Cost-effectiveness of UGT1A1 genotyping in second-line, high-dose, once every 3 weeks irinotecan monotherapy treatment of colorectal cancer
69	Costa-Scharplatz et al.	2007	Cost-effectiveness of pharmacogenetic testing to predict treatment response to angiotensin-converting enzyme inhibitor
70	van den Akker et al.	2006	Cost-effectiveness of pharmacogenomics in clinical practice: a case study of thiopurine methyltransferase genotyping in acute lymphoblastic leukemia in Europe
71	Hughes et al.	2004	Cost-effectiveness analysis of HLA B*5701 genotyping in preventing abacavir hypersensitivity
72	You et al.	2004	The potential clinical and economic outcomes of pharmacogenetics-oriented management of warfarin therapy: a decision analysis
73	Pichereau et al.	2010	Cost-effectiveness of UGT1A1*28 genotyping in preventing severe neutropenia following FOLFIRI therapy in colorectal cancer

Index

Note: Page numbers in *italics* indicate figures, and page numbers in **bold** indicate tables in the text

5-fluorouracil (5-FU) 89, 91
*6 rs1801160 A risk allele 91

abacavir 95
aboriginal peoples 8, 61, 62
academic/university medical centres 78–79
academic versus non-academic medical institutions 114–115
Acquaviva, K. D. 30
activism 15, 73
admixture 29
adverse drug reactions 17, 20, 81, 88, 89–90, 98, 101, 113
African 10, 12, 31, 32, 54, 58, 91
African American 4, 12–14, 17, 19, 57, 73, 91, 95
algorithm 52, 108; automatic "race corrections" and 80; biases 14; diagnostic 13; dose algorithms 91, 95–96, 98, 100; race/ethnicity-adjusted 18; racialized 123; surname-matching 56
allele frequency 30, 65; prevalence 29, allelic frequency variations 16, 66, 72; *see also* genetic differences and genetic variations
allopurinol 89–90, 95
Almaguer, T. 8
American Medical Association 6
Amster, E. J. 11
ancestry informative markers (AIMs) 50, 55, 56, 64, 65, 67, 110
Andreasen, R. 50
anti-racist racialism 31

arbitrariness of race 28, 32, 105; and imprecision of race/ethnicity 105
Asian 19, 31, 37–42, 55–57, 59–62, 67, 91, 93–97, 100, 110, 115, 120–122; East Asian 38, 39, 93, 95, 100; Northeast Asian 59; Southeast Asian 62, 90
Au, L. 2
autism 5
availability of resources 43, 74, 75, 108

Bach, P. B. 56
Baluran, D. A. 7, 66, 120
Banton, M. 7
Barclay, M. 90
barriers to personalized precision medicine 120
basic research 49
Beal, A. C. 12–13
best research practices 112
Bevacizumab 83
Bhopal, R. 100
biases 10, 13–14, 29, 30, 105, 117, 122: confirmation bias 63–64, 119
BiDil 73
BIM (B cell lymphoma-2-like 11) polymorphism 39, 122
biological/genetic determinism 6, 10, 16–17, 28–29, 50–52, 54, 56, 62–63, 66, 72, 74, 110–112, 115–116, 121–120; biological determinism of race 18
biomarkers: clinical 4, 72; disease 36; -driven disease 41; genetic 34, 36–40, 43–45; pharmacological 4, 89–93, 96, 98; *see also* genetic biomarker

biomedicalization of race 19
bio-piracy 16, 74
Black 5, 11, 13, 57, 62
Bliss, C. 44
Boas, F. 10
Bonham, V. L. 4
Bowser, R. 88
British 11, 61–62, 94
British-colonial legacy 94
Brown, M. 7, 10
Burchard, E. G. 32, 45
Bustamante, C. D. 45

California Cancer Registry 52
Canadian Medical Association 89–90
cancer 1, 20, 77; 5-fluorouracil for 91–92; allopurinol for 89–90; breast 28, 59, 80, 91; care 17–19, 122; causes 5–6; drugs 89–92; gastrointestinal 91; germline mutations 91; head and neck 91; lung 36–38, 41, 43–44, 122; nasopharyngeal 35–36; precision medicine for 107, 109, 118; risk factors 5
cancer precision medicine 1, 18, 107
Cardiovascular Disease Risk Estimator 13
Caucasian 110, 115, 120, 122; European 91; Irish 8, 96; non-Caucasian 8, 62; Polish 96
Caudle, K. E. 91
Caulfield, T. 16
census categories 31; Asian 19, 31, 37–42, 55–57, 59–62, 67, 91, 93–97, 100, 110, 115, 120–122; CMIO (Chinese, Malay, Indian, Others) 62, 94; Hispanic/Latino 8, 13, 19, 52; Mexican 8, 31; U.S. Census 61; visible minority 8; White 8, 10–11, 13–14, 32, 57, 100
Chan, S. 4, 72
Chinese 9, 11, 19, 36, 38, 41, 52–53, 55–62, 65, 74, 89–91, 93, 94, 98, 115, 122
Chinese-Malay-Indian-Others (CMIO) categories 62, 94
Chronic Kidney Disease Epidemiology Collaboration 14
classificatory ambiguity 32, 106
cline 65; clinal 65; clinally 65
clinical application: clinical decision-making 42, 43–45, 72–73, 89, 116, 119; clinical guidelines 12, 98; clinical outcomes 97; clinical recommendations 98; clinical utility 89

clinical/medical decision-making see medical decision-making
clinical trials 8, 18, 34–35, 43–46, 49, 54, 109–110, 119, 122; genetics-driven 40; N-of-1 112; recruiting suitable human subjects for 37–40; of risk-based breast cancer screening 28; scientific research to 32; statistically meaningful 38; translation process to 33; US-based 92
clinical value 113
clinician-scientists 43, 49, 52, 61, 66, 67, 89, 93, 101, 106, 107, 111, 120, 121, 123; see also stakeholders
clopidogrel plavix 99–100
Collier, R. 123
colonial expansion 10
colonial history 105
colonialism 9–12, 17–19, 67, 105, 121; British 62, 94; European 51
confirmation bias 63–64, 119
conflation of race and genetics 51, 88, 106
constructivists 16
cost 29, 99; -benefit ratio 76, 77; -effectiveness studies 20, 89, 92–93, 111, 118, 121, 132–137; estimations 76; excessive 83; of genetic sequencing 18; healthcare 76, 114; model 74; molecular-based drugs 76–77; potential 31; precision medicine drugs 83; of prescription drugs 16
cost-benefit ratio 76, 77
cost-effectiveness studies 20, 89, 92–93, 111, 118, 121, 132–137
country of (family) origin/nativity 54
Crompton, S. 17
cultural background 55
cutaneous adverse drug reactions (CADRs) 89–90
cystic fibrosis 5

Da Silva, R. G. L. 2
data 32, 40, 119; accessing 67, 121; big 49; collection 1, 53, 56, 112; empirical 66, 109; generation/capturing 2; genetic 3, 64, 71, 98, 114; genomic 49, 111, 123; interview 18–19, 33, 39, 44, 52, 57, 65–66, 74–75, 82, 89, 92–93, 100, 117, 119, 122; medical 80–81; molecular 3; pharmacogenetic toxicity 95–96, 98; privacy 81, 114; qualitative 20n1, 43, 122; race-based 43, 56; race/ethnicity-based 75;

racialized/ethnicized 15; Singapore-centric databases 4; whole-genome sequencing 3
databases 52, 92, 110; Chinese Millionome Database 3; genomic 49; National Cancer Institute's Surveillance, Epidemiology, End Results (SEER) program 52; Singapore-centric 4
datasets 49
degree of acceptance of race as a proxy for genetics 33
Department of the Attorney General 100
diagnostic algorithms 13
diabetes 1, 31
diet 30, 37, 97–98
diet-drug pharmacokinetic interactions 98
differences: biological 10; cultural 7, 11; between individuals 2; measure of 9; physical 7; racial 11; *see also* racial differences
differential rate of diffusion 78
differential treatment 105
dihydropyrimidine hydrogenase (DPD) deficiency 91–92
discrimination 105; insurance 82; genetic discrimination 30, 73, 81–83, 114; racial discrimination 106, 109, 116
disease 1–4; biological characteristics of 72; biomarker-driven 41; cardiovascular 13, 122; diagnosis/prognosis and treatment 28; etiology 6; genetic 30, 37, 74, 112–113; genetic markers for 15, 34, 38; heart 44; immunity towards 11–12; insurance coverage for 82; kidney 14, 90; occurrence of 11, 29, 31, 35–36, 50–51; phenotype 39; probability 111; racialized statistics of 36; rates 29; respiratory 14; risk 12, 59, 61, 66, 81, 114, 123; susceptibility 36, 66, 72, 75, 81, 114–115, 117, 119, 123; treatment of 2, 107
diversity in genetic research 49
DNA sequencing 2
Dobzhansky, T. 50
Donaldson, L. 100
donor DNA 63
dose requirements 4, 72
drug: 5-fluorouracil 91–92; allopurinol 89–90; cancer 89; cost of 83; development 109; dosage 42, 91, 95–96, 98, 100; effectiveness 123; efficacy 15, 20, 39, 88, 98, 111, 113, 119; marketing 73, 99; metabolism 97, 98; metabolizing enzymes 31; molecular-based 76–78, 114; prescription 4, 16, 89; providing miracle 99; racialized 45, 106; reactions 123; response 29, 37, 72, 75, 88, 98, 100, 115–117; safety 88; *see also* adverse drug reactions; drug toxicity
drug efficacy 15, 20, 39, 88, 98, 111, 113, 119; genetic testing for 113
drug metabolism 97, 98
drug response 29, 37, 72, 88, 98, 100, 115–117
drug toxicity 42, 88–89, 100–101, 117, 119, 123; 5-fluorouracil 91–92; clinical trials and 38–39; drug safety 88, 91; genetic susceptibility to 67, 109, 113, 120; genetic testing for 89, 96, 98, 109, 113; genome-based 89; as multifactor phenomenon 97–98; pharmacogenetics/pharmacogenomics 88–101, 111; polygenic nature of 98; race/ethnicity-based 95–96; and racialization 89–93, 97, 100, 111; racialized 94, 96, 99–100; racialized/ethnicized risks of 96, 101; risk estimates 96; risks 39, 96–97, 99, 101, 113; subjective interpretation of risks 96–97; tests 97, 111, 113
Duffy antibody 12
Duster, T. 8, 31, 66

environmental factors 72, 98, 111, 113, 123
epidermal growth factor receptor (EGFR) 14, 18, 37–41, 76, 78, 122
equity: access to healthcare 30, 82–85; diversity, equity and inclusion in clinical trials 66; social inequalities 15, 30, 118
Epstein, S. 31, 44
errors in diagnosis and treatment 29, 88, 105
essentialists 16
estimated glomerular filtration rate 14
ethnic and racial population groups: arbitrary definitions of 93
ethnicity *see* race/ethnicity
ethnoracial population groups 57–59, 60–61, 65–66, 91–93, 110–111; Chinese 65; genetic differences between 57–58, 66; genetic

heterogeneity within 59, 66; genetic similarities between 66; no clear genetic distinction between 58–59
European 90, 91, 93–94
European conquest 61
Evans, W. E. 98

factors 43, 45, 72; causative 30, 31, 112, 117; correlational 11; cultural 5, 29, 88; environmental 98, 111, 123; genetic 29, 31, 79, 88, 97, 111, 123; genomic 79; modifiable risk 36; non-genetic 31, 90, 97–98, 113; political 16; societal 16, 73; socioeconomic 5, 16
fallacy of racialism 119
false positives 32
family history 45; -based estimates for disease susceptibility and drug responsiveness 75, 117; -based methods 67, 120; as proxy for genetics 113
family-history based estimates 75
financial burden: on patients 73, 75, 76, 78, 114
financial resources 75–78, 108, 111, 118; on the health systems 76–77, 82
folk racial categories 50
French 50, 61
Fujimura, J. H. 5, 15, 51, 63
Fullerton, S. M. 45
funding 11, 15, 83

gabapentin 98
Gans, H. J. 119
Garcia, R. 5
gene 17, 36, 38, 51, 98; coding 100; DPD 91; encoding 41; environment interaction 59; target 39; variants 91
gene-environment interaction 59
generalizability 32, 66, 110
genetic allele 59, 62–65, 101, 105; frequencies of 59, 62–65, 101; prevalence of 105
genetic and non-genetic factors 97
genetic basis of differences 106
genetic biomarker 36–38, 45; disease-causing 34; hypothetically causal 40; prevalence of 39; testing for 43
genetic clustering study 50, 51, 63, 64
genetic data privacy 81, 114
genetic determinism 101, 112
genetic discrimination 30, 73, 81–83, 114

genetic diversity 6, 39, 45, 49, 51–52, 56, 65–66, 106, 110, 112, 118
genetic/genomic sequencing 2–3, 18, 63, 76, 114
genetic heterogeneity/homogeneity 58, 59, 66, 110–111; within ethnoracial population group 59, 66, 110; within racial/ethnic group 111
Genetic Information Nondiscrimination Act (GINA) 81, 114
geneticization of health 6
geneticization of race/ethnicity 16
Genetic Non-Discrimination Act (GNDA) 81, 114
genetic predisposition 17, 58
genetic profiles (of patients): access to 6, 67, 80, 81; claims on genetic sovereignty 16, 74; of the Hawaiian population 99–100; of the Japanese population 16, 66, 91
genetic risk 2, 31, 81–82
genetic structure 31
geneticists *see* scientific research
genetic testing 4, 17, 32, 43, 72, 114; based on race/ethnicity 41; decisions 41; for drug efficacy 113; drug toxicity 109, 113; for drug toxicity 89, 96, 98, 109, 113; errors in 123; genomic 76, 78; for germline mutations 81; incorporating 96; interpretation of genetic testing results 32; pharmacogenetic testing 89; results 80, 82; socioeconomic impact of 82
genetic variation 28, 51, 63, 95–96, 98, 109
genome 57–58, 115; -based clinical decisions 119; -based precision medicine 1–2, 6, 17–19, 109, 111, 118–119; -based toxicity 89; Human Genome Project 28, 121; sequencing 2–3; variation research 1, 110, 119; -wide association studies 15
genome wide association studies (GWAS) 15
genomic malpractice litigation 123
genomic science: global scale of 18; persistence of race in 16; race and 44, 49; racialization in 14–17, 52–57, 110; research 15
genomic sovereignty 16
genotype 92
genotypic/phenotypic ambiguity 106

142 Index

genotypic/phenotypic variations 72, 98
geography 16, 39, 54–55, 65–66, 72, 93; *see also* race-making
germline mutations/variants 80–81, 88, 91, 100
Ginsburg, G.S. 108
Goh, D. 9
Gonzalez-Sobrino, B. 6
Goodman, A. H. 10
Goss, D. R. 6
Gould, S. J. 10
governance of medical data 80–81

Han Chinese 89–90
Hardimon, M. O. 50
Harmon, A. 17
Hartigan, J. Jr. 52
healthcare 3, 13–14, 17, 19, 49, 71, 76–82, 84, 90, 114, 123
healthcare costs 76, 114
healthcare policy *see* policy
healthcare providers 14, 19, 71, 111
health disparities 6, 30, 32, 105; inequalities 6, 15, 30, 32, 82–84, 105, 111, 118; racialized health disparities/racial disparities in health 6
health inequalities 82, 84, 111, 118
health insurance 5, 76, 77–78, 81–82, 114
health outcomes 3, 14, 30, 31, 51, 66, 67, 73, 82, 97, 123
Health Science Authority (Singapore) 41, 89–90
health systems: multi-payer 76–77, 82, 108, 114; single-payer 76–77, 82, 114
heritage 54, 93
heterogeneity of resources 71, 82
HLAB*5801 allele 89
Hoskins, P. J. 83
HSA *see* Health Science Authority (Singapore)
human and informatics resources 78–80, 108, 111, 118
Human Genome Project 1, 28, 121
Hung, S. I. 89
Hunt, L. M. 2, 12, 14
hyperbilirubinemia, risk estimation of 12–13
hypersensitivity reactions 90

identity politics 17
implicit biases 13, 29
implicit racial/ethnic bias 105
Indians 41, 52, 55, 56, 58–59, 91, 93–94

indigenous people 61
individualized medical treatments/individualized care 2
individualized medicine 72
Indonesian 56–57
informatic tools 79, 115
in-group/out-group differences 67, 121
inherent contradiction in precision medicine 20, 28, 32, 33, 44–45, 71, 99, 107, 110, 112, 119, 122
insurance: access 77; coverage 78, 82; discrimination 82; health 5, 76, 81, 114; policies 77–78; premiums 81–82
interchangeable use of "race" and "ethnicity" 19, 118–119
interdisciplinary endeavors 79, 109, 112
interdisciplinary/multidisciplinary teams 79
intermarriages 58–59, 61, 95–96; interethnic marriages 94; interracial/interethnic marriages 42, 113; interracial marriages 29
International Haplotype Mapping Project (HapMap) 63

Jackson, M. 16., 57
Jain, K. K. 107
James, J. E. 28
Japanese 16, 55, 62, 66, 72, 90–92
Jarjour, S. 90
Jewish 8, 10, 54
Johnson, H. R. 11
Joseph, G. 28

Knerr, S. 118
knowledge gap hypothesis 82
knowledge transfer 79
Koenig, B. 109
Koreans 55, 62, 90
Kreiner, M. J. 2, 12, 14

Lan, P. C. 7
Lee, S. S. 44, 100, 106
legal and infrastructural resources 80–82, 108, 111, 118
legal implications 89
legislation 80–81, 114
legislative environment: GINA (Genetic Information Nondiscrimination Act) 81, 114; GNDA (Genetic Non-discrimination Act) 81, 114
Leong, L. W.-T. 94

leprosy 11, 12
Lewontin, R. C. 51
Lindor, R. A. 123
Livingstone, F. B. 51, 65
lung: cancer 18, 36–38, 41, 43, 122; function 14; Non-Small-Cell Lung Cancer 122

Maglo, K. N. 65
malaria 5
Malays 9, 11, 35–36, 41, 52–58, 60, 62, 90–91, 93–94
Manolio, T. A. 45
Marchant, G. E. 123
market forces 16, 106
market pressures 16
materials for race-making 57, 67, 121
McCarthy, J. 107
McCleery, I. 10
medical decision-making 8, 20, 28–29, 33, 34–35, **34**, 45–46, 71, 107, 116, 122; biological difference into 96; in clinic 32, 40–43; clinical trials to 122; concerning adverse drug reactions 20; contexts 46; domains 35; drug response to guide 72, 75, 105; errors in 123; genomic information in 18; race/ethnicity in 95–96, 109, 116; stage 35; usage of race in 119
medical education/training 12, 18, 73, 96, 116–117, 152–153; see also medical decision-making
medical specialists and equipment 79, 115
medical treatment 2, 4, 6, 29–30, 32, 74–75, 77, 81–82, 88, 107, 109, 115
Mendelsohn, B. 107
microarrays 63
Middle Eastern 13, 52, 91
migration/globalization 29, 58–59, 61, 62
Miles, R. 7, 10
Mintz, M. 30
minority ethnoracial groups 5, 8, 15, 32, 44, 49, 60–62, 73, 111, 118; see also race/ethnic groups
misdiagnosis 5, 41
mixed race/parentage 37, 94, 123; racial origin 53
modifiable risk factors 36
Moinester, M. 6
molecular-based drugs 76–78, 114
molecularization of race/ethnicity 19, 44, 51, 66, 105–107, 112
molecular reinscription of race 18–19, 31, 44, 51, 63, 66, 105–107, 111–112, 118; see also relative resources model
molecular tumour boards 17
Morning, A. 15., 63, 64
multi-factor phenomenon 97–98, 101
multigenerational ancestry/generational descent 50, 52, 53–55, 56, 58, 64, 67
multipayer public health system/co-pay system 77, 108, 114
mutation 40; acquired somatic 18, 81; BRCA 80; EGFR 38, 39, 41, 76, 78; genetic 39, 88; germline 80, 81, 88, 91, 100, 114; homozygous 91

name/surname 52, 55–56, 65, 67, 110, 120, 121
National Cancer Institute 52
national population categories 61
National Institute of Health (US) 15, 16, 44, 74, 118
National Precision Medicine (NPM) strategy 3
National Registration Identity Card (NRIC) 53, 93–94, 110
neutropenia 96
NIH see National Institute of Health (US)
N-of-1 trials 112
non-genetic factors 31, 90, 97, 113
Non-Small-Cell Lung Cancer (NSCLC) 122–123

Oh. S. S. 45
Omi, M. 51. 7, 61
one-size-fits all 2, 4, 99 organization of study populations and/or results 115
Ossorio, P. 8
othering 10, 61, 62

Parker, H. 19
patent applications and approvals 17
pathologizing of race 105
patient-centered care 43
patients': impact of biomedical practices 1, 3, 4, 6, 11, 13, 14, 18–20, 29, 33, 38–44, 53, 55, 57, 71–83, 89–92, 97–98, 105, 108–115, 122
Persian 9, 95
personalized precision medicine 18–20, 83–84, 93, 112, 119; access to 114–115, 117–118; adoption of 113, 116; barriers of 73, 80–82, 120; financial resources 75–78; human

144 *Index*

and informatics resources 78–80;
implementation of 71, 74, 108;
legal and infrastructural resources
80–82; physicians' ability to practice
75; resources to realize 75–83; *vs.*
racialized medicine 71–74, 106
pharma 16, 99
pharmaceutical companies 3, 16, 31, 73,
83, 98–100
pharmaceutical firms 89, 99
pharmacogenetic/pharmacogenomics
88–89, 101; 5-fluorouracil 90–91;
allopurinol 89–90; Asian and
Caucasian 93–95; cost-effectiveness
studies 92–93; and pharmaceutical
companies 98–100; precision
medicine 92–93; race/ethnicity 92–93;
toxicity data 95–98
pharmacogenetic testing 89, 96, 98
pharmacogenomics: pharmacodynamics
17; pharmacokinetics 17, 98
pharmacogenomic studies/
testing: pharmacogenomic drug
efficacy studies/testing 111;
pharmacogenomic toxicity studies/
testing 111
pharmacological research 4
phenotype 29, 39, 51, 53
Phillips, K. A. 108
Phimister, E. G. 14–15
Plavix 99–100
policy: against discriminatory practices
in biomedicine 112–114; on
classification of national population
117–118; on immigration 62
political boundaries 94
Popejoy, A. B. 45
population groups: ethnoracial 57–59,
60, 61, 65–66, 93, 110–111; genetic
differences between 63; human 10,
51; selection/sampling for clinical
trials 37–40, 43–45
population specific alleles 50
population stratification 12, 56, 67, 121
Pothier, K.C. 107
pragmatic racialism 31
Prainsack, B. 108
Precision Health Research, Singapore
(PRECISE) 3
precision medicine: cancer precision
medicine 107, 109, 118; genome-
based precision medicine 1–2, 6–8,
17–19, 109, 111, 118; personalized
precision medicine (*see* personalized
precision medicine); racialized
precision medicine 19–20, 71–75,
83, 84*n*1, 106, 108, 113, 118–120;
stakeholders of 16, 19, 31, 67, 73,
106, 108, 113, 116–118, 120–121;
translational precision medicine
33–45, 109, 112; *see also* precision
medicine initiatives
precision medicine initiatives: All of
US research program 2; Brazilian
Precision Medicine Initiative 2;
Canada's Personalized Medicine
Signature Initiative 3; China
Precision Medicine Project 2, 3;
Chinese Millionome Database 3;
GenomeCanada 3; Million Chinese
Genomes Project 2; National
Precision Medicine strategy 3;
Precision Health Research, Singapore
(PRECISE) 3; U.S. Precision
Medicine Initiative 2, 3
predictive pharmacogenomic testing 99
prejudice 6, 30, 88
prenatal genetic tests 17
preventive health care 2
Price, M. J. 100
probability sampling 122
profitability 76, 83
profit-making agendas 89, 99
public health systems 76–77, 82, 108,
114; multi-payer public health
systems 76–77, 82, 108, 114; single-
payer public health systems 76–77,
82, 114
public policy: NIH Policy and Guidelines
on the Inclusion of Women and
Minorities as Subjects in Clinical
Research 74, 118
Purushotam, N. S. 9

race/ethnicity: arbitrariness and
imprecision of 105; as biological
4–5, 7, 10–11, 15–19, 31, 44,
49–52, 55, 60–61, 63–66, 100,
106, 110–111, 116, 121, 123;
as biologically determined 6, 10,
50, 93, 121; as diachronic and
synchronic variable 121; as diagnostic
shortcut 12, 73, 116; drug toxicity
95–96; genetic testing based on 41;
medical decision-making\medical
education in 109, 116; mixed 37,

94, 123; molecularization of 19, 44, 51, 66, 105–107, 112; molecular reinscription of 18–19, 31, 44, 51, 63, 66, 105–107, 111–112, 118; operationalization of 63, 67, 121; pathologizing of 105; as proxy for biology 6; as proxy for genetic diversity 6, 45, 49, 56, 112; as proxy for genetic diversity and equity 45; as proxy for genetics 1, 6, 16, 28–33, 35, 42–43, 52, 71, 73, 107–109, 113, 121; relative resources theory 19, 71–84, 111, 119–120, 122–123; as residual category 15, 73; as social construct 15–16, 32, 49–51, 55, 56, 57, 60–62, 65, 106, 110, 117, 123; as sociopolitical construct 51; as stepping stone 6, 37, 106, 117

race-based genetic studies 28–29

race-based medicine 11, 13–14, 28, 72, 106, 117; defined 4, 105; harmful practices of 18, 123; problems with 5–6, 13, 109, 111, 118–119; replacing 108

race-conscious medicine 123

race correction 13, 14, 80, 123; and algorithms 123; ethnic adjustment 13–14, 80, 123

race-making 55–57, 67, 117, 120, 121; see also racialization

race positivity 32

racial differences: in allelic frequencies 17, 30, 66, 72; in disease occurrence 29, 31, 35–36, 51, 72

racial/ethnic biases 13, 105

racial/ethnic categories 8, 19, 32, 35, 42, 60, 65, 67, 112–113, 115–116, 121; classificatory ambiguity of 106; conventional use of 72–73, 105–106; framing of cost-effectiveness studies using 118; in genetic research 15; incorporation 7; political factors, role of 16; reliance on 106

racial/ethnic disparities in health 106

racial/ethnic minority 5, 15, 32, 49, 110–111, 118

racial formation 61–62

racial hierarchies 50

racialization 1, 18–20, 64–67, 107–108, 113; 5-fluorouracil 91; ancestry informative markers (AIMs) race 50, 55, 110; appearance race 65, 110; country of family origin/nativity race 54, 65, 110; defined 6–7, 109, 118–119; deracialization 107, 118, 119; differential 7, 67, 120–121; factors fueling 73; of genetic differences 57–58; of genetic variants 111; in genomic science 14–17, 52–57, 110; geographical race 14, 65, 110; health economists in 118; inconsistencies between different ways of racialization 56, 65; issues with the different ways of 55–57; materials for 52–55; of medicine 10–12; of medicine in colonial contexts 10–12; in medicine in contemporary times 12; misinterpretation of 117; name-surname race 52, 55–56, 65, 67, 110, 120–121; of national census categories 8–9; National Registration Identity Card race 53, 93, 94, 110; occurrence of 115, 119–120; parental/grandparental race 65–66, 110; of pharmacogenomic drug toxicity 89–93, 97, 100, 111; of population sample/patient 52–55; of precision medicine 1, 7, 18–20, 71–84, 107, 108, 110, 117, 118–121, 123; racialized drugs 45, 94, 106; racialized guidelines 45; racialized implicit biases 29; racialized statistics 33, 36–43, 45–46, 73, 123; racializers 107, 109; racially/ethnically framed probability statements 111; relative resources and 119–120, 122; in science (or, scientific racism) in colonial contexts 9–10, 12, 20, 109; self-reported race 13, 65, 110; in translational precision medicine 33–43, 109–110

racialized 18, 115–116, 122–123; drugs 45; drug toxicity 94, 96, 99–100; ethnicized data 15; format 111; guidelines 45; health disparities 6; implicit biases 29; national census 8; patient's identity 52; pharmacogenomic studies 89–93; populations 44, 52, 61, 106; precision medicine 19–20, 71–75, 83, 84n1, 106, 108, 113, 118–120; probability statements 75; spirometry 14; statistics 33, 36–43, 45–46, 73

racialized health disparities 6

racialized probabilities 75, 113

racialized statistics 33, 36–43, 45–46, 73, 123

racial profiling 1, 20, 30, 88, 109, 118, 122; in clinical care 13; defined 4; persistence of 19; problems with 5–6; reliance on 29
racial stereotyping/stereotypes 6, 30, 88
racial variations 31; in disease prevalence 36; in genetic frequencies 59
Rajagopalan, R. M. 5, 15, 49, 50
Reardon, J. E. 52, 112
regulatory frameworks 80, 81, 114
relative resources model: financial resources 75–78; human and informatics resources 78–80; legal and infrastructural resources 80–82
relative resources theory 19, 71–84, 111, 119–120, 122–123
Relling, M. V. 98
representation 32, 66, 73, 109, 112, 118
Research, Innovation, and Enterprise (RIE) 3
residual category 15, 73
resource heterogeneity 114
resources 2, 4, 30, 38, 107; availability of 43, 74, 75, 108; financial 75–78, 108, 111, 118; heterogeneity of 71, 82; heterogeneous 114; human and informatics 78–80, 108, 111, 118; legal and infrastructural 80–82, 108, 111, 118; medical 11; misallocation of 6; power 49; relative resources theory 19, 71–84, 111, 119–120, 122–123; saving 39
risk 89–90, 113–114, 117; adverse drug reactions 17, 113; allele 31, 91; of being biologically inaccurate 29; cancer 5, 28; disease 12, 59, 61, 66, 81, 114, 123; drug toxicity 39, 96–97, 99, 101, 113; estimates 96; estimation of hyperbilirubinemia 12–13; genetic risk 2, 31, 81–82; of genetic discrimination 73; health 109; modifiable 36; subjective interpretation of 96–97
risk alleles 31, 91
risk prediction model 97
risk profile 58
Root, M. 6
Rosenberg, N. A. 51
Ross, L. F. 57
Rumbaut, R. G. 8

SCARs *see* severe cutaneous adverse drug reactions
schizophrenia 11

Schork, N. J. 112
Schwartz, R. 28
Science and Technology Studies (STS) 20, 44
science communication 115–116
scientific racism 9–10
scientific research 44–46, 54, 71, 107, 109–110, 115, 118–119; to clinical trials 32; diversity and representation in 112; genetic biomarker in 34–35; proxy for genetics in 52; race in 33
screening 28, 75, 82, 90
SEER *see* Surveillance Epidemiology, End Results (SEER) program
self-identification 53, 57, 67, 120
self-reports 4, 13, 29, 53, 55, 57, 65, 67, 72, 110, 120
severe cutaneous adverse drug reactions (SCARs) 89–90
Sheldon, T. A. 19
Shim, J. K. 44
Shostak, S. 6
sickle cell anemia 17
single nucleotide polymorphism (SNP) 63
single-payer public health system 76, 77, 82, 114
skin color 11
smallpox 12
Smart, A. 12
snowball sampling 122
SNP chip 64
SNP map 63
social decision 56
social determinants of health 6, 51, 66, 116
social justice 15, 31, 44
socioeconomic factors: cultural factors 5, 29, 88; economic factors 5; environmental factors 5; lifestyle factors 5; social determinants of health 6, 51, 66, 116
somatic mutations 18, 81, 88
sovereignty over DNA 16, 74
spirometry 14
stakeholders of precision medicine 16, 31, 73, 106, 108, 113, 120–121; health economists 19, 67, 107, 109, 111, 116, 118, 120–121; journalists 115–116; clinicians/physicians/ medical doctors 7, 113, 116, 117– 118; public policy makers 117–118; scientists 115, 116–117
Stamp, L. 90

Stevens-Johnson syndrome (SJS) 89
stigmatization 105
stratification 19; approaches 3; of healthcare services 77; population 12, 56, 67, 121; precise method for 37
studies/testing 111; *see also* pharmacogenomic studies/testing
subjective evaluation of drug toxicity risks 113; interpretation 96–97
Surveillance, Epidemiology, End Results (SEER) program 52, 56
systematic review 13, 89, 92, 132–137
systemic racism 14

Takezawa, Y. 16, 66
targeted drug therapies 3
Thais 55, 60, 90
Thompson, D. 61–62
Tichenor, P. J. 82
Toh, D. S. L. 98
toxic epidermal necrolysis (TEN) 89
Travassos C. 28
treatment 5, 28, 33, 100, 113; cancer 44; decisions 31, 111; difference in 11; differential treatment 6, 12, 105; EGFR-TKIs 122; guiding 4, 42–43; individualized 72; medical 2, 4, 6, 29–30, 32, 74–75, 77, 81–82, 88, 107, 109, 115; options 77, 82; overtreatment 14; personalized 6; recommendations 77; of respiratory diseases 14; US FDA-approved 3
treatment/therapeutic decisions 42
tuberculosis 11

van Staveren, M. C. 92
visible minorities 8, 61–62
visual/appearance/look/phenotype 53
visual assessment 29, 67, 121
visual identification 53, 57

Walko, C. 17
Ward, E. 5
warfarin 4, 72, 98
Weiner, K. 12
Williams, D. R. 28
Winant, H. 7, 51, 61
World Economic Forum 3

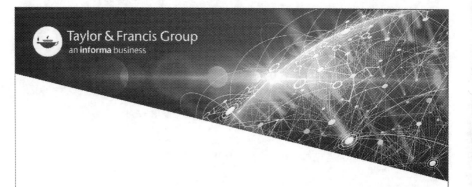